Christian school administrators often have to [...] teachers trained in different educational mo[...] grounds, and parents with enormous expectations. Attempting a strategic plan often becomes a dream-only, drawer-lining exercise in futility for Christian schools—but *Rethinking Strategic Planning* may change that. Dr. Pue provides a rational foundation for a solid plan with actionable steps. I can't wait to have my board read this!

Erin Hart, Administrator, Three Rivers Christian School, Longview, WA

————◦————

This book is a must read for any Christian school thinking about going through a strategic planning process. Dr. Pue writes from a position of experience and not just theory. Having gone through the strategic planning process with him, I can say that he doesn't talk about anything in the book he didn't actually require of us as we went through this process with him. In this book he lays out a very succinct and concrete way to walk through the process and gives a rationale for each step. Not only does Dr. Pue come from a position of experience, but he gives relevant biblical examples of why Christian Schools should go through this process. Throughout the book he continually makes the case that God requires excellence in all we do. I would highly doubt that after reading this book you could argue otherwise.

Dan Kuiper, Administrator, Valley Christian High, Chandler, AZ

————◦————

For those who believe that change is inescapable but improvement is optional, Dr. Pue's explanation of strategic planning will be encouraging, thought provoking, and compelling.

Brian Modarelli, Head of School, Christian Heritage School, Trumbull, CT

————◦————

Alan Pue for years has brought clarity and direction to Christian schools seeking strategic thinking. In this practical and engaging book, Alan guides all administrators and board members through a grounded process of school improvement that is focused on growth and best practices. Alan's work here echoes the sons of Issachar referenced in I Chronicles: he is a man "who has understanding of the times, and knows what we ought to do."

Barry Giller, Head of School, Charlotte Christian School, Charlotte, NC

Where was this book 20 years ago when I needed it? This book should be in every Christian school leader's library. Alan Pue artfully emphasizes the "new" nature of strategic planning and compels leaders to create a dynamic, ongoing process of planning. This book is written in common-sense language and provides practical tools and planning protocols to guide the leader. Most importantly, it is integrated with Scripture and biblical concepts that anchor the process and provide spiritual understanding for the reader who is questioning whether or not strategic planning is a biblical concept.

Cindy Dodds, Executive Director Emeritus, Penn Christian Academy, Butler, PA

———o———

"Rethinking" is the approach which must be brought to the strategic planning process today. This vital process has become diluted and complicated by overexposure. Dr. Pue simplifies and clarifies the "essentials" by posing the right questions versus formulaic answers. Furthermore, he has well articulated the critical balance between our dependence on God's sovereignty and our obligation to act wisely.

Bryan Miller, Director of Leadership Development, ACSI

———o———

As he did in writing *Rethinking Sustainability*, Alan Pue has created an important resource for Christian schools! Drawing from the work of Peter Drucker, Jim Collins, Joel Barker, Chip and Dan Heath, Patrick Lencioni and many others as well as his own vast experience with Christian schools, and fueled by his own passion for the Christian school movement, Dr. Pue not only provides a road map for the process of strategic planning, but also challenges us with the urgency of engaging in this process. The future of the Christian school movement depends on leaders who are willing to ask the hard questions, tackle the challenges head on, and courageously seek God's vision for our schools. This book is a great tool for equipping leaders with the *why we must* and the *how we can* effectively lead our schools through this process.

Elsie R. Wright, Former Head of School, Barrington Christian Academy, Barrington, RI

RETHINKING
Strategic Planning
for Christian Schools

Alan Pue

purposeful design®
p u b l i c a t i o n s

Colorado Springs, Colorado

RETHINKING
Strategic Planning
for Christian Schools

Alan Pue

Purposeful Design Publications is the publishing division of the Association of Christian Schools International (ACSI) and is committed to the ministry of Christian school education, to enable Christian educators and schools worldwide to effectively prepare students for life. As the publisher of textbooks, trade books, and other educational resources within ACSI, Purposeful Design Publications strives to produce biblically sound materials that reflect Christian scholarship and stewardship and that address the identified needs of Christian schools around the world.

The views expressed in this publication are those of the author, and they may not necessarily represent the position of the Association of Christian Schools International.

Unless otherwise noted, all Scripture quotations are taken from the Holy Bible, English Standard Version, Copyright © 2001 by Crossway Bibles, a division of Good News Publishers.

Scripture quotations marked KJV are taken from the King James Version.

Scripture quotations marked NASB are taken from the New American Standard Bible®, Copyright © 1960, 1962, 1963, 1968, 1971, 1972, 1973, 1975, 1977, 1995 by The Lockman Foundation. Used by permission.

Scripture quotations marked NIV are taken from the Holy Bible, NEW INTERNATIONAL VERSION®. Copyright © 1973, 1978, 1984 by Biblica, Inc. All rights reserved worldwide. Used by permission of Biblica, Inc.

Printed in the United States of America

20 19 18 17 16   1 2 3 4 5

Pue, Alan
    Rethinking strategic planning for Christian schools
    ISBN 978-1-58331-554-5 Catalog #6659
    eISBN 978-1-58331-373-2 Catalog #e6659

Designer: Mike Riester
Editor: John Conaway

Purposeful Design Publications
A Division of ACSI
PO Box 65130 • Colorado Springs, CO 80962-5130
Customer Service: 800-367-0798 • www.acsi.org

Contents

Foreword

"When you get to a fork in the road … take it!"   —Yogi Berra

There are times when our schools are at a crossroads. When we find ourselves there, ambiguous advice like Yogi's famous quip leaves us chuckling but perplexed. At times like this we tend to look for answers, when what we really need is help identifying the right questions. We need a plan, but how do we get there? The whole planning endeavor can feel like we are hugging a mattress—we can't seem to find any handles!

When our school leadership sensed our "crossroads" moment, we turned to Dr. Alan Pue to lead us through a strategic planning process. It was a six-month journey during which he helped us identify where we were, assess our opportunities, and seek God's plan for the next few years. The process did not create a platform dominated by the agenda of a few vocal advocates. It proved to be a team approach full of hard work, deep thought, discovery, and renewed passion for what the school could become.

During our planning experience, Alan occasionally mentioned that he was engaged in writing this book. His commitment to writing is always driven by his passion to share what he has learned about this critical process with as many Christian schools and ministries as possible. Alan's blend of personal experience as a Christian school student, coach, teacher, and administrator, coupled with his rich knowledge of the related research, equips him to connect with the challenges we face in planning for the future of our schools. He is keenly aware of the stewardship responsibility attached to his knowledge and experience, and he has produced a book that offers a thoughtful path to more effective ministry.

One of the great challenges of leadership is carving out the time to read, reflect, and synthesize the flood of information on leadership topics. The necessity of marinating all of this in biblical truth for its proper application in the Christian school requires both private thought and collaborative discussion. There are no shortcuts to this process. There are, however, folks who have gone before us who have been involved in this pursuit over the years, and we would be wise to benefit from them.

This book offers the perspectives of one who has read widely, thought deeply, and has practiced the craft of planning in hundreds of ministry settings. The opportunities to engage countless leaders in substantive discussion on this topic have provided Alan with access to both the reflective thought and practical implementation experiences of many. His many hours on airplanes provide the reading time that those of us running a school can only dream about!

But as valuable as expertise and strategies are to the planning process, I would remind us of the last piece of counsel provided by Alan to our school's task force. The initiatives had been identified, the goals listed, and the way forward established. In the end he reminded us all that "we must go forward on our knees."

As we have pursued building teams to implement the initiatives identified in our planning process, we have also increased our focus on prayer. Proverbs 19:21 (ESV) reminds us, "Many are the plans in the mind of a man, but it is the purpose of the Lord that will stand." Planning and implementing plans are some of the more challenging aspects of leadership. But in reality, the process of planning and implementation provides the most substantial benefit for an organization. The experience of prayerful, intentional planning, execution, assessment—and repeat cycle—can be transformative. After all, the goal is not a plan in a notebook on a shelf in the accreditation visiting team workroom. It is a living, breathing, morphing journey that results in changed lives and the extension of the kingdom for the glory of God and for our own good.

I know of no other book specifically aimed at equipping us to do strategic planning in the Christian school. We are all indebted to Alan Pue and to Purposeful Design Publishers for providing this contribution to the leadership literature. You will want to read it, mark it up, share it with your leadership team, and reflect on its implication and application. It is a never-ending growth process for us all, because as Yogi said, "It's never over till it's over!"

Mike Sligh, Headmaster
Lakeland Christian School
Lakeland, FL

Preface

I was your worst nightmare—the student you never want to see walk into your classroom. I was also your greatest opportunity—the opportunity to demonstrate that Christian schooling and those who pursue it as a calling really can make a difference in the life of a child, even one as broken as I was. Let me tell you part of my story.

In the spring of 1963 I arrived home from school one day; there, sitting just off the street by my house, was my dad's pickup. Now that wasn't all that uncommon. He often parked his truck in that spot. What was unusual, and a bit disturbing, was the load of furniture and suitcases occupying space normally reserved for his tools. When I went into the house, there in the living room I found my mom, my dad, and my brother waiting for me. It was a pretty somber scene. My dad asked me to sit down, and then he and my mom announced to my brother and me that they were getting a divorce. It was not a good moment.

Divorce is not at all unusual today; a lot of your kids come from single-parent homes. But in 1963, in a Baptist church, it was pretty rare. I remember my dad getting up, hugging my brother and me, and then walking out to his truck. At that moment he essentially disappeared from our lives. I can only recall seeing him twice during my high school years. Life in our household had changed in a fundamental way.

Kids react to the break-up of a family in many different ways. My immediate and continuing response was anger. My poor mom really didn't know what to do with me. She'd never been in the workforce before, and now she was responsible for not only parenting but for fully providing for two teenaged sons, neither of whom was in the least concerned with her emotions or the financial challenges that divorce always brings. Every day was an unpleasant battle; every day angry shouts echoed off the walls of our home. So in desperation, I am sure, she decided to enroll me in the Christian school sponsored by our church.

Our pastor, Dr. Al Janney, was among the pioneers of the emerging Christian school movement. In 1960 he founded the Dade Christian School, which at that time was housed in the facilities of the New Testament Baptist Church in the heart of downtown Miami. In 1963 the school added a ninth-grade class, so I became a member of what would be the first graduating class of DCS, the class of 1967.

No one has ever been a more reluctant student. I showed up for classes on the Tuesday after Labor Day 1963 with one goal in mind: to get expelled as quickly as possible. And when I got hold of the school's handbook and read it, I quickly concluded that getting expelled would be easy. All it required, according to the text of that little booklet, was earning twenty-five demerits. And since you could earn a demerit for doing something as simple as chewing a piece of gum during the school day, I reasoned, "Twenty-five days, twenty-five pieces of chewing gum, and I'm outta here!

What I had not counted on was this thing called grace. The staff members of the school went out of their way to help me make a good transition. I didn't care, however; I just wanted out. It is amazing how anger and fear can cloud the judgment of a teenaged boy. So I continued to push the limits, and by the first of November I had managed to accumulate twenty-four demerits—just one short of my goal. The final blow came on a Friday afternoon bus ride while returning to the school from the local YMCA, where we had physical education classes. While en route to the school I got into a fight on the bus with one of my classmates. According to the handbook, fighting was an automatic 10 demerits, so I was suddenly well over the line.

I wasn't even thinking about that minor detail, however, as I got on the bus to head home that afternoon. And believe me, I never mentioned anything about the fight to my mom.

The next morning, Saturday, I was out mowing the grass when into our driveway pulled Dr. Verle Ackerman, who was the executive pastor of the church and served as the liaison between the church and the school. Dr. Ackerman calmly got out of his car, dressed as he always was in a suit and tie, called me over, and said, "Alan, you need to come inside. I need to talk to you and your mom." I immediately knew I was in trouble.

My mom was as surprised as I at Dr. Ackerman's visit. I suspect, however, that she was not at all surprised at what he had to say. Once in our living room, Dr. Ackerman looked at my mom, shared with her what had happened on the bus the previous day, and then told her that a decision had been made to expel me from school. As you can imagine, my mom did not respond well to that message. He then continued with these words: "Lois, I want you to know that as soon as I heard what had happened I went Dr. Kreft (the administrator of the school) and said to him, 'Look, you don't know what's going on in this kid's life. You're not going to expel him from school. I will accept responsibility for him.'" I'll never forget what happened next as long as I live. Dr. Ackerman leaned over, pointed his finger in my direction, and said, "Alan, you are mine, and I will not let you fail!"

That's the moment my life changed forever, and that's why for over forty years I have invested my life in this thing we call Christian schooling. When Christian schools do what they exist to do, and do it with excellence, changed lives are the result. Think about our remarkable opportunity. We get to engage in the work of spiritual, intellectual, and personal transformation in a way that nobody else in this country gets to do. That's not to say that there are not a lot of ministries focused on working with children and young people. It's just that none of them have the access and opportunity that we in Christian schooling do.

Here's the problem, however. It is much more difficult to do that work well today than it was back in1963 when I began attending Dade Christian School. The culture has shifted dramatically; the curriculum has become much more complicated; the expectations of parents and students have skyrocketed; and the church, which has never fully embraced the Christian school, seems even less inclined to do so. You can't just show up every day and declare that you love kids and succeed. It takes more, much more, to deliver quality Christian schooling—all the while making adjustments to curriculum and instructional strategies in response to all that is happening in the world around you. Good intentions and hard work are essential to your success as a Christian school; they are just not enough.

I discovered that truth very early in my career as head of a Christian school. No one was more committed to Christian schooling than I was, but in five brief years I watched—and watched is the operative word here—a healthy K–12 school with an enrollment of nearly 400 students decline to the point that we opened the 1984–85 school year with a mere 118 students in grades pre-K–6. It was devastating. There were days I could hardly work up the energy to head to campus. And while much of what happened was the result of events beyond my control, I felt like an utter failure. Fortunately, I had two very positive resources available to me, both of which were soon to have an enormous impact on how I viewed my role as head of school and how I was to fulfill that role.

The first resource was the doctoral program in which I was enrolled at the University of Delaware. It was a new program designed with school leaders in mind. Through this program I was introduced to a different way of looking at leadership in a school context, as well as to some very insightful individuals like Peter Drucker, who challenged much of what I believed about the role of a leader.

Perhaps no one puts it more clearly than John Kotter. He writes, "I am completely convinced that most organizations today lack the leadership they need. And the shortfall is often large. I'm not talking about a deficit of 10% but of 200%, 400%, or more.... This is not to say that untalented, unenergetic people occupy managerial positions. The typical case is just the opposite, with bright, experienced, and hardworking individuals, some quite extraordinary, almost all trying to do what they believe is right. The problem is that far too few of these people are providing the leadership that is increasingly needed in business, government, everywhere" (1999, 1–2).

Kotter then goes on to tell us why the leadership problem has become so challenging. "What is clear is that the increasingly fast-moving and competitive environment we will (and now do) face demands more leadership from more people to make enterprises prosper. Without that leadership, organizations stagnate, lose their way, and eventually suffer the consequences" (Kotter 1999, 2). Far too often, I've seen exactly what Kotter describes—hence, a primary motivation for writing this book.

The second resource was the community in which our school was located. Wilmington, Delaware, and environs was home to a number of world-class businesses, including the DuPont Corporation and Hewlett-Packard. Many of those who attended our church were employed by world-class companies, and they were familiar with much of the growing literature on effective organizational leadership. One of the men in our church lent me a video series that was making the rounds at DuPont at the time. It was titled *Paradigms: The Business of Discovering the Future*, and was narrated by Joel Barker. I'd never heard of Barker, but the videos so impressed me that I purchased and devoured the book that was a companion to the series.

In both the book and video series, Barker made an observation that grabbed my attention: "In the last twenty years, all of Western society has passed through extraordinarily turbulent times. We have been living in a time when fundamental rules, the basic ways we do things, have been altered dramatically.... These dramatic changes are extremely important because they have created in us a special sense of impermanence that generates tremendous discomfort" (Barker 1993, 21–22).)

He then went on to say that if we truly want to break free of paradigms that keep us from anticipating and innovating, we've got to learn a new way of thinking. Sitting in the debris of a broken school, I felt hope for the first time that things could be different, that the school could once again excel at the work to which we had been called.

I must confess that I didn't share my thinking with a lot of people. I didn't try to enlist the help of our board. As the saying goes, I kept my cards close to my vest. What I did do was to put into practice much of what I was learning. Remarkably, in a relatively brief period of time the situation at our school began to change—and change quite dramatically. Where there had been decline, there was growth. Where there had been a demoralized staff, there was now an energized staff. Not every problem was solved immediately, but a sense that we could address our challenges had replaced an I-don't-know-if-we're-going-to-make-it mentality.

What I hope to share with you in this book is not some magic formula. It is hard work. It will require enormous effort and a willingness to invest the necessary resources. It will require you to examine, and in some cases discard, the current paradigms that shape how you "do" school. It won't be easy. You will be asking people to surrender cherished ideas of how best to accomplish your common calling. Because this can be the cause of much pain, I will focus the entire last chapter on the challenge of change. What I have to share in this book can, however, help you "excel still more" in pursuit of God's calling.

Introduction

John Craig, who for many years served as director of ACSI's South-Central region, best captured what I try to do in working with schools. He once introduced me with these words: "Alan works with schools to *help them better become what God has called them to be.*" That's it. That's exactly what I try to do. It's why I'm writing this book. It's what Paul means when he encourages the church in Thessalonica to "excel still more" (1 Thessalonians 4:1, NASB). To do that, however, you've got to find and maintain that balance. You've got to learn to be both "wise as serpents" and "harmless as doves."

To help you accomplish the task of finding and maintaining that balance, I have structured the book with two major divisions.

In the first section of the book I will address these foundational concepts:

1. A rationale for strategic planning—the why behind the what

2. A description of strategic planning—what it is and what it is not

3. A discussion of the principles, both biblical and practical, that should shape how you approach the process

In the second section I will address the process itself—the questions you must ask and answer if you are to successfully complete your task of strategic planning. Here are some of those questions:

• *Are we ready to engage in this process?* In other words, are we healthy enough as a school to tackle the task of strategic planning, knowing that during the course of this process we are going to shed light on everything we are doing as a school?

• *Who should be part of our team?* Excellence produces excellence; therefore, how do we find people with the right qualities to help us engage in this process?

• *What is nonnegotiable?* This is the defining piece, and it is foundational to everything that follows.

• *What is our current reality?* You can't move into the future until you fully understand your current reality. This is not an easy task because it requires a level of objectivity that is hard to achieve in any organization.

- *What is most important right now?* No organization can take on an endless number of initiatives. Thus you've got to carefully choose where you will invest your time, energy, and resources.

- *How can we best achieve our goals?* This is the action-planning part of the strategic plan, during which you will build a roadmap from your current reality to your desired future.

- *How can we best ensure that all of our efforts make a real difference over time?* Any quality planning process will lead to changes in how you do what you do and perhaps even changes regarding who you are. How you address the natural resistance to change will in large part determine the long-term success of your planning efforts.

In addition to the book text, we have provided a number of downloadable supporting documents. Go to https://www.acsi.org/tradebooks/psr/6518 to access these documents, which include forms, templates, and worksheets. You'll find them especially helpful if you use this book to train your team.

As a bonus, we have included an appendix featuring an excellent resource article by Dr. Lynn Swaner: "Needs Assessment for Christian Schools." This article provides in-depth insights that will help you better understand and apply the insights in chapter 8: "What Is Our Current Reality?"

As with my book *Rethinking Sustainability*, this book is focused on the basics. There are a number of fine books that will immerse you in greater detail and introduce you to more sophisticated concepts than you will find in the pages of this book. The bibliography at the end of the book will introduce you to some of those books and the authors whose experience and insight will prove most helpful to you. My goal here is to pique your interest while giving you enough helpful ideas to get you started. This is but the first step in what I hope will be a continuing journey for you and your school.

A final thought before we jump into our topic. It is easy in Christian organizations to lose the balance between the work that only God can do and the work that we must do. This is a topic we will explore in much greater detail in chapter 3. For now I'd like to make some observations.

The Old Testament books are organized into five categories. The Pentateuch (the first five books) is called the Law. The History books, beginning with the book of

Joshua and concluding with the book of Esther, are an account of the nation of Israel from the time they enter the Holy Land through their captivity in Babylon and return. Then there are the Major Prophets and the Minor Prophets, so called because of the length of the text rather than the importance of their content.

Placed right in the middle of the Old Testament is the Wisdom Literature, and right in the middle of the Wisdom Literature is the book of Proverbs. Derek Kidner gives us insight as to the purpose of Proverbs in the introduction to his excellent commentary: "The samples of behavior which [Proverbs] holds up to view are all assessed by one criterion, which could be summed up in the question, 'Is this wisdom or folly?' This is a unifying approach to life, because it suits the most commonplace realms (like how to purchase a boat—my note) as fully as the most exalted" (Kidner 1964, 13).

Here is reality. We live in a fallen world, and if we are to succeed at what we are called to do we must work at maintaining that balance between dependence on God's sovereignty and our obligation as prudent men and women to act wisely and well. It's when we lose that balance that we experience the kinds of problems that can be life-threatening to an organization committed to fulfilling God's purposes in the world.

The Pilgrims provide a compelling illustration of what can happen to the best of people when that balance is lost. In his fascinating account of the Pilgrims and their epic journey to the New World, Nathaniel Philbrick (2006, 17–18) makes an observation that is descriptive of many followers of Jesus Christ today. He writes, "The members of [Pastor John Robinson's] congregation knew each other wonderfully well, but when it came to the outside world they could sometimes run into trouble. They were too focused on their own inner lives to appreciate the subtleties of character that might have alerted them to the true motives of those who did not share in their beliefs. Time and time again during their preparations to sail for America, the Pilgrims demonstrated an extraordinary talent for getting duped."

I want to help you find and maintain the balance Proverbs calls us to and that the Pilgrims seemed to ignore. It is one of my primary motivations in writing this book.

We don't live in a world in which our efforts have no meaning. We are beings created in the image of God, and we have been given the capacity to see beyond current reality, the wisdom to make necessary changes in how we can best fulfill our calling, and the capacity for the courage necessary to make tough decisions along the way. Don't squander those remarkable gifts. Use them to *better become what God has called you to be and to excel still more.*

PART ONE

Foundations of Strategic Planning

The Why Behind the What

Behind every what there is a why. We may not always fully understand the why, but there is always a why. There is a reason, for example, why you get up every morning and head off to work, wherever that may be. For some it might be as simple as, "I've got to make enough money to cover my living costs." Or you could be driven by something a bit less materialistic. For example, if you have chosen to lead a Christian school you might do so because you feel a sense of calling or a desire to impact the lives of children.

The same is true of me. There is a reason I get up at 3:30 in the morning some 30–35 times every year to make the 45-minute trek to Denver International Airport to catch a 6:00 AM flight to Somewhere, USA—and it isn't for the frequent flyer miles. The why behind that what is easy for me to explain. Christian schooling changed my life—and not just mine, but the lives of countless others around the world as well. Like you, I want to see Christian schools remain effective in their work of life transformation. That's why I do what I do, and it's why I'm writing this book.

In fact it was while reading through Paul's first letter to the church in Thessalonica that I came across a passage that crystallized the why behind what was to become The Barnabas Group, Inc. Consider these words. "Finally then, brethren, we request and exhort you in the Lord Jesus that as you received from us instruction as to how you ought to walk and please God (just as you actually do walk), that you excel still more" (I Thessalonians 4:1, NASB). It was the phrase "that you excel still more" that caught my attention.

It wasn't as though those in the church of Thessalonica were failing to live godly lives. In fact, Paul strongly commended them with these words: "Now as to the love of the brethren, you have no need for anyone to write to you for you yourselves are taught by God to love one another; for indeed you do practice it toward all the brethren who are in all Macedonia" (1 Thessalonians 4:9–10, NASB). Yet he again encourages them to "excel still more."

That's what I want you to do. I want you to "excel still more." I have no doubt about your desire to do good, to effectively engage in the work of transformation, and to prepare your students for the challenges you know they will face. And I have no doubt about your willingness to invest the energy necessary to achieve all you hope to accomplish in the lives of your students. I've learned, however, that good intentions and hard work, as essential as they are, are never by themselves enough to achieve excellence. You've also got to think wisely, plan creatively, and then act effectively. Strategic planning done right can help you do that.

In chapter 2 I'm going to define what I mean by strategic planning. Before we go there, however, it is my goal to explain the why behind the what. Strategic planning done well is hard work. To succeed you must own the process, and to own the process you must fully grasp what is at stake in the process. So before we go any further together I want you to ask and answer the following question: "Why in the world do I want to do this thing called strategic planning?" Without a satisfying answer to that question it will be hard for you to sustain the level of effort essential for any quality planning process.

A Little Research

During the years that I served as an adjunct faculty member in the doctoral program at Columbia International University, as part of a class project I had my students do research on Christian schools and strategic planning. Most disconcerting to me, as I read through those research reports, was the fact that my students struggled to find Christian schools that had actually chosen to engage in any kind of strategic planning process. As I sifted through what my students reported, I discovered four primary reasons that were given for why strategic planning was not a priority.

1. *Cost.* We don't have or don't want to spend the resources necessary to do strategic planning.

2. *We don't see the need.* We are doing OK without strategic planning.

3. *Time commitment.* We already have too much on our plates to even consider adding a strategic planning process to all we are doing.

4. *A failure to see any true benefit.* We just aren't sure that the end result will be worth all of the effort and cost.

For those choosing to move ahead with a planning process, the number-one reason—the why behind their what—was the desire to pursue accreditation. Since a completed strategic plan is a necessary prerequisite for accreditation, most schools that chose to engage in a planning process did so in response to that requirement. Unfortunately, at least in my estimation, such motivation often leads to a minimalist approach to the planning process. It simply becomes another box to check on the way to a successful conclusion of the accreditation process. To do justice to the strategic planning process you need a more compelling rationale. Providing that more-compelling rationale is the primary purpose of this chapter.

In considering the why question I've identified five primary reasons why every Christian school should engage in strategic planning efforts. Some of these reasons will evoke a "Well, of course" response. Some, however, might be a bit more thought provoking. For me all are crucial reasons if we are to fully anchor our thinking and efforts to a sound biblical foundation. So, let's take a look at some of the whys behind the what of strategic planning.

Strategic planning allows you to
• set the course for your school;
• stay the course when things get tough;
• sustain your school financially, now and into the future;
• serve the church as full partners in fulfilling the Great Commission; and
• show God's glory to a watching world.

Let's briefly consider each of those reasons.

Set the course

What does it mean to "set the course?" I don't know if you're a fan of J. R. R. Tolkien's books, but when the *Lord of the Rings* trilogy came out I was one of the first in line at the theater. Since reading the trilogy many years ago I had been waiting for someone to make a film that was worthy of that text. Peter Jackson managed to pull it off. I think I've watched all three of those movies at least a dozen times. So when *The Hobbit* series came out a few years ago, I was once again one of the first in line.

I love the story of Bilbo Baggins, that meek, unassuming hobbit who wants nothing more than to live his simple, quiet life but who instead ends up heading out on a dangerous quest with a group of unlikely companions. One of the fascinating parts of this story occurs when Bilbo and the dwarfs find themselves hopelessly lost in Mirkwood Forest, where they are attacked by some rather large, hungry spiders.

Even though they are able to fend off this vicious attack, fear and despair grip the hearts of the entire group. It is then that Bilbo does something completely out of character for a hobbit. While everyone else seems paralyzed by the events they've just experienced, he acts. He climbs to the top of a nearby tree from which he is able to see beyond the limitations imposed by the dense forest into which they have wandered. With the horizon in view he is able to point the way forward.

That's what leaders do. Indeed it is a fundamental obligation of leadership. Leaders, in a sense, are called to climb the tree, look to the horizon, and say, "That's where we need to go." In essence that is what you do in a strategic planning process. Now leaders can't fully do this on their own. Leadership is a team sport. That's why when David ascended to the throne as king of Israel, one of the first things he did was to put together his leadership team. On that team were "the sons of Issachar, men who understood their times, with knowledge of what Israel should do" (1 Chronicles 12:32, NASB). You need people like that on your team.

Leaders, however, have a crucial role to play in the planning process. They are the instigators. They are the ones who understand the importance of climbing the tree, of pointing the way forward. No quality leader, however, will stay safely ensconced in the tree and simply point to the horizon. True leaders know that they must come down from that elevated position and humbly walk through the forest with their team. Leaders who stay in the tree and simply say "Let's head in that direction" will never get their team or their organization where it needs to go. Fail in this fundamental obligation and you will doom your school or your organization to continued mediocrity. Worse, as an organization, you will never fully fulfill God's calling.

There are those who will respond to what I have just said by declaring, "God directs our school. We simply follow His lead." That may sound good in theory. In the real world, however, we have a more active role to play. How your leadership responsibility intersects with God's sovereignty is a mystery I doubt any of us will fully understand on this side of eternity. It does seem, however, that when a difficult task needs to be accomplished, God typically raises up a leader who, like Bilbo, is able to see beyond the current horizon and is adept at mobilizing people as they move toward that horizon. Think Moses, think Joshua, think David and Nehemiah, and in the New Testament think Peter and Paul. While this is not intended as a book on leadership, I can say without apology that leaders matter—a lot!

Stay the course

As Solomon reminds us, "Where there is no prophetic vision, the people cast off restraint" (Proverbs 29:18). To fully grasp the import of those words we've got to better understand the meaning of the word *vision* as it's used in the text. Solomon does not employ the word here, as we often do, to speak of what we hope to become. Rather, the usage is more akin to our concept of a constitution, a document that serves as an objective frame of reference for those times when lots of different voices are urging us to move off in any number of new directions. Those voices seem the loudest during times of momentous transition such as our current reality, an era General Stanley McChrystal has memorably termed an era of "unpredictable complexity" (2015, 54).

I think Peter Drucker has best captured our current transitioning cultural landscape with the following observation: "Every few hundred years throughout Western history a sharp transformation has occurred. In a matter of decades society altogether rearranges itself—its worldview, its basic values, its social and political structures, its arts, its key institutions. Fifty years later a new world exists. And the people born into that world cannot even imagine the world in which their grandparents lived and into which their own parents were born." (Drucker n.d.). Wouldn't you agree that we are living in just such a time?

Here's a bit of historical context from my own experience. For many years my great aunts lived what was essentially a 19th-century agrarian lifestyle. They had no electricity and therefore no TV and no refrigeration. When they cooked a meal it was on a wood-burning stove. They also had no indoor plumbing. During the day that lack of plumbing necessitated a visit to what was called an outhouse, and at night required the use of a chamber pot. (Ask your children or grandchildren to describe a chamber pot. I'm pretty certain that they will have no idea what you are talking about.) A visit to the ranch was quite an adventure for my brother and me, but in the 1950s many people still lived in similar circumstances.

That is no longer the case. We live in a world where a handheld device called a cell phone can gain you access to more information in an instant than my grandfather could access in a lifetime. And imagine how the people of my grandfather's generation would respond to what the culture at large, or in the church for that matter, considers acceptable in terms of lifestyle. It isn't that all of the changes we've experienced over the last fifty years have been bad. I love my little Apple laptop. But it has, without question, created more than a bit of turbulence.

And actually there is nothing wrong with a little turbulence. It certainly keeps you focused. The real challenge with turbulence, however, is the way it can push you off course if you aren't careful. It happens all the time to organizations, especially when there is a lack of clarity about key concepts such as purpose, mission, core values, and nonnegotiable beliefs. Creating clarity is, therefore, a key part of any strategic planning process and a major reason for engaging in the process. During a strategic planning process you in essence create or confirm what becomes your North Star, which then provides you with the compass you will need for traversing any challenging context without losing your way. In other words, you are able to stay your course.

Permit me a final thought on staying the course. As we will explore in chapter 7, one of your great challenges will be learning to identify what is absolute, nonnegotiable, and unchangeable at your school—and what is open to discussion. Failure to distinguish between those two categories will either leave you vulnerable to unhealthy change during which you give away what is essential or will lock you into out-of-date practices that will doom you to mediocrity or worse.

Sustain the school

As I argue in my book *Rethinking Sustainability*, you simply cannot sustain a quality Christian school if the only resource at your disposal is the income you generate through the tuition you charge your students. It's just not possible. Though I do believe that your tuition rate should be sufficient to cover all of your operational costs, there are more expenses related to providing a quality education than those relating to your day-to-day operations. For big-ticket projects such as new facilities, major renovations, financial aid, and endowments you need large gifts from major donors, and those major donors tend to be people of wealth.

Here is a question, however, that I'm sure has gnawed at you a bit over the years: Why do so few people of wealth give significant gifts to Christian schools? I think that I can provide an answer to that question. Over the years there are two things I've learned about people of wealth. First, wealthy people seldom actually *give* their money away. Rather, people of wealth *invest* their money, and they invest in Kingdom work the same way they invest in the stock market. They ask this question: "Where can I get the best return on my investment?" A major reason, therefore, why people of wealth are reluctant to give money to people in ministry, including to those who lead Christian schools, is this: they don't trust you enough to invest their money in what you are doing. That's just the simple, sad fact of the matter. They think you're wonderful people. They think you're hard-working people. They think you care deeply about kids. They just don't think you're very good at what you do. They don't trust you.

Another thing I've learned about wealthy people is that they don't give to *someone else's* passion. They make gifts to organizations with which *they* share a passion. Sadly, not many people are all that enthusiastic about Christian schooling. They love evangelistic programs. They will give generously to helping at-risk kids or to feed hungry children or in response to the need for disaster relief, but K–12 Christian schools are pretty far down on their list of what matters most. I have no real research to back up what I am about to say, but most of the people I have observed in the evangelical world don't really know enough about Christian schooling to develop a fervency for it. They are largely uninformed about the real purpose of Christian schooling, and what they do know does not ignite their passion.

Your task, therefore, is twofold. First, you've got to deliver what you do with unmistakable excellence. That is the only way you will ever build trust in the minds of wealthy people. And second, you've got to infect them with your passion.

Now what does that have to do with strategic planning? The answer to that question is simple. When you plan wisely, when as a result of that planning process you carefully identify key strategic initiatives and create a sound action plan on how best to implement and achieve those strategic initiatives, and when you effectively implement that plan and are able to demonstrate to people the impact your plan is having on your ability to deliver your mission, then—and only then—are people likely to say, "That's a thoughtful leader. That's a person who knows what he or she is doing. That's a ministry worthy of my trust and of my investment."

And by the way, while you are sharing your what—your mission—and how your strategic plan is allowing you to deliver that mission with greater excellence, that's when you will be able to share again and again the why behind the what. That's a context in which you get to infect others with your passion.

Serve the church

Here are a few questions I would ask you to pose to your pastor at some time.
1. What is Jesus asking of us when He tells us to "make disciples"?
2. What is the primary purpose of education as viewed by most people in modern American culture?
3. What is the primary purpose of education as revealed in the Scriptures?
4. How do the answers to questions 2 and 3 align or not align with each other?
5. Why does that matter?

Now pose those same questions to yourself. If there is much overlap in the answers your pastor gives to those questions and the answers you give to those questions, I will be surprised.

I would argue that education properly understood is discipleship properly understood. Thus, I believe the church and the school share a common purpose: both are called to make disciples. Many of my colleagues in the church or in the Christian school would not agree with that assertion, however. For most pastors, schooling exists in one sphere (the academic and intellectual sphere), and the church in another—the spiritual-formation sphere. And while there is some overlap, the two spheres are essentially unconnected in any formal sense. Pastors and parents who follow that line of thinking view schools as primarily institutions designed to prepare students for a productive life in the world of commerce and as a mission field in which Christian kids are able to share their faith with their secular friends.

In reality the real missionaries in any school system are the teachers, not the students—a point of view, by the way, that was endorsed by none other than the father of progressive education, John Dewey (1897): "I believe that every teacher should realize the dignity of his calling; that he is a social servant set apart for the maintenance of proper social order and the securing of the right social growth. I believe that in this way the teacher always is the prophet of the true God and the usherer in of the true kingdom of God." Until pastors and parents grasp that truth they will continue to ignore the reality that schools don't simply exist to teach reading, writing, and arithmetic. They also exist to teach the meaning of Truth itself and how students should employ their understanding of Truth in every aspect of life.

One of the primary tasks of the Christian school leader, therefore, is to carefully develop a message that clearly connects education and discipleship in a compelling, convincing, thoroughly biblical way. Until Christian school leaders are able to do this it will remain difficult, if not impossible, for schools to build strong partnerships with local churches and church leaders or to overcome the power of the cultural message that education is primarily the "passport to privilege" (Garber 2007, 69).

The task of the teacher in a Christian school is to help students learn to "take every thought captive to obey Christ" (2 Corinthians 10:5) and to do so because they believe that the "fear of the Lord is the beginning of knowledge" (Proverbs 1:7). Teachers in the public system also teach about what is true and good and beautiful. They are not, however, going to do so from the perspective that God is the author of what is true and good and beautiful. Even Christian teachers in the public system— given the restrictions, real and imagined, placed upon them—will find it hard to do more than try to be a good example of Christlikeness. Christian content is off the table. Try to bring the Scriptures into any discussion in any public school classroom and the likelihood of a reprimand or even a lawsuit increases dramatically.

This reality is historically, by the way, largely a problem only in the American evangelical world. Go to most other places in the world and you will find a vibrant partnership between the Christian school and the evangelical church. Indeed, even here in the U.S. that same kind of partnership has existed in both the Roman Catholic Church and many churches from the Reformed tradition. By and large it has only been the free churches in the U.S., most often located within the evangelical tradition, who have disconnected education and discipleship.

Education, as noted above, is not simply about reading, writing, and arithmetic. It is equally about the transformation of life. It has always been that way in every school system that ever existed throughout human history. What goes on in the local public school is not just an objective presentation of the facts of history, science, literature, and mathematics. It is, by any honest definition, discipleship for life. The question that every parent and every pastor must ask and answer is this: Who do we want discipling our children Monday through Friday during school hours? It is a question, however, that they seem reluctant to ask.

During the strategic planning process you will be asked to answer questions such as these: Who are we? What are we called to do? In any process I lead I will push very hard for you to think both biblically and practically as you answer those questions. Strategic planning at its best is not about business as usual. Rather, it forces you to carefully examine all of your assumptions, all of your foundational principles, all of your common practices. In so doing I believe that you will find a far deeper and broader overlap between the spheres we have too casually separated and labeled education and discipleship. When you clearly explain that overlap, you increase the probability of making a compelling case for a stronger partnership between church and school—a partnership that benefits both.

Show God's glory

Ask anyone from the Reformed tradition to tell you the chief purpose of man in the world and you are likely to hear this question and answer from the Westminster Shorter Catechism:

> Question 1: What is the chief end of man?
>
> Answer: The chief end of man is to glorify God and to enjoy him forever.

In fact, it's not just those from a Reformed background who use that language. Our praise songs are filled with admonitions to glorify God. Just what does it mean, however, to glorify God? How, in a very practical sense, can we actually bring glory to God? Ponder that for a moment. I suspect we could have a lively conversation around that phrase. This mustn't be, however, just a theoretical conversation. Fulfilling that obligation is, I believe, at the heart of what it means to be a follower of Jesus Christ.

My own thinking on this subject was challenged and changed many years ago while in a study of the Gospel of John. Consider these familiar words from the first chapter of that

Gospel: "The Word was made flesh and dwelt among us, (and we beheld his glory, the glory as of the only begotten of the Father,) full of grace and truth" (John 1:14, KJV). If you are like me, you'd probably want to know what John means by the word *glory* in that context. If he had said we beheld that Jesus was a certain height with dark hair and a full beard, we could easily grasp that. But he doesn't give us any kind of physical description. Rather he uses a word that most of us don't fully understand, but one that is clearly intended to communicate something significant.

John returns to this concept of glory in chapter 17 of his Gospel, in which he records the prayer that Jesus prayed in the garden of Gethsemane the night before His crucifixion. Pay careful attention to what Jesus says: "I glorified you on earth, having accomplished the work that you gave me to do" (John 17:4).

Here Jesus tells us that He did something very important during His ministry on earth: He glorified His Father. In his commentary on John, James Montgomery Boice gives us some insight into this language and why it matters so much. He writes, "What does the phrase 'the glory of God' mean anyhow?... in this association the glory of God was obviously linked to God's attributes.... In this formulation God's glory consists in His intrinsic worth or character ... all that can be known of God is an expression of it" (1983, 69). Therefore, when the disciples beheld His glory it means that the disciples beheld His character, which was the character of God. It is one way of saying that if we have seen Jesus, we have seen the Father.

If we then as followers of Jesus Christ are to fulfill our responsibility to glorify God, we must do so by visibly manifesting the qualities of God before a watching world. As Jesus reminds us in Matthew 5:16, "Let your light shine before others, so that they may see your good works and give glory to your Father who is in heaven." Thus one way we can glorify God is by doing "good works."

Paul broadens that meaning a bit when he instructs the members of the church at Corinth with these words: "Whether you eat or drink, or whatever you do, do all to the glory of God" (1 Corinthians 10:31). In other words no matter how humble the task, you can do it in such a way that it brings glory to God. You can do it in such a way that people "see" God in your actions. To glorify God, therefore, is to do anything in such a way that your deeds provide an accurate reflection of the nature and character of God.

For example, God is love. Therefore, anytime I demonstrate God's love to another person I am showing God's glory. God is compassionate. Therefore, anytime I act with compassion toward a person in need I am showing God's glory. Give a cup of cold water in the name of Christ and you bring Him glory. Extend forgiveness to someone and you show God's glory to that person.

God is love. God is compassion. God is forgiveness. He is all of those things, but His nature extends far beyond those qualities. He is also remarkably creative, as even a cursory glance at the world around us reveals. Thus when we act creatively we show God's glory to the world. Yes, as a result of the Fall, creativity can be used to bad ends, but using our God-given gifts in creating beautiful music like Bach did (as John Elliott Gardiner observes in his book *Bach: Music in the Castle of Heaven*) is showing God's glory as much as if we were sharing the gospel in words.

Listen to how Gardiner describes how Bach viewed his music: "[Bach] saw both the essence and practice of music as religious and understood that the more perfectly a composition is realized both conceptually and through performance, the more God is immanent in the music" (Gardner 2013). Spend time listening carefully to a Bach cantata and you'll grasp what Gardiner is saying and what Bach was trying to communicate. The same is true of your school. The more perfectly a Christian school realizes its mission, the more God is immanent in that mission.

At the risk of running afield a bit, permit me an observation about how our failure to understand this crucial theological truth can negatively affect our efforts in making disciples. Think of how often we speak to our students of God as Creator, of God as the designer of the universe, of God as great and good. Think of the powerful and positive images we hope to inculcate in the minds of our students. Now ask yourself this question: What do they see of God's creativity, of His majesty, of His goodness in the facilities that house your school, in the teaching skill of their teachers, in the personal interaction among faculty, staff, students, and parents? I wonder about the impact that consistent inconsistencies in those arenas have on our students. If you don't you should, because I suspect they have a huge impact on how our students view God.

In his book *The Evidential Power of Beauty*, Thomas Dubay (2009, 1) makes this thought-provoking observation: "Every human person is drawn to beauty.... But few of us seem to be aware that the beautiful packs a power not only to fascinate but also to convince a mature and honest mind of solidly grounded truth." Ponder on that a bit as you walk about your campus and visit your classrooms.

Now consider another aspect of God's nature: He is strategic in everything He does. Nothing He does is done haphazardly, nothing is done reactively, nothing is sloppy, nothing is off-the-cuff. God was not caught by surprise when Adam and Eve chose to pursue their own interests rather than the instructions of their Creator. The Flood was not simply a matter of pique. The Exodus was not God suddenly awakening to the plight of the Israelites after a long period of slumber. Nor was the Incarnation a spur-of-the-moment decision. As the apostle Paul instructs us, "But when the fullness of time had come, God sent forth his Son, born of woman, born under the law" (Galatians 4:4).

Paul's usage of the Greek word for *time* in this text speaks not of a simple moment in time but of an epoch-making event. The Incarnation was an event to which God literally directed all of history. The birth of Christ was not only a historic event but a strategic one as well.

If we are to represent our Creator well, which is what we must do to show His glory, then we must learn to act creatively as well as compassionately, strategically as well as justly. In so doing we increase the probability that we will do what we are called to do not only with love but with excellence as well. In doing both we more fully show God's glory.

I'd like to pose one final question at this point. So what? So what if we don't engage in strategic planning? Does that mean we can't pursue our purpose and fulfill our mission? To answer that question let me pose another. How badly do you want your kids to see Christ in you—to see a full, robust, truly biblical image of Christ in you? Or are you satisfied with having them catch a vision of Christ that is frail, flawed, and flimsy? I am convinced that one of the things that drive kids from faith is the one-dimensional representation of Christ they too often see on a daily basis while attending school. I believe it leads them to conclude that Jesus is a good guy but kind of out of touch with the realities of life in this high-tech, culturally diverse world we inhabit. Don't believe me? Ask your kids this question: Who's the smartest person in the room—the person to whom you go to first for answers to your most perplexing questions? I'd be curious at their responses.

Not a Magic Bullet

There are lots of problems that planning alone can't solve. Some schools are so broken that any attempt at a legitimate strategic planning process would do more harm than good. It would be like the person who is 150 pounds overweight and decides to suddenly take up jogging. A heart attack, not weight loss, is the most likely outcome of that decision. There are even times when I have suggested to a school board that the best possible course of action would be to close the school.

Most schools, however, can derive great benefit from a well-designed, effectively led strategic planning process. The starting place for any process, however, is recognition of the why behind the what. Get that right and you'll find yourself more willing to make the kind of investment of time, energy, and resources essential to any strategic planning effort. With the why in place, it's time to move on to the what. What is this thing called strategic planning? That is what we will explore in our next chapter.

2

What Is Strategic Planning?

Years ago I was asked to consider accepting the call to pastor the church that sponsored the Christian school where I served as head. I was reluctant to do so for a number reasons, one of which was the reality that at the time I was a full-time head of school, a doctoral student at the University of Delaware, and oh, by the way, a husband and father. There were then, as now, only twenty-four hours in a day, and I couldn't see having enough time in any given day to fulfill all of those responsibilities responsibly.

A second concern was what I knew was a potential cause for conflict over ministry philosophy. I saw the role of the church in the world and the means for fulfilling that role in a very different way than some of the key deacons in our church. The pastoral search team was persistent, though, and after much prayer and discussion with my wife I decided to accept the call—with one proviso. Before the congregation would vote to issue a call I wanted permission to preach a series of sermons in which I would outline my ministry philosophy. If the church body was in accord, I told the search committee and the deacons, then I would accept the call.

So, I preached my series, outlining in as clear terms as I thought possible my philosophy of ministry, and at the end of that series the church members voted to call me as pastor. All went well for about eighteen months or so—I think they call it the "honeymoon." Then things began to unravel. During one brief period of about a month or so we lost a large number of long-time members. Not only did attendance decline, but giving as well. As I suspected, many of those defections were a response to what some perceived as the wrongheaded direction in which I was leading the church.

During one particularly tense deacon's meeting, one of the long-time leaders in the church launched into an attack on my leadership, really into the direction of my leadership. In frustration I responded to a rather stinging rebuke with these words: "I don't understand why everyone is so angry. I clearly told everyone what I thought we as a church ought to be doing before you called me as pastor. All I'm doing is what I said I would do. Why are you so angry?" I'll never forget the response. "Alan, that's not what we thought you meant when you talked about discipleship."

As I look back on those days I would have to confess that my leadership tended to be a bit autocratic and that I didn't always respond to differing opinions in a gracious manner (hence, by the way, my continuing fascination with leadership and planning). I did, however, learn a huge lesson. Conflict is often the inevitable result of misunderstanding. Until there is clarity—a concept to which we will repeatedly return—about what we mean by what we say, there is always a high degree of probability that there will be confusion and conflict.

Here's a little exercise to illustrate my point. Use the word *fast* in as many different ways as you can. I suspect you might be surprised at the number of options you will discover. For example you could write, "I've decided to go on a fast." Or you might say, "The glue held the paper fast to the wall." Then again, you might talk about how fast you used to be able to run the 100-yard dash. Same word, very different meanings. That is a key reason why it always makes sense to clarify what you mean by a particular word or a phrase.

Strategic planning is one of those phrases that have been used in so many ways that the meaning has become obscured and frequently misunderstood. My goal in this chapter is, therefore, to define strategic planning in a very specific way. I suspect that there will be those who will disagree with part or all of my definition, and that's OK. After reading dozens of books on the topic I have concluded that there is no standard description with which everyone will agree. There are, however, common elements in all of those definitions that I will try to incorporate into my description of strategic planning.

What It's Not

Let me begin by explaining what strategic planning is not. First of all, it is not what I call situational planning. Situational planning is what you must do when an unexpected crisis occurs. It is by its nature reactive. For example, it's what you do in response to a sudden, unanticipated decline in enrollment or to the unexpected resignation of a beloved faculty member or to bad press arising from the moral failure of a faculty member. None of us can anticipate every possible event. Sometimes we are simply caught unaware and must respond wisely. This is when situational planning is needed.

As in any other decision-making context, situational planning requires that you seek clarity by asking good questions. Philip Mudd in his fascinating book *The Head Game* (2015) provides these examples:
• What is the problem?
• What are your "drivers"—the important characteristics that define your problem?
• How will you measure performance?
• What about the data collected in relation to the defined problem?
• Are you missing any important information? (Schermer 2015)

To those questions I would add the following:
• What do we know about how we got to this situation?
• What can we learn from what has happened?
• Were any of our core values violated along the way?

The purpose of situational planning is not to attribute blame. Rather it is to solve the immediate problem and to do so in a way that helps you avoid facing the same problem at a later time.

Only God is omniscient, so we will never fully eliminate the need for situational planning. I do believe, however, that strategic planning done well will reduce the times that we are caught off-guard or unprepared. As Solomon reminds us, we can avoid nasty surprises if we just do a little proactive planning. Read carefully these words: "The prudent sees danger and hides himself, but the simple go on and suffer for it" (Proverbs 27:12).

Another concept that has gained popularity over the last few years is the practice of scenario planning. In a scenario planning process you take a look at what you are doing and ask, What if? What if we did this instead of that? What if we did it this way instead of that way? What if we started this program and eliminated that program? The number of inquiries you could make are nearly endless. The idea is to continually assess what you are doing and look to enhance your efforts. It is a great exercise for that purpose.

Many proponents of scenario planning would argue that the world is moving too fast to take the time for strategic planning. Things change with such speed that anything so cumbersome as strategic planning is a waste of time. Scenario planning, they would argue, allows an organization to make tough decisions in a more timely fashion, and that in turn allows the organization to act more nimbly in times of rapid change.

There is more than a kernel of truth in that observation. Organizations do need to stay nimble and, as we will see, must be able to adjust to frequently changing realities. I suspect that much of the negative feeling about strategic planning, however, flows from a misconception that strategic planning is just another name for what we used to call long-range planning. Strategic planning certainly begins with a sense that the horizon for any organization is a bit further out than the next quarter. It also acknowledges, however, that a five-to-ten-year horizon is probably too distant, recognizing the difficulty any organization encounters when trying to maintain long-term continuity in the face of continually shifting priorities. Strategic planning done well provides, I believe, the right balance between nimble action and the hedgehog concept Jim Collins discusses in his book *Good to Great* (2001).

I believe that organizations benefit from both scenario planning and strategic planning. Leadership teams need to go away frequently to ask the what-if question. But they also need to step away periodically to ask the fundamental questions that are posed during a sound strategic planning process. Those questions probe more deeply and explore more widely than simply asking, What if? They will be questions that go to the heart and core of what an organization claims to be and what it believes it must do well to fulfill its reason for being.

With that as background, let's begin to explore the concept called strategic planning.

It's the Process, Not the Plan

I confess I am a fan of the Star Trek series. I've always loved science fiction, and the thought of hurtling through space in search of exotic places and thrilling adventures has always appealed to me. I think that is why the opening words of the original Star Trek series so captured my imagination: "Space, the final frontier. These are the voyages of the starship *Enterprise*. Its five-year mission: to explore strange new worlds, to seek out new life and new civilizations, to boldly go where no man has gone before."

In one sense that is your mission. You are searching for a place you've never been, for a future that is different from, and hopefully better than, your present. You are on a journey to discover what can be.

For many years I would explain to people that strategic planning is akin to building a bridge from your current reality to your preferred future. Over time I have come to realize that the bridge building illustration is too static. Strategic planning is certainly about moving from your current reality to a preferred future. Your preferred future, however, is never—or at least I believe it should never be—a final, fixed place.

I now encourage people to think of strategic planning more as a journey. You do start from a fixed place, but there is no final, single, set destination. Rather there are a series of goals you will need to achieve as you continually move toward your ultimate objective of "better becoming what God has called you to be." In that sense the strategic planning process is a bit like sanctification in the life of the believer. Achieving spiritual maturity is a lifelong journey, not a static moment in time. You, me, all of us are constantly being formed more fully into the image of Christ (Ephesians 4:10–17).

That is why I so resonate with the phrase "the process is the plan." I first heard that phrase years ago when serving as the provost at The Master's College. We had asked Dr. Bruce Lockerbie to assist us in development of a new strategic plan. I had led earlier planning efforts at TMC, and I believed that we needed to add a bit of objectivity to this new round of planning. Thus a decision was made to engage Dr. Lockerbie to serve as the facilitator for our planning efforts.

It was during the first meeting with our task force that I heard Dr. Lockerbie declare, "The process is the plan." Actually it was not a completely new concept to me, but it is one I have come to more fully appreciate over the last few years. David Brooks, in his wonderful new book *The Road to Character*, gives us some insight into this idea of planning as process from the life of Dwight Eisenhower. Brooks tells us that a key to Eisenhower's success was his fanatical commitment to "preparation and then adaptation" (2015, 63). Of planning Eisenhower often would say, "The plans are nothing, but the planning is everything." This echoes language from Jim Collins' best-seller *Good to Great*: "Plans are useless but planning is priceless" (2001, 123).

Now I don't fully agree with the sentiment that plans are useless. Quality plans are hugely helpful. We all know, however, that conditions on the ground are going to change—sometimes dramatically—and those changing conditions will impact our ability to deliver even the most carefully constructed plans. That is why Eisenhower's choice of the words "preparation" and "adaptation" are so critical. As we continue through this book it will be my goal to emphasize both practices. Here is the key, however: You can't adapt a plan that you have not created; nor can you successfully adapt a plan that has been created with a static mind-set in place. True strategic planning is always dynamic in nature, meaning it is more a way of thinking and behaving than it is a project to be completed.

Perhaps that is why I identify with the following definition of strategic planning: "Planning is not an event. It is a continuous process of strengthening what works and abandoning what does not, of making risk-taking decisions with the greatest knowledge of their potential effect, of setting objectives, appraising performance and results through systematic feedback, and making ongoing adjustments as conditions change" (Drucker 2008, 4).

Every phrase in that definition is carefully chosen by Drucker to assist his readers in discovering a new way of thinking about planning. Here are some of my thoughts:

1. Planning is not a singular event; thus, don't think that a weekend away with your leadership team or your board constitutes strategic planning. It takes much more time than a two-day retreat to develop a sound strategic plan.

2. Because it is a continuous process, you have not completed strategic planning once you have created a strategic planning document. That document becomes a plan of action that helps focus your efforts and use of resources, but—as has already been noted—changes are likely to be made along the way.

3. Strategic planning does not begin by asking what needs to be fixed; rather, it begins by asking what we already do well. Too many organizations spend too much time, money, and energy trying to fix what's broken while failing to make appropriate investment in what they already do well. Don't ignore your weaknesses, but always focus on your strengths.

4. Strategic planning cannot eliminate all risk, but it can reduce risk through quality research that asks probing questions about what is, what we already know, what we don't know, and what we must learn if we are to make wise decisions.

5. And finally, while strategic planning is about identifying and implementing important initiatives, it is also about ensuring that those initiatives actually accomplish desired goals. Thus every action plan must have a built-in means for evaluating progress and performance.

In the following chapters it will be my goal to help you understand how to bring Drucker's concepts to life in your school or organization. There is another key concept, however, that we must explore at the outset.

Strategic Planning Is a Process of Discovery

Yes, strategic planning is a process, but it is not a process during which your goal is to create a new vision for your school. Rather it must be a process during which you discover the vision God already has for your school. If you are to do this, however, you must begin with this presupposition: God is the author of vision—not us.

This truth is made clear in countless texts of Scripture. Consider just a few.
- "Come now, you who say, 'Today or tomorrow we will go into such and such a town and spend a year there and trade and make a profit—yet you do not know what tomorrow will bring. What is your life? For you are a mist that appears for a little time and then vanishes. Instead you ought to say, 'If the Lord wills, we will live and do this or that.' As it is, you boast in your arrogance. All such boasting is evil" (James 4:13–16).
- "Do not boast about tomorrow, for you do not know what a day may bring" (Proverbs 27:1).
- "The heart of man plans his way, but the Lord establishes his path" (Proverbs 16:9).

What do all of those passages have in common? In each we are reminded that we are utterly dependent on God. This is a truth that properly understood should produce in all of us a sense of humility. Leaders matter, but God matters more. Nothing we hope to accomplish will be possible apart from God's sovereign grace. As Solomon reminds us, "The king's heart is a stream of water in the hand of the Lord; he turns it wherever he will" (Proverbs 21:1).

What is equally apparent in each of these passages is that planning is a good thing. The Scriptures never condemn planning. Indeed we are repeatedly encouraged to make wise plans. Consider the following:
- "In everything the prudent acts with knowledge" (Proverbs 13:16).
- "The simple believes everything but the prudent gives thoughts to his steps" (Proverbs 14:15).
- "Without counsel plans fail but with many advisors they succeed (Proverbs 15:22).
- "By wisdom a house is built, and by understanding a house is established" (Proverbs 24:3).

The problem is not the act of planning. The problem is hubris: the assumption that it is our wisdom, our actions, our efforts alone that create success. And frankly, if you are good at planning and implementation and good at mobilizing people, it is likely that you will experience success—for a while. Continuing success in fulfilling a God-given call, however, requires more. It requires acknowledgement that there are always factors beyond our control that will impact our efforts at building a strong school or organization, that those factors don't arise from random chance but through divine purpose, and that we are always dependent on God's grace no matter how clever our plans or how effective our efforts.

Thus I believe that it is not a leader's job to *create* a vision for the organization he or she leads. Rather it is the duty of a leader, and his or her team, to *discover* the future God has already designed for the organization and then to *align* all of the organization's efforts to that end. Much harm has been done in the pursuit of human-created vision. Whenever I hear someone say, "God has given me a vision for this ministry," I fear for the future of that organization.

That is not to say that leaders don't have a huge role to play in developing and shaping the plans that will be a guide into the future. In fact, I believe that vision first takes root in the heart of a leader. I believe that for two simple reasons. First, as I have already noted, I believe that God works through leaders and that He raises up leaders to be catalysts through which organizations can fulfill their calling. Second, I believe that leaders simply spend more hours in any given day or week thinking about the organization they have been called to lead.

If leaders are doing their job as they should, they are constantly asking the "what if" questions that underlie scenario planning while continually reading and researching and asking the "how can we get better at this" questions. More importantly, they are also praying and pondering and pursuing the mind of God. I don't know if *consumed* is the right word to describe a leader, but I would say that any leader worth that title is deeply engaged in not only the day-to-day operations of the organization they lead but, like Bilbo Baggins (see chapter 1 of this book), understand the importance of climbing the tree and looking to the horizon.

What leaders must avoid, however, is the impulse to believe that their ideas about next steps for an organization are, without question, God's ideas about those next steps. A sense of genuine humility and a spirit of grace are essential if the leader is to avoid pushing an agenda that may have many good points but may contain destructive ideas as well.

David Brooks illustrates that kind of humble leadership from the life of Dwight Eisenhower. He writes, "Eisenhower learned to master procedure, process, teamwork, and organization. He learned the secrets of thriving within an organization. 'When I got to a new station I would look to see who is the strongest and ablest man on the post. I forget my own ideas and do everything in my power to promote what he says is right…. Always try to associate yourself closely and learn as much as you can from those who know more than you, who do better than you, who can see more clearly than you'" (Brooks 2015, 63). The leaders who can't believe that anyone knows more than they do, or that there is no one who can do better or see more clearly than they, invariably lead their organizations into a ditch—or worse, over the edge of a precipice.

It is generally true that leaders do spend far more time thinking about the organizations they lead than anyone else. As head of school I was constantly thinking about the future, about what would make us a better school, about what we needed most to do. Early on, however, my thinking was not as disciplined as it needed to be and was often unrestrained by reality. Strategic planning adds a necessary dose of both discipline and reality to how we think about what makes the most sense for our school or organization at any point in time. More importantly, as we will see in chapter 6, it provides appropriate restraint to those who would claim to be the authoritative voice of God about the future of the school.

A compelling vision for "what could be" is essential for an organization. To remain mired in the mundane realities of the moment is a formula for continued mediocrity. That vision, however, must be discovered, not dictated. The strategic planning process when done properly will help avoid the tendency of strong leaders to simply decree the future.

It Is a Process During Which You Will Be Asked to Answer Key Questions

Strategic planning as a process is not really all that difficult. It does not require a superior intellect or some kind of special insight. What it does require is a willingness to engage in hard work, the discipline to stay on task when inevitable distractions arise, the humility and grace we have already noted, a high degree of objectivity (which can be hard to achieve without the help of a qualified, experienced facilitator), and a willingness to ask and answer a lot of tough questions about yourself and your current context. An important goal of any strategic planning process, therefore, is to keep asking questions until, as Peter Drucker observed, you are able to make "risk-taking decisions with the greatest knowledge of their potential effect" (Drucker 2008, 5).

From the 30,000-foot, big-picture perspective there are six questions that I always use during the planning process. These are big-category questions that provide a helpful structure for the planning process. Within each of these categories there are numerous other questions that will be posed, with the goal of creating clarity about what is most important and what will bring focus to all of your efforts. In part 2 of this book we will explore together how best to answer each of these questions. At that time we will dig deeply while focusing specifically. My goal at this time is simply to identify those big-category questions and give a brief explanation of each.

Question 1: Are we ready?

While strategic planning doesn't require superior intellect, it does require a certain level of organizational health. Schools that exhibit signs of long-term financial instability, poor staff morale, or significant staff turnover should address those problems prior to choosing to engage in any strategic planning efforts.

Strategic planning, done right, requires strenuous effort on the part of the entire staff and will shed light on every aspect of the school. If there are systemic problems in the school they will be exposed, and they can often derail planning efforts early in the process. Therefore, I highly recommend that schools engage in some kind of self-examination prior to engaging in a strategic planning process. In chapter 5 we will explore this topic.

Question 2: Who should be on our team?

Planning is a team effort. As Solomon reminds us, "Plans are established by counsel" (Proverbs 20:18). No one in recent years has said it better than Jim Collins: "If you have the right people, with the right character, they will do everything within their power to build a great organization because they simply cannot imagine settling for anything less" (2001, 41). Identifying and recruiting those exceptional people will be one of the most important tasks a school must undertake in preparation for the planning process.

At its heart, strategic planning is a process that unleashes the efforts of exceptional people in fulfillment of a crucial task that is directed toward this common purpose: that you better become what God has called you to be. This is important. Your strategic planning process will only be as effective and successful as the people who are on your strategic planning task force. That's why we're going to spend all of chapter 6 focusing on one thing: how to choose your task force. Without the right people, your efforts will be wasted.

Question 3: What is nonnegotiable?

With a quality team in place, the first task you must undertake is deciding what must never change about your school. By its nature a strategic planning process will push you toward making many changes at your school. What it must not do is push you off course. This is an opportunity for you to confirm what is essential, what is crucial, what truly defines who you are, and what you hope to accomplish. Those are your nonnegotiables. That is the theme of chapter 7. To get at what is nonnegotiable I use the following questions:

• Why do you exist? *Your purpose.*
• What are you going to do in response to your purpose? *Your mission.*
• How will you behave as you seek to fulfill your mission? *Your values.*
• What are your foundational beliefs (both biblical and philosophical)?
• Are you committed to excellence?
• Who is your customer? Whom has God called you to serve?
• What are you committed to accomplish in the lives you are called to serve?

Many schools already have detailed mission statements. So I'm often asked, Do we really need to reengage these questions? The answer I give is always the same. Yes, you must, for three reasons.

1. Words tend to lose their meaning over time. If nothing else, this activity will force your leadership team and task force to clarify and recommit to what you believe is most important.

2. Though it is hard for leaders to admit to this reality, many if not most people affiliated with your school couldn't tell you the mission of the school, much less identify the core values that you believe should characterize your school, even if their lives depended on it. This is an opportunity to ensure a better understanding of, and support for, those key aspects of your school.

3. This part of the process will force you to not only clarify what is nonnegotiable at your school, but it will also force you to examine the extent to which those nonnegotiables actually align with your everyday practice. Without alignment of purpose and practice, your school can never achieve true integrity. And as we will see, without integrity you can never attain what you hope to achieve.

Question 4: What is your current reality?

As Jim Collins observes, "Yes, leadership is about vision. But leadership is equally about creating a climate where the truth can be heard and the brutal facts confronted. There's a huge difference between the opportunity to 'have your say' and the opportunity to be heard. The good-to-great leaders understood this distinction, creating a culture wherein people had a tremendous opportunity to be heard and, ultimately, for the truth to be heard" (2001, 74).

Facts, as someone once observed, are stubborn things. What if major employers in your community just cease operations? Or what if the demographics in your area begin to skew toward people of retirement age and your enrollment begins to decline? No amount of marketing is likely to alter those realities. If the average household income of the families in your school is below national averages, it is going to be difficult to increase your tuition 30 percent no matter what you decide in your strategic planning process. If your faculty and staff turnover is consistently high based on national norms, then deciding to build a new classroom building is probably not the wisest course of action. You just can't pretend that real problems don't exist. Unless and until you are willing to "tackle the tyrant" (Eppler 2003)—a phrase we will explore at length in chapter 8—it is probably best for you and your school to avoid a genuine strategic planning process.

It takes courage and a high degree of objectivity to face reality. That is hard to do on your own. The forces pushing back against your efforts can be powerful. That is why I encourage schools to consider employing the services of a capable, experienced consultant to help lead your planning process. That person will see what is hard for you to see (or to admit even if you see), will ask the tough questions you will be reluctant to ask yourself, will force you to fully answer those questions, and will hold you accountable for what you have agreed to do. An objective viewpoint is invaluable.

Question 5: What is most important right now?

This is the vision question. Remember, however, that vision is not simply about more, about bigger, about greater. It is about doing what you are called by God to do with ever-increasing excellence to ever-growing impact in the lives of those you are called to serve.

To that end, during the planning process you must do the following:
• Prioritize from among all of the options that will surface during this process.
• Avoid the temptation to focus first on solving for your weaknesses.
• Resolve instead to focus on current strengths, gifts, and passions.
• Identify which of all your choices are likely to have the greatest level of impact, for the greatest number of people, for the least amount of money, over the shortest period of time.
• Establish whether there is anything that would prove costly down the road if you don't address it now.

Doing the above is harder than you might think. There will likely be as many opinions and priorities as there are people on your task force. A sound strategic planning process will, therefore, include tools for helping people set aside those personal agendas in pursuit of God's vision for the school. In chapter 9 we will explore ways to accomplish the goal of deciding what is most important right now.

Question 6: How will we achieve our goals?

I love this quote: "In the end, a vision without the ability to execute is probably a hallucination" (Case n.d.). That quote reminds me of the lyrics from an old 1960s song by Dusty Springfield. (I'm sure all of my younger readers will remember it well!) It goes something like this: "Wishing and hoping and hoping and dreaming." That pretty well sums up the planning and implementation strategy employed by too many schools and organizations. As another well-known saying goes, "Wishing won't make it so."

To implement any plan, you must develop a thoughtful, realistic plan that takes into account these issues:
• Who is responsible?
• What will it actually cost, and how will it impact financial realities at our school?
• What is our timeline?
• What impact will this plan have on our current resources?

- What impact will this plan have on our current staffing?
- What impact will this plan have on our current facilities?

Implementation will also require focus, hard work, frequent meetings to check on progress, a flexible spirit, and most of all a willingness to be transparent and accountable. Nothing happens without intentional effort—nothing. A well-designed implementation plan will provide the road map. You will have to provide the intentional effort. You will also need to develop a strategic financial plan. Much more on that in chapter 10.

Other Questions

If you are a wise person, you are struggling with another question about now. You will want to know the scope and sequence of this process. And if you are the head of school or a member of the school board, you will want to know just how this process is going to impact your life. So, let me answer those questions.

Remember: the process is the plan. Strategic planning is not the work of a weekend, a week, or a month. In my experience a fully mature process will require about six months to complete.

If Anything Can Go Wrong ...

A final "let's get real here" thought. Strategic planning—even when done well by competent, committed people—is inevitably a messy, messy process. Murphy (as in Murphy's Law) has a point; if anything can go wrong, it will go wrong—and at the worst possible time. We live in a fallen world, with all of the consequences that truth implies. No matter how many you pull, those weeds keep coming back; despite our best efforts, the car refuses to run; and the order you placed for those new computers, the ones you needed yesterday, are once again on back order. Fallenness is not an excuse for lazy thinking, poor preparation, or failure to follow through. But it is naïve to think that unexpected problems won't arise—and as Murphy reminds us, at the worst possible time.

Because this is so, success in strategic planning will require enormous resources of patience, incredible flexibility, and the ability (as one of my early mentors taught me) "to maintain the inner calm." Getting angry, expressing frustration, and berating staff are all counterproductive to the goal of better becoming what God has called you to be.

I want you to jump into this process with enthusiasm, understanding, and—perhaps most of all—with a calm awareness that all will not remain calm. If you can adopt and maintain those qualities, you can succeed at this thing called strategic planning.

I have tried my best to help you understand the why and the what of strategic planning. Before we jump into the how, I want to identify and describe some of the rules of the road that should shape the what and the how of strategic planning. That is my goal for chapters 3 and 4.

Rules for the Road, I

Several years ago I had the opportunity to visit Jakarta, Indonesia. I don't know if you have ever been to Jakarta or Mexico City or São Paulo or Tokyo or any other large international city. If so, you'll likely smile as I tell you this story. Jakarta is one of the most frightening places in the world to drive, or ride in, a car. I remember on one occasion we were inching along in the middle of six lanes of traffic and (I'm not making this up) I looked out of my window to see right next to our car an entire family—mom, dad, and two kids—all on a single motorbike. It was an astonishing but, as I looked around, common situation.

At the time good friends of mine, Gary and Paula Miller, were living just outside Jakarta. Gary was serving as chancellor of the largest Christian university in Indonesia and had invited me to spend a few days with him and Paula. On our way from Jakarta to his home, as I was remarking about the traffic, he told me a story designed, I think, to create even more tension than I was already feeling. He related how during one trip into Jakarta he had observed a rather bad accident involving several cars and a number of injuries. Traffic stopped completely and was likely to remain so for a long time. Gary could see no way that police or emergency vehicles would be able get anywhere near the site. As he was wondering what would happen next and how long he would be sitting there in traffic, people jumped out of their cars, removed the injured, carried them to the side of the road, and then moved the cars to the median. The people got back into their cars, and traffic began move again. Gary had just witnessed one of the "rules for the road" in Jakarta.

No matter where you live, no matter the size of your city, there are rules for the road—rules that govern how you, and hopefully everyone else, will behave behind the wheel of a car. There are stop signs, red lights, speed limits, signs to direct you on and off the freeway, and white lines down the middle of the road to keep drivers in their respective lanes. Without those rules you would have chaos—or worse, carnage. The same is true when you engage in a strategic planning process. Without appropriate rules for the road it will be difficult to achieve anything of lasting value, and there is increased likelihood of chaos and carnage of a different kind that can derail your planning efforts. In the next two chapters it is my goal to identify some of those rules of the road and provide enough detail to keep the planning process moving along in a positive direction and timely fashion.

Through Three Lenses

In this chapter we are going to explore some biblical principles that I believe absolutely must shape your process. Then in subsequent chapters we are going to take a look at some proven practices culled from a variety of sources. In so doing my primary goal is to engage in a bit of what we call biblical integration. To help us achieve that goal I am going to continually look at the planning process through three distinct lenses: the lens of history, the lens of culture, and the lens of Scripture. My intent in pulling together all three threads is to create a sound, thoroughly biblical, and eminently practical approach to strategic planning.

The lens of history is a reference to our own personal history, to our school's history, and to history in general. For example, all of us have participated in planning efforts. As a consequence, all of us have experiences that now impact how we view any planning effort. If you've had a bad planning experience, it will most certainly shape your thinking about current planning efforts in a less-than-ideal way. Likewise, if you have had a positive encounter with planning efforts, that experience will influence you as well. We simply cannot ignore events from the past— affirmative or harmful—nor should we. In either case, positive or negative, our past experiences will inevitably shape our current behavior.

Equally influential are current cultural ideals and practices. So powerful an influence is culture that Paul warns us to avoid being crushed into the mold of the world (Romans 12:1–2). So dominant is the influence of culture that we often just assume that everyone everywhere sees things the way we do. That kind of thinking is quickly challenged the minute we step outside of our own country. For example, how differently might we approach the strategic planning process here in the United States than would a school leader in South Korea? In America the idea of recruiting a broad cross-section of the school's constituency might not seem unusual at all. In

Korea's more hierarchical culture it might seem strange, even unwise. That is just one example of what we might discover when looking through the lens of culture. And by the way, each school has its own culture. I've been in schools where the only people who ever have any input into whatever is going to happen are the board members. So when I present my idea of strategic planning to them, I've got to take that cultural reality into account.

Finally, we have to look through the lens of Scripture. If I heard it once I heard it a thousand times growing up: the Scriptures are our final rule of faith and practice, our final authority. Sadly, at least in my opinion, it seems that we've lost a bit of that certainty. We have far more confidence in Jim Collins than we do in Nehemiah, for example. As we will see, however, God has given us "all things that pertain to life and godliness" (2 Peter 1:3). So we're going to look carefully at applicable biblical principles.

A Unique Hybrid

Before we jump into a discussion of the biblical principles that I believe must shape the planning process, I'd like to share a concept with you that I think will help us understand a bit better why the area of executive leadership (of which strategic planning is a part) can be such a challenge for Christian school leaders. I was discussing this situation with the strategic planning task force at Dayton Christian school a couple of years ago when the chair of the board, Dr. Geoff Goff, shared a diagram he had drawn while listening to me. It was an insightful illustration.

Education

Christian schools as organizations are indeed an interesting hybrid. A Christian school is an educational organization, a ministry organization, and a business. You cannot long survive, much less thrive, until you understand and embrace that reality.

Business   **Ministry**

I suspect most of us get the education part of that diagram—at least I hope we do. And most of us in Christian schooling understand the powerful ministry component of our schools. As to the business part of that equation, however, I think we enter into our task woefully unprepared. I'm in Christian schooling because of the ministry that had taken place in my life, and I was eager to give to my students what I had received. Prior to accepting my first leadership job, I had also earned a master's degree in administration and supervision. So I thought I had a pretty solid grasp of the educational component of my job. What I didn't know, however, was business. And worse, I didn't know that what I didn't know would have such a harmful impact on my leadership.

I didn't have a clue, for example, about marketing or resource development; I didn't really understand that either was necessary. I didn't know much about building a leadership team, creating a budget, or crafting a strategic plan. It was all a mystery. As a consequence I watched as our school began to slide into irrelevance. Fortunately, before all was lost, God in His grace provided exceptional opportunities—including my doctoral program at the University of Delaware and the insight of truly godly, capable men like Dr. Bruce Lockerbie—to set me on a journey of discovery: the discovery of what could be when we did the right things well.

Another valuable resource was the fascinating little book titled *Paradigms: The Business of Discovering the Future*, authored by Joel Barker. (I referred to this book in the preface.) Though written over 20 years ago, it still resonates today. If you have ever used or heard someone use the phrase "We've got to examine our paradigms," you can thank Joel Barker. He took the idea of paradigms out of the scientific world and introduced paradigms into the world of business. It was, at the time, a revolutionary thought. It certainly helped me understand how my personal history and culture had had such an impact on my thinking—and how paradigms could keep people locked into an unhealthy way of looking at the world around them and the role of their business, whatever that business might be. His insights gave me the encouragement I needed to change the way I thought about my responsibility as head of school.

In introducing me to the business of paradigms, Barker also helped me understand what was crucial to my school's success. It had been my passionate desire to offer an exceptional educational experience to our students, and to do so in a powerful spiritual context. One is not more important than the other. Indeed, I understood that a person truly in pursuit of God will not only hunger and thirst after righteousness, but will also seek God with the whole mind as well. Intellectual development is not a barrier to spiritual growth; rather, when done appropriately, it is an impetus to spiritual formation.

What I came to realize was the need to pursue excellence in business with fervor equal to my pursuit of academic and spiritual excellence. It is really this simple: without sufficient resources it is nearly impossible to provide a quality education. And furthermore, as Barker pointed out (1993, 11), it is difficult to achieve success as a business unless you are able to do three things well:

• Anticipate the future.
• Innovate in response to the changes you see coming in the future.
• Deliver everything you do with excellence.

So important are those three behaviors that Barker said they were the price of admission to the marketplace (1993, 111). Do all three well and you are likely to experience success. Do them poorly and you are likely to limp along, increasingly frustrated and ineffective. Given the importance of our mission and given our obligation to the One who has called us to that mission, it seems to me that we need to carefully consider all three of those elements as we ponder how best to deliver our mission. In the following chapters we will explore in detail what it takes to anticipate, innovate, and deliver our mission with excellence. At this time, however, I want to return to the primary purpose of this chapter—the biblical principles that must shape all our efforts.

Godliness in Working Clothes

The Old Testament Scriptures are arranged into five major thematic categories. The first five books are what we call the Pentateuch, the Law. In those books we have the early history of humankind and of the people of Israel. We are also provided with an extensive review of the laws that were meant to govern God's people in the land of promise. The second major section of the Old Testament is what is called the Histories. In this section, beginning with the book of Joshua and concluding with the book of Esther, we have the account of God's people from the time they arrived in the land of promise through their return from exile. It is in these books that we find accounts of people like Joshua, Gideon, Ruth, Samuel, David, Solomon, Esther, and Nehemiah. The final two sections contain what we call the Major and Minor Prophets. Those descriptors speak to the length of each book rather than to the nature or quality of the content. Every prophet had important messages to deliver to the people of God.

Set right in the middle of the Old Testament is a section we call the Wisdom Literature. These are the writings that help us make sense of life. The book of Job contains some of the deepest philosophical discourses you will find anywhere.

The book of Psalms helps us better understand the nature of God and the role of worship in our lives. Ecclesiastes is perhaps one of the most interesting sociological research studies ever undertaken. It is both bleak and hopeful in its assessment of life "under the sun." Song of Solomon helps us grasp the meaning of intimacy in a way few authors have ever been able to do. In the middle of all of this wisdom is that most practical of all books, Proverbs. In studying Proverbs we learn, as Derek Kidner observes, how to put "godliness into working clothes." Read carefully what Kidner has to say about the Proverbs. "... the book is largely concerned to show that the godly man is in the best sense a man of affairs, who takes the trouble to know his way about, and plan his course realistically" (1964, 37).

So as we consider biblical principles that should shape our thinking on and practice of strategic planning, many of them are going to come straight out of Proverbs. I am going to encourage you to listen carefully to what Solomon has to say to us about how we should decide what is best for the schools we lead. In the process I am confident that we are going to discover that what was true 3,000 years ago still has application to us today, because "There is nothing new under the sun" (Ecclesiastes 1:9). As we jump into this discussion I'd like us to begin with what I believe is the most critical of biblical principles: "Behold, how good and pleasant it is when brothers dwell in unity" (Psalm 133:1). Fail to understand this principle, and the planning process is likely to descend into a painful battle over competing priorities.

That They Be One

Here's our first challenge. It's been a challenge for humankind since the Fall. If there are two people in the room, there is inevitably the potential for conflict. This fact of life under the sun is revealed most powerfully in the Gospel accounts of events in the "upper room" where our Lord and His disciples had gathered to celebrate the Passover. To get a sense of what was most prominently on their minds as they made their way into the upper room, read Luke 22:24–30. It seemed that the focus of their conversation was on the question of who would sit at the right hand and who would sit at the left hand of Jesus when He ascended to the throne of David— something that the disciples thought He would do soon. It was a conversation focused on position and power, as so many of our conversations are today.

The response of our Lord to that contentious conversation was remarkable. As each of the disciples was finding a place at the table, jockeying for position, He found a basin of water that had been placed in the room so that a servant could use it to wash the dirt and grime from the feet of guests. A more unappetizing task can hardly be imagined. Upon locating the basin, Jesus girded Himself as would a servant and began, one by one, to wash the feet of His disciples. As He did so silence descended upon the room— the kind of uncomfortable silence we've all experienced when someone does something unexpected, embarrassing, or extraordinary. That silence remained unbroken until Jesus reached Peter, who declared quite authoritatively, "You shall never wash my feet" (John 13:8). *Always* and *never* are words to be used sparingly, but they communicated well what was in Peter's mind. Some who read that text might be tempted to cut Peter a break, suggesting that he simply didn't think it appropriate for Jesus, the master, to be washing the feet of a common disciple. And perhaps that was part of what influenced Peter to speak with such force. I suspect, however, that there was much more at work here. I suspect that Peter fully understood the implications of what Jesus was doing. I think Peter recognized the point Jesus was making about position and power. Here was servant leadership at its clearest.

Not much has changed in 2,000 years. Everybody wants to be in charge. Everyone wants to control the process so as to ensure a preferred outcome. My use of the words *everyone* and *everybody* is purposeful. We might use different strategies to push for our agendas, but it is utter foolishness to ignore the dynamics at work in typical planning or decision-making processes. It is crucial to remember, however, that in the strategic planning process we're not trying to create a vision. We're not trying to push an agenda. Rather, our goal is one of discovery. We want to discover God's vision—a singular vision—for our school.

I think the greatest barrier to our ability to reach the world with the gospel of Christ is our lack of unity. It destroys churches, it destroys schools, and it almost always begins with conflicting agendas. So when beginning a task as challenging as strategic planning, you've got to begin that process by committing to the biblical principles that need to shape that process. Let's begin to unpack some of those principles.

We Serve a Sovereign God ...

I suspect that if we were to poll all the readers of this book, we would find conflicting opinions about how God works His sovereign will in the world. I suspect, however, that most would agree with this simple idea: We must pray as if everything depended upon God, and we must work as if everything depended on us. Nowhere is that idea more beautifully illustrated than in the book of Nehemiah.

When we first encounter Nehemiah he is talking with his brother and some friends who had just returned to Babylon from a fact-finding trip to their ancestral home, Jerusalem. So devastating was the news that we are told Nehemiah "sat down and wept and mourned for days" (Nehemiah 1:4). It is in reading Nehemiah's prayer that we discover some of the hallmarks of great leadership.

First of all, Nehemiah accepted responsibility for the tragic situation in Jerusalem even though he personally had nothing to do with the downfall of the city. Leaders always accept responsibility for problems, even those they inherit—unlike so many in leadership today! How often do we hear a leader pointing at a predecessor while suggesting that the leader's current problems are the result of the other person's failures? While that may be accurate from a historical point of view, no true leader blames others for the problems the leader needs to solve. Second, before they plunge into the problem, true leaders take the time to pray and ponder. More on that later. Third, they take account of and employ all the resources at their disposal. Note that at the end of chapter 1 Nehemiah shared this thought with the reader: "Now I was cupbearer to the king" (1:11). Quite a resource, when you think about it for a moment.

Chapter 2 opens six months after the visit of Nehemiah's brother. Nehemiah had been pondering the situation, asking himself this question: What would I do given the opportunity to return to Jerusalem? Now the text doesn't explicitly tell us that fact, but it is an inference we can easily draw as we listen to the conversation unfold between Nehemiah and King Artaxerxes.

To understand what follows it is important to note that six-month passage of time because something unusual happened on the twentieth day of the month of Nisan. On that day as Nehemiah was engaged in serving the king, Artaxerxes suddenly turned and made an interesting observation: "Why is your face sad, seeing you are not sick? This is nothing but sadness of the heart" (2:2). What makes this observation and the timing of the observation so interesting to me is what the text tells us about his behavior in the presence of the king over the previous six months: "Now I had not been sad in his presence" (2:1). In other words Nehemiah had worked very hard at keeping his personal pain out of the workplace—great advice to all of us, and even greater advice for those working with someone whose displeasure with your performance could end with loss of a job or, as would have been true in this case, something far worse.

Now note the direction the conversation took. Nehemiah's first reaction may have been fear (he offered a silent prayer to God before answering). Speaking truth to power is always a difficult task. However, his answer to the king was brilliant and clearly demonstrated that he had been thinking on this issue for, well, six months.

He began by using an analogy that was culturally relevant and would most certainly have piqued the king's interest. The Persians worshiped their ancestors. To hear that the tombs of Nehemiah's forefathers had been desecrated would have immediately pricked the heart of the king. (Just a quick word on speaking to parents and donors: Don't ignore the heart. You will need to make a compelling, rational case for your cause, but you must first win the heart.)

With Nehemiah's words ringing in his heart and mind, the king then posed a remarkable, unexpected question: "What are you requesting?" To this question Nehemiah responded with a specific request: I want to return to rebuild the city of my fathers and oh, by the way, I need two very important things from you: resources and authority (2:4–8).

This is exactly the point at which God's sovereignty and Nehemiah's responsibility met. God did what only God could do: He opened the eyes and heart of the king. Nehemiah did what only he could do: he prayed, pondered, planned, and prepared to walk through the door that God would open. Manipulation of others—a temptation to all of us in pursuit of something worthwhile—always short-circuits God's work, and it always ends badly.

Knowing that God is sovereign should increase our trust that in the end, if we fulfill our obligation to pray, ponder, plan, and prepare, then God will fulfill His purposes through us. As you read the following familiar words, be encouraged that God is always at work as you continue to seek and serve Him: "Trust in the Lord with all your heart, and do not lean on your own understanding. In all your ways acknowledge him, and he will make straight your paths." (Proverbs 3:5–6)

... Who Has Spoken

Recently a prominent pastor who is known for some rather controversial beliefs was a guest on a talk show with Oprah Winfrey. During their conversation this pastor made an observation that went something like this: "The Bible was written thousands of years ago in the context of a culture quite different from ours in 21st-century America. To believe that we can take the Bible literally or live our lives according to such ancient principles is unwise." At one time those kinds of remarks would have created a tsunami of criticism. In this case, those comments created barely a ripple of response.

In his book *The Great Omission*, Dallas Willard (2009, 18–19) made an observation that should give us pause.

> A short while ago I led a faculty retreat for one of the better Christian colleges in the United States. In opening my presentation, I told the group that the important question to consider was what Jesus himself would say to them if he were the speaker at their retreat. I indicated my conviction that he would ask them this simple question: Why don't you respect me in your various fields of study and expertise? Why don't you recognize me as master of research and knowledge in your field?
>
> The response of these Christian professionals was interesting to observe, to say the least. Some thought the question would be entirely appropriate. Many were unsure of exactly what I was saying. Quite a number responded with, "Are you serious?" The idea that Jesus is master of fields such as algebra, economics, business administration, or French literature simply had not crossed their minds—and had a hard time finding access when presented to them.
>
> That brings out a profoundly significant fact. In our culture, and among Christians as well, Jesus Christ is automatically disassociated from brilliance or intellectual capacity. Not one in a thousand will spontaneously think of him in conjunction with words such as "well-informed," "brilliant," or "smart."

Perhaps you are tempted to think that way as well. After all, the world we inhabit does look much different than the world inhabited by Solomon 1,000 years before the birth of Christ, or the one in which the apostle Paul traveled and taught, or even the one in which your parents and mine lived. Is it really possible to believe that words written 2–3,000 years ago still make sense today?

The answer to that question depends, I believe, on what you believe true of God the Creator and of Christ our Savior. For me the answer is simple. If God is indeed sovereign, then He is the Master of time, able to see the beginning and the end and every point in between. Thus when God spoke He spoke in a transcultural and transhistorical way that is always applicable if we but take the time to think with care about the words we read in Scripture. Unfortunately there are far too many people, including far too many pastors, who are willing to concede that God has spoken but has done so in an unintelligible way. Certainly we need to approach the Scriptures with humility, care, and proven methods of interpretation. To suggest, for example, that God left us unable to provide wise counsel to people suffering painful personal problems until Sigmund Freud arrived on the scene is to ascribe to God qualities that reduce Him to the level of, say, the Wizard of Oz.

When the apostle Peter writes, for example, that God's "divine power has granted to us all things that pertain to life and godliness, through the knowledge of him who called us to his own glory and excellence" (2 Peter 1:3), he is not suggesting that God has given us a limited vision of what it means to live as a follower of Jesus Christ in the world. Instead he is reminding the Church that in knowing the mind of God we can see clearly the realities of the world.

When the author of Ecclesiastes draws our attention to the fact that "there is nothing new under the sun," he is not suggesting that there will be no technological innovations or increases in knowledge. Rather, he is surely sharing with us that people's behavior will always be consistent with their nature. I am hugely grateful for all of the insight I have gained by reading authors such as Jim Collins, Peter Drucker, Patrick Lencioni, and Harry Beckwith. If, however, I only had the book of Nehemiah to give me insight into how leaders ought to think and behave, I would be well served.

We must look through the lens of history. We must consider the lens of culture. All we see, however, must be viewed finally through the lens of Scripture.

... Who Made Us in His Image

In a book that made a profound impact on my thinking and life, *Being Human: The Nature of Spiritual Experience*, Ranald Macaulay and Jerram Barrs make this powerful observation: "The expression the image of God means simply 'made like God' ... To say this does not mean that man was completely like God. There were differences of course: man was a limited, a physical creature, male and female, who was totally dependent on the Creator not only for the origin of his existence, but also for its continuation. Nevertheless, though unlike God in important ways, man was like God.... Like God, we relate to everything personally—he is creative and so are we: we are given dominion over the earth—a dominion intended originally to be benign and so to reflect God's own dominion" (1998, 13–14).

The implications of that observation are significant—staggering, even. When God created humankind He placed within us the qualities and characteristics we associate with the Creator. God is love, and He placed within us the capacity for love and then calls us to love one another. God is grace, and He placed within us the capacity for grace and then calls us to extend grace to others. God is relational, and He placed within us the capacity for relationship and then gives us a living laboratory in which we can exhibit both love and grace in relationship.

God is also creative and strategic. The creation we inhabit gives testimony to God's creativity. Join me on a walk through any major airport in the world and we see evidence of God's endless creativity. Take a stroll in any national park or gaze into any microscope or telescope and be blown away by God's creative genius. God's creativity, however, is not just for show. It all has a purpose. God is neither arbitrary nor reactive. He is always purposeful, and as beings created in His image, called to reflect that image in an accurate, robust manner, we too must act in a manner that is both creative and strategic. To do otherwise as school leaders is not only to doom the schools we lead to continued mediocrity, but it is to distort the image of our Creator. Nothing we can do will have a more negative impact on our students than that.

... Who Gives Us Enormous Freedom

I took two courses in graduate school on education and the law. As a consequence I was required to do some research in a law library. Have you ever been in a law library? What you see are hundreds and hundreds of volumes containing case studies on tort law, constitutional law, family law, property law, and on and on and on. The legal system in our country is a morass of nearly indecipherable language and conflicting opinions about how the law must be applied in any given case. Perhaps that is all necessary to keep evil at bay in a fallen world. However, when the church (as did the Pharisees of Jesus' day) chooses to enslave itself to false ideas of holiness or flawed ideas of how best to do the work to which we have been called, we quickly find ourselves wandering in a wilderness from which there seems to be no exit.

When God redeems us, He restores us to our true purpose. In fulfilling that purpose we are to be about the business of managing His creation in a manner that best reflects His image to a watching world. To ensure that we are able to fulfill our purpose He gives us the capacity to think wisely—and by that I mean biblically—and to then execute with excellence all He has called us to do. And amazingly, He gives us wide latitude in how we go about doing all that we have been given to do.

Consider the task of teaching our students how to read. It's certainly a crucial task—so crucial in fact that we might expect to find a long discussion of the topic somewhere in Scripture. But of course we don't. To listen to advocates of various methods that can be employed to teach reading skills, however, you might be forgiven for believing that method A beats method B because it is how God intends for us to teach reading. For some, the gospel of phonics nearly rises to the level of the gospel of redemption.

Our task is to fulfill the duties given us by God. One of those responsibilities includes the education of our children. To fulfill that obligation we are free to utilize any methodology that does not violate a clear teaching of Scripture, does not violate a legitimate legal statute, does not violate any ethical standard, does not do direct harm to our students, or does not simply ignore quality research or effective practice. Beyond that we are absolutely free to pursue any methodology we believe will best accomplish our goal of teaching students to read.

We could use any number of other examples, but permit me to draw our attention to the task at hand: strategic planning. As I noted in chapter 2, there are dozens if not hundreds of books on the topic and literally thousands of articles in professional and popular journals. The advice on how to proceed is nearly endless. In one sense I guess I could be accused of simply adding to the confusion. Hopefully I'm creating a bit of clarity, but some might disagree. Of one thing I am certain: there is no single best way to proceed with planning efforts. And while I believe strongly that there are principles that must shape the process and practices that have proven effective over time, I must confess that there is no single way to approach the planning process. You are free to incorporate my ideas or to ignore them. That freedom is God's gift to us.

In another far more crucial context, the apostle Paul reveals to us an essential truth: "Let no one pass judgment on you in questions of food and drink, or with regard to a festival or a new moon or a Sabbath" (Colossians 2:16). That same principle applies here. I hope you will consider all I have to say in this book, but you are free to choose a different approach or pursue a different path. You are free.

... Who Exemplifies Exceptional Effort

I love the phrase God exclaims at the end of each day of creation: "It is good!" How often at the end of a day or at the conclusion of a project are we compelled to shout, "Wow, now that was good!"? You might argue, "But, Alan we are not God. Wouldn't it be a bit presumptuous to simply declare that something we have done is good?" Not really. We often stand at the end of a concert and clap wildly as a way of expressing our appreciation for something well done. We've all, at some time, been in the presence of excellence and felt compelled to respond to what we have seen, heard, or experienced. The shame is that such occurrences seem to be so rare.

Excellence of effort, however, should not be rare. Rather, because we are beings created in the image of God and called to express that image in the most common of events, excellence should become increasingly commonplace. I love how the apostle Paul puts it. Writing to the church in Corinth, he encourages the members there to insert the very nature of God into the most mundane of activities. "So," he writes, "whether you eat or drink, or whatever you do, do all to the glory of God" (1 Corinthians 10:31). He then concludes his thoughts with this simple phrase: "Be imitators of me, as I am of Christ" (1 Corinthians 11:1). That would be the same Christ who as the second Person of the Trinity was able to observe at the end of every day of creation, "It is good."

If we want our kids to believe what we say about God, then we've got to demonstrate those characteristics we want them to embrace and live out in their lives. Do you want your students to believe that God is the author of beauty? Then show them beauty. Do you want your students to believe that God does everything with excellence? Then do all you do with excellence. Do you want your students to think with discernment? Then let them see you thinking and acting with discernment. Like it or not, we are called to be imitators of Christ. And like it or not, our students are more likely to embrace what they see in us than what they hear from us.

... Who Promises His Continued Presence

I want to conclude this chapter with this observation. As I noted earlier, I'm sure that there is a wide variety of theological persuasions among those who will read this book. I grew up in an independent fundamental Baptist church. For many years I attended a Presbyterian church. Now I attend a Brethren church. I suspect some who will read this book come from a more charismatic theological background.

I discovered something, however, a few years ago that has had a profound impact on me when it comes to the strategic planning process—indeed, when it comes to all of life. As pastor, I started taking our leadership team away for periodic retreats. We would head out of town late on a Thursday afternoon and spend all of Friday and much of Saturday in prayer, study, and planning. I must confess that early on I approached the prayer part in a pretty perfunctory way. You know what I mean. We would open our time in prayer and then maybe spend a few minutes going around the table praying for this person or that situation.

Over time we started heading out twice a year. Once was a planning retreat; once was a study retreat. For one of our study retreats we decided to tackle the topic of worship. This was back in the late 80s or early 90s, at a time when the "worship wars" were beginning to heat up and churches were being torn apart. I had long been a student of the Psalms, but was really struggling to figure out how best to engage in public worship. So I acquired some books, distributed them to our elders, and gave them instructions to read the books and be prepared for a healthy discussion. For our study retreat we would typically go away in January and head down to Rehoboth Beach in Delaware. (Who goes to the beach in January? The answer is no one. And because nobody goes to the beach in January it's really inexpensive.) As I was planning for this particular retreat, one of the men in our church, Kerry Jones, who was the director of Campus Crusade at the University of Delaware, came to me with an invitation. "Alan, we have Jim Irwin, the former astronaut, speaking at Crusade this Thursday night. Before that, however, he is coming to our house for dinner. Why don't you bring Linda and the kids and join us? I think it would be a fun evening for you guys, and who knows if you'll ever get to meet a real live astronaut again."

Wouldn't you guess, the night Kerry had invited us to dinner was the same night that we were to gather in Rehoboth Beach, and since I've not yet mastered the skill of being in two places at once I told Kerry that I couldn't make it that night. He just looked at me for a moment and then pulled the trump card from his deck with these words: "So you want to tell your kids that they are going to miss dinner with an astronaut because you've to be at a meeting with the elders?" Zing! Then came zing number two: "You don't think that the guys can make it without you for a few hours?" I folded at that point. So I told the guys, "Go on down, I'll join you later, we'll get together about ten o'clock and have a bit of conversation in preparation for our day together on Friday."

Only it didn't work out quite that way. During the course of that day I developed a terrible head cold. So by the time I made it to the hotel where we were meeting I told the guys, "Look, you do whatever you want to do tonight. I'm taking medicine and going to bed. I'll see you in the morning." So off I went to my room, where I took my drugs and tried somewhat unsuccessfully to sleep.

The next morning after a long, hot shower I managed to make it to breakfast. Ever see the movie *The Invasion of the Body Snatchers*? There is a scene where a character is talking with his next-door neighbor, but then realizes it's not really the next-door neighbor; there's just is something odd about the person. Well, that's exactly what I felt like when I walked into the room that morning. Nobody made eye contact with me; everybody seemed kind of different.

Right away I was thinking that since I told them to do whatever they wanted to do, maybe they got together and decided to fire me. So I sat down for breakfast, and everyone was very quiet, very subdued. After about five minutes of that, I said, "OK, guys, what in the world is going on here?" At that moment they got real quiet. Finally the chairman of our elder board said, "Alan, you told us to do whatever we wanted to do. So we thought since we had been studying about worship that we would spend some time in worship. We started out by singing some hymns and worship songs."

He then continued, "After singing for some time we decided to pray. And then we sang some more and then we prayed some more and we sang some more." I'll never forget what he said next. "And then God came." Now that's not actually theologically accurate because God was already present. It's just that, as we learn from the life of Elijah, sometimes we've got to get quiet to hear Him speak. God simply refuses to shout at us to get our attention. Rather, we are instructed to "be still." It is then that God is able to make His presence known. The frenetic activity that many consider essential for connecting to God is most often counterproductive.

I love how Eugene Peterson describes prayer: "Prayer means that we deal first with God and then with the world. Or, that we experience the world first not as a problem to be solved but as a reality in which God is acting.... If we skip the prayer, or allow ourselves to be stampeded into activities other than prayer, we end up in [a] tragic impasse." He then goes on to say, "Anything creative, anything powerful, anything biblical, insofar as we are participants in it, originates in prayer" (1987, 40–41).

For far too many of us, prayer is much like a lucky rabbit's foot, a lucky token we use to sanctify what we are doing. I hear this all the time: "OK, we need to open our meeting in prayer. John, why don't you pray." Prayer thus becomes a perfunctory activity in which we engage. God doesn't want perfunctory; He desires our passion. He pleads for us to recognize His presence. When you engage in strategic planning, you cannot do it simply as an activity or even a process. It is an act of worship, and in every meeting you need to spend the time to say, "Lord, we are here bowing before You, in Your presence, seeking Your face."

Prayer and praise are crucial to every planning effort because in prayer and praise we are reminded of God's presence and directed into His presence. Why does that matter? It matters because we can never do all that God calls us to do without His presence. Indeed when I read the Scriptures I am struck by how often God calls people to truly difficult tasks at just the moment they have slowed down enough to seek His presence.

Think of Moses in Sinai beseeching God for a sign of His presence. Think of Isaiah, who in the year King Uzziah died went into the temple to pray and saw a vision of God, who then called him to a remarkably difficult task. Think of the disciples on that hillside in Galilee to whom Christ promised His presence until the end of the age. Think of Barnabas and Saul, who together with the other leaders of the church in Antioch stepped aside for a time of worship and into whose worship God spoke, calling them to a very difficult work.

I believe this with all of my heart. You simply cannot know God's heart or His vision for the ministry you lead until you have taken the time to step aside, to be still, and to hear the voice of God. That is hard for one person to do. It is much more difficult when there are a couple of dozen people in the room. It is difficult. It is also an indispensable element of any planning process that is designed to discover God's vision.

Rules for the Road, II

Let me ask you a question. Your answer to this question would give me a good idea of the decade in which you were born. Here we go. Did you ever own a Kodak Brownie or Instamatic camera? You know, the kind with film. The kind you had to physically turn a knob in order to advance the film. The kind with no zoom, no wide-angle, no adjustments at all. The kind that when you were finished taking your pictures you had to remove the roll of film from the camera and physically take it to a drug store or Kodak kiosk to get the film processed (unless, of course, you had your own darkroom). Then you had to return to pick up the prints, having waited several days only to discover that you cut the head off of your girlfriend or boyfriend. Do you remember?

How about the last time you actually used a camera of any kind? Or took film to that kiosk? Or actually placed a print into that ancient historical data storage device called a photo album? Today it is point and shoot with your smartphone, where everything is digitally stored for instant or (depending on the size of your storage capacity) nearly instant viewing. There is a small chance that a minute number of you still remember the Brownie camera by Kodak. A larger number will recall actually using a camera with film. Your kids and grandkids will only know such devices from a trip to a museum or from a discovery while on an archeological expedition digging through the junk in your closet or attic.

Now let me tell you a story. In 1881 George Eastman, a former bank clerk from Rochester, New York, obtained a patent for a dry-plate process for taking photographs. Soon after, he developed a film made of paper that quickly evolved into the celluloid film still in use today. The first Brownie camera hit the market in 1898 with a price tag of $1. Film sold for 15 cents a roll.

In 1997 Kodak (as the company started by George Eastman had come to be called) had reached a market peak of $31 billion—lots and lots of money back then. By 2011, however, its market capitalization had dropped below $2 billion, and in January of 2012 Kodak filed for bankruptcy. Few heritage businesses have declined so sharply, so quickly. And like the American steel industry, when Kodak collapsed so did the city in which it was born. Today Rochester is a shadow of what it once was.

So, what happened? It's simple, really. As Chip and Dan Heath point out in their book *Decisive*, "Kodak's executives were trapped in autopilot; they were coasting with the momentum of past choices" (2013, 223). Sadly, the story of Kodak is not at all unusual. In his book *How the Mighty Fall*, Jim Collins (2009) explores in some detail the fall from prominence of such iconic companies as Circuit City, Motorola, A&P, Merck, Zenith, Scott Paper, and Rubbermaid—all brands that I am sure you recall.

I suspect that if you took just five minutes you could add to that list the names of businesses, schools, and churches that at one time were thriving but that are now nonexistent or struggling to survive. I know I can.

Here is a sobering truth: Make enough unwise decisions, respond poorly to changing realities, fail to even consider how those changing realities could impact your school or organization, and anyone, including those reading this book, could be next to fall. It doesn't have to be that way, however. You can become adept at making good choices, at responding wisely in a timely fashion—but only if you are willing to develop a better way of thinking, deciding, and acting. Strategic planning done well can not only help you identify what's most important right now, but by engaging in the process you will develop that better way of thinking, deciding, and acting so necessary to continued success.

As I noted in chapter 1, we are living in an era of chaotic discontinuity—and not just chaotic discontinuity or even disruptive technology, but what Larry Downes and Paul Nunes (2014) call "devastating innovation." Just a quick review of history will reveal that people, organizations, and entire cultures have often faced such disruptive innovation, often with catastrophic results. Consider these examples:

• Egypt developed the wheeled chariot and became the most powerful nation in the known world, then fell.

• Assyria learned to smelt iron, conquered all of its neighbors, including Egypt, then itself fell to emerging technology.

• The English longbows made suits of armor obsolete, then they were made obsolete by rifles.

- Think iron ships versus wooden ships, steam versus sail, nuclear versus steam.
- Consider the impact that a single invention—the printing press or the automobile or the airplane or a tiny circuit made of silicon—can have on the entire history of the world.

I think you get the picture. Change, even radical change, isn't new; but when it arrives, it almost always arrives unannounced, creating the kind of massive disruption to which Downes and Nunes refer. That is why business as usual can quickly put you out of business. It is, therefore, the responsibility of every leader to help his or her organization anticipate the future, innovate in response, and then deliver everything they do with excellence. And please remember: you are a business.

Let's see if I can raise the level of urgency just a bit. Here's an interesting quote from a disconcerting article from the January 9, 2014, edition of *The Wall Street Journal*: "The American political class has long held that higher education is vital to individual and national success.... Yet despite such exhortations, total college enrollment has fallen by 1.5% since 2012. What's causing the decline? While demographics—specifically, a birth dearth in the mid-1990s accounts for some of the shift, robust foreign enrollment offsets that lack. The answer is simple: The benefits of a degree are declining while costs rise."

You may be breathing a sigh of relief. "After all," you might be tempted to say, "we are a K–6 or K–12 school, not a college or university. Those statistics don't apply to us." Oh, but they do. Your costs continue to rise, and attempts to slow increases almost always backfire because they impact your ability to deliver your mission with excellence. Don't forget Joel Barker's observation about excellence.

More challenging, however, is the overall—and to me, quite stunning—lack of interest in Christian schooling among evangelicals, both parents and pastors. Using a bell curve, we could describe the attitude toward Christian schools as ranging from tepid support on one end of the spectrum to outright hostility on the other end, with the majority of pastors and parents bunched in the middle—having adopted an attitude of "everyone is free to do that which is right in their own eyes"— something they would never do with attitudes toward things like church attendance, giving, prayer, or evangelism.

It has always struck me as fascinating that the pastor of the typical evangelical church would never consider inviting a committed secularist to teach Sunday school or lead a small-group Bible study but seems to have no problem exposing the children and teens of the church to that same person Monday through Friday at the local public school. The reasons for this are complex. The results, however, are only too real. At present only a small percentage of evangelical Christian parents choose Christian schooling as an option for their children. That makes your task even more daunting.

In response to that underwhelming support, your school must develop a reputation for unmistakable excellence. It must become a school that the parents in your community simply can't ignore or dismiss. That won't happen by accident. It will require a sustained process of learning to think and act wisely and well—a quality that a well-done strategic planning process can help you achieve. So, let's begin taking a look at those rules.

As You Begin

As I noted earlier, the strategic planning process itself is not all that complicated. Common sense, quality research, careful analysis, development of a reasonable tactical plan, and a willingness to be held accountable are essential; a high IQ and an MBA are not. Work hard, answer the tough questions, and stay focused. Do that, and you are likely to succeed.

There are, however, some tough challenges you must be prepared to face during this process. Let me describe a few of those challenges.

1. We do live in an era of chaotic discontinuity.

When the world is transforming as rapidly and radically as it is today, effecting real change in your school—change that makes sense and doesn't lead you into a box canyon—is tough. That is why many people criticize strategic planning efforts as futile. It is never futile, however, to ask good questions of yourself and your organization. It is only futile when you get trapped in autopilot, as the Heaths observed about the folks at Kodak. Strategic planning must always be driven by a sense of urgency. We do not live in a business-as-usual world; thus our planning efforts should not have the feel of business as usual.

2. Organizations and the people in them tend to respond poorly to change.

This is a topic we will explore in greater detail in chapter 11. Suffice it to say at this point that most people, most of the time, struggle with change.

Strategic planning done well will inevitably result in change—sometimes significant change. Indeed, if your planning process does not lead to real change it was not done well. People intuitively know that. They understand that strategic planning means change. Thus you must be prepared to make a sound case for both the process and the outcomes of the process if you hope to win the support of your staff and constituency.

3. You live in a "whirlwind."

Chris McChesney, Sean Covey, and Jim Huling capture this reality so well in their book *The Four Disciplines of Execution*: "The real enemy of execution is your day job! We call it the whirlwind. It's the massive amount of energy that's necessary just to keep your operation going on a day-to-day basis, and, ironically, it's also the thing that makes it so hard to execute anything new. The whirlwind robs from you the focus required to move your team forward" (2012, 6).

To succeed at the strategic planning process you must learn to manage the reality of the whirlwind. It isn't going away. It isn't going to abate. Today may be a 10 on the whirlwind scale, and tomorrow may find you in calmer winds, say a 4 or a 5; but it is highly unlikely you'll ever experience a 2 or a 3 except on that rare day in mid-July or late December. Here are some thoughts on living life in the whirlwind:

- Don't let yourself become the answer to every person's problems. Create an appropriate chain of complaint and insist that everyone follow the appropriate protocols. Only under the rarest of situations should you be the first person anyone calls.
- Create eye-of-the-storm times throughout your day. Management by walking around remains a crucial leadership task. Visibility is immensely important. A bunker mentality is hugely harmful. Like teachers who crave and value a bit of quiet prep time during the day, you need to build those times into your day.
- Develop and maintain an appropriate accountability process for your staff. In some cases, beyond an administrative assistant or two, you are the staff. If that is the case, you've got to start with you. In Patrick Lencioni's book *The Advantage*, McChesney, Covey, and Huling's book *The Four Disciplines of Execution*, and General Stanley McChrystal's book *Team of Teams*, you'll find helpful suggestions on how to do that well.
- Find time to "be still and know that I am God." As both David and Elijah discovered, God simply refuses to shout above the noise of the whirlwind. I'm an early morning person, so as a school head my time to listen for God's voice was scheduled early. Fortunately, I had a wife who allowed me to do that. You may find later in the day or

evening a better time. Whatever the time, you must guard it jealously. There are lots of guides to quiet time. Find one that helps you learn to be still.

4. Hope is not a policy, nor is it a helpful strategy.

During Barack Obama's first campaign for president his slogan was "hope and change." I was always deeply troubled by that slogan, asking answers to two questions: How is hope a legitimate strategy for solving the immense, complicated problems we face as a nation? and, Change from what to what? At no time in the campaign did he really answer either question, and when he did his answers simply raised more questions. It was a brilliant political strategy since people were free to provide their own answers. It was, however, in my opinion, a less-than-satisfactory policy strategy.

Kathleen Parker, a syndicated columnist for the *Orlando Sentinel*, described it well: "Hope is not a policy.... We all learn eventually that hope only takes you so far. The rest is hard work and clear thinking." In a sense, what I am hoping to help you better understand by introducing you to the concept of "rules for the road" is how you can become better at the clear-thinking part. You will need these "rules for the road" throughout the strategic planning process. More importantly, you will benefit from them in every aspect of your leadership.

Invest the Time

Here is reality. Organizations often lack, or are unwilling to invest, the time necessary for quality planning or problem-solving efforts. As a result, strategy-development processes are adapted to fit the limited time and resources available, resulting in short, periodic discussions of the issues and alternatives. Such limited processes are unlikely—in fact, very unlikely—to produce truly creative solutions to difficult problems or innovative approaches to new opportunities.

I continue to be astounded by how many schools believe that a Saturday away once a year will suffice in developing a sound, truly strategic plan. Forgive me for stating my thoughts in such strong terms, but it is foolhardy, self-deceiving, and utterly preposterous to believe that you can set the strategic direction of a school during a single eight-hour meeting. You can certainly go away for a day and engage in a healthy scenario-planning exercise that may prove beneficial, but a strategic planning process will require a lot more of the board and leadership team of a school.

I would recommend the schedule of meetings outlined in Patrick Lencioni's book *Death by Meeting* (2007) as a model for you to follow for your ongoing thinking and planning efforts. He recommends five kinds of meetings:

- **A daily stand-up meeting lasting no more than fifteen minutes.** This meeting should focus exclusively on sharing necessary information about the day with one another. This can be with your senior staff or with your faculty. (A wise leader will ensure there is always coffee and tea!)
- **Weekly tactical accountability meetings.** This is not the time for strategic or philosophical discussions. This is where you evaluate progress and make necessary revisions to your plans. It is also where you hold one another accountable, and in my experience real accountability is a sorely lacking quality at many schools.
- **Monthly professional development.** We have forever called these teacher in-service days, and hold them maybe once a quarter. Wrong name, insufficient time. Every month you should schedule at least a half day to focus on one thing: helping everyone get better at delivering the mission God has given you. As administrators you will need to focus on that arena. Teachers will need to focus on the classroom. There are all kinds of resources—from videos to books to conferences to "experts"—available to help you accomplish this task. Work with your team to create a focus for each month, perhaps a focus for the entire year. Make it worthwhile, and your team will rise up and called you blessed.
- **Quarterly strategic-planning or scenario-planning days.** This is something for you and your leadership team. If your team is small, get together with the leadership of another school in your area. Doing that will help with another concept I will introduce in a minute: networking. During these meetings you do not spend time addressing tactical issues. During these meetings you ponder, you dream a bit, you climb the tree and look to the horizon. These meetings will be far more profitable if reading assignments are given in preparation for each meeting. Focus your efforts. Don't just choose articles or books haphazardly. Focus your energies. Two additional thoughts: anyone who comes unprepared doesn't get to engage in the conversation, and if you have staff members who repeatedly come to those meetings unprepared or refuse to appropriately engage, replace them.
- **Yearly getaway on your own to "clear the mechanism."** You need time away to clear your mind of all the daily issues that claw away at your consciousness. Jesus did it. He often headed into the wilderness for time away. If you don't take time away, you will soon find yourself worn away.

Prime the Pump

To keep the water flowing from an old-fashioned hand pump often required a priming process. The same is true for the flow of ideas. If we are not careful, our well will dry up. You've probably heard the phrase "He's gone to that well once too often." That is what happens when we don't prime the pump. Keeping yourself fresh while deepening the pool of ideas from which you can draw is not difficult. It does require you to invest your time and energy into some very specific activities—some of which I'll address briefly here and some of which I will unpack as we continue through our rules for the road.

• **Read.** You've heard it many times: "leaders are readers." They are. If you're not reading, that says less about your complicated schedule than it does about your understanding of leadership. Read widely. Don't just read books on leadership; also read books about leaders. Read biographies; read history; read about educational theory and practice. Read about current events, theology, and spiritual formation. Read about sports, economics, and world affairs. Subscribe to and read *Harvard Business Review*, *Wired*, *The Wall Street Journal*, *The Chronicle of Philanthropy*, and at least one good educational journal. Refuse to become a one-dimensional person. By the way, if you don't know what to read, peruse the book reviews in *The Wall Street Journal*, *World Magazine*, *Christianity Today*, ACSI's *Leadership Matters*, and even the *Sunday New York Times Review of Books*.

• **Research.** Ask yourself, What interests me? What do I need to know to help me be a better person and leader? What do I need to know to help me help my school "better become what God has called us to be"? Ask yourself those kinds of questions and then develop a research strategy. Let's say you are struggling to understand the current and coming impact of technology on schools and schooling—both the positive impact and the negative impact, for there are always two or more sides to every issue. Find the books and articles that will help you think through this issue. Identify schools and school leaders who seem to be wrestling with this issue and contact them. A sixty-minute phone call can point you in a number of interesting directions. Get your faculty, staff, board, and perhaps even knowledgeable parents involved in your research.

• **Read with a second set of eyes.** Electronic readers like the Kindle have become very popular and are certainly very convenient. Like Captain Picard of the starship *Enterprise*, however, I just like the feel of a book in my hand. It isn't just the feel, however, it is the ability to underline and write notes—to actively interact with the text—that I find so valuable. Research tells us that the kinetic activity required to underline and write helps the mind to engage more deeply with the text and then to recall more vividly what we have read (Carr 2011, 90). I never read without a pen in my hand. It is my second set of eyes.

- **Reflect and journal.** In his book *Where Good Ideas Come From*, Steven Johnson observes, "... the snap judgments of intuition—as powerful as they can be—are rarities in the history of world-changing ideas. Most hunches that turn into important innovations unfold over much longer time frames.... Because these slow hunches need so much time to develop, they are fragile creatures easily lost to the more pressing needs of day-to-day issues" (2011, 77). That is why so many of history's greatest thinkers kept what we today would call a journal. Writing down your thoughts gives you the opportunity to revisit them, to nurture them, and to watch them develop into something of great value. Consider how often the psalmists call us to meditate on what we read. Journaling is a means to meditation. Without it we tend to lose what we have read. Unfortunately, journaling has lost cachet as a practice. We are poorer as a result.

Network

As Solomon reminds us, "Without counsel plans fail, but with many advisers they succeed" (Proverbs 15:22). This doesn't just apply to formal decision-making or planning processes. It equally applies to our efforts to prime the pump. As Steven Johnson observes, "The trick to having good ideas is not to sit around in glorious isolation and try to think big thoughts. The idea is to get more ideas on the table." He further notes that "most ideas come into the world half-baked, more hunch than revelation. Genuine insights are hard to come by ... so most great ideas first take shape in a partial, incomplete form. They have the seeds of something profound, but they lack a key element that can turn the hunch into something truly powerful. And more often than not, that missing element is somewhere else, living as a hunch in another person's head" (2011, 42).

None of this should surprise us. It is simply the practical outcome of how God has designed us. We are all gifted, but our gifts are complementary rather than complete. As the apostle Paul instructs us, "For the body does not consist of one member but of many.... If the whole body were an eye, where would be the sense of hearing? If the whole body were an ear, where would be the sense of smell?... The eye cannot say to the hand, 'I have no need of you,' nor again the head to the feet, 'I have no need of you'" (1 Corinthians 12:14–17). None of us is wired to see the whole picture. We need one another. Develop a network. Move outside of your own team. Don't let fear of competition keep you from doing that.

Assemble a Virtuoso Team

Networks are often made up of people from outside of your school. In this section I am asking you to focus on the team you will build to help lead your school. I am less interested in names on an organizational chart than I am in complementary talents, personal character, thoughtful insight, and a shared passion not only for the mission of your school but for achieving that mission with excellence. I like this description of a virtuoso team:

• A small group of people (5–7) …
• Who assume collective responsibility, meaning that they don't need external compulsion to get them focused on the task at hand …
• To achieve a common objective (which implies that the make-up of a team can change over time depending on the task at hand) …
• In a climate of trust (essential, as with all teams) …
• Able to master conflict, the inevitable result when bright, talented people struggle together to find the best route to a successful conclusion to the task at hand (You will seldom achieve a quality outcome without some level of conflict.) …
• While thinking and acting creatively. (Creative, thinking people will clash with one another. Conformity kills creativity.)

These are the people you want to take with you for those quarterly strategic-planning or scenario-planning meetings. These are the people who will help you discover good books and articles. These are the people with whom you'll enjoy sharing a late afternoon or evening cup of coffee or tea. These are also, however, the people who will resent being asked to participate in shapeless, unfocused, poorly planned meetings with no discernible purpose. Don't waste their time. Don't squander their gifts.

Build the Box

You cannot begin a journey (and strategic planning is a journey) without asking three fundamental questions: What is our starting point? What is our destination? What is our reference point for our journey? When you build the box you answer questions 1 and 3. If you don't, you will surely wander off course. As Eric Fromm observes, "True freedom is not the absence of structure but rather a clear structure that enables people to work within established boundaries in a creative way" (cited in Eppler 2003, 108). We will devote an entire chapter to this critical topic.

Identify the "Real Problem"

In his fascinating book *The Wright Way*, an examination of the problem-solving process employed by the Wright brothers, Mark Eppler uses a colorful phrase—*tackle the tyrant*—to explain how Wilbur and Orville were able to discover a solution to a problem that had eluded some of the most brilliant minds in human history (2003, 61).

It has been my observation that far too much of our effort in planning or problem solving is expended in searching for solutions to symptoms of deeper, more entrenched problems. We do that, I think, because we don't really understand how to see beyond the symptom and discover the underlying problem. We also are sometimes unwilling to dig beneath the surface for fear of what we might find, intuitively understanding that the real problem will take much more effort and time to address than we are willing to invest. So we end up putting bandages on life-threatening wounds or taking aspirin to relieve our fever rather than facing up to the possibility of a more serious condition.

In chapter 8 we will set about to consider the question, What is our current reality? To give us a bit of a head start, let me list some of the tasks and attitudes we must employ if we are to do that well.

To Tackle the Tyrant We Must ...

Imagine what could be

To do that you've got to regain a bit of the wonder you and I more frequently experienced as children. I love how Walt Disney put it: "Around here we don't look backwards for very long. We keep moving forward, opening new doors and doing new things, because we're curious ... and curiosity keeps leading us down new paths" (cited in Heath and Heath 2013).

Too often, as someone wiser than me once observed, the horizon for most people is the edge of the rut into which they have most recently fallen. Don't let that be you. Get out of your office. Identify some great schools and make arrangements to visit them. Ask the leaders of those schools how they identified the biggest obstacles to success. Find out what they did to turn things around. And don't limit your visits and inquiries to other schools. You've probably got a number of successful business owners in your school, people who've had their own tyrants to tackle. Talk to them. Listen to them. Learn from them. They will become some of your greatest supporters.

Surrender our memories

Nothing will derail a problem-solving or planning process faster than these words: "We tried that once and it didn't work." The fact of the matter is that people seldom did what they think they did, and if they actually tried something they seldom fully understood what they were doing or how best to do it. We've all been guilty of this.

I've often been given advice that I dismissed out of hand because "I'd already tried that once," only to discover that in reality I'd missed a crucial step or left out a key ingredient or completely missed a cultural context. It is kind of like the first time my wife baked a cake in Denver. She forgot the part about the impact of elevation. At 5,280 feet, cakes don't rise the same way they do at sea level.

To surrender your memories, you've got to be intentional. Here are some suggestions:

• Acknowledge your assumptions. We all have them. Assumptions, however, like assertions, are nothing more than personal opinions. All of us are entitled to our opinions and assumptions, but none are binding on anyone else, and typically they blind us to legitimate alternative ideas. To be successful at problem solving, all assumptions must be publicly stated. Simply create a list of assumptions on a whiteboard. Once they have been uttered in public, you now have the opportunity to examine and (where necessary) challenge those assumptions.

• Admit to your agendas. As with assumptions, we all have them. Agendas, however, create greater opportunity for mischief because we will use whatever power or leverage we can muster to advance our agendas. And because agendas are often hidden, they tend to mask the why behind the what of people's actions and decisions. As with assumptions, agendas must be brought into the light so that they can be examined.

• Discuss previous experiences and how those experiences are shaping our thinking now. It is from our personal experiences that arise statements like "We tried that once and it didn't work." By now you are probably beginning to get a sense for what must happen. Get those experiences out in the open. Acknowledge the power of experience to shape how we see things and how what we see makes us feel. Those feelings are real, but they must never be allowed to derail or dead-end our conversations. Ask questions like these:

  ◦ How would you describe the context of your experience?

  ◦ How is this current context the same? How is it different?

  ◦ What do you know now that you wish you had known then?

  ◦ Looking back on that experience, what would you have done differently?

  ◦ What external forces were at work then that are the same today? What other external forces are active today?

○ What were some internal forces at work then that are the same today? What other internal forces are active today?

○ What about the people involved? How are they the same today? How are other people different today?

• Identify your greatest fear. Some fears are legitimate. Some are not. All, however, can be paralyzing, so get them out in the open and address each with the same level of seriousness.

Be willing to embrace divergent thinking

School leaders must reject the tyranny of the OR and embrace the genius of the AND. Jim Collins discovered this key principle at work in those organizations and companies that achieved and maintained greatness. He describes it this way. The tyranny of the OR is "the rational view that cannot easily accept paradox, that cannot live with two 'seemingly' contradictory forces or ideas at the same time. The tyranny of the OR pushes people to deliver things that must be either A or B. Instead of being oppressed by the tyranny of the OR, highly visionary companies liberated themselves with the genius of the AND—the ability to embrace both extremes of a number of dimensions at the same time. Instead of choosing between A or B they figure out a way to have both A and B" (2001, 198).

Organizations embrace the tyranny of the OR all of the time and still deliver their mission with excellence. I've seen it in Christian schools all across the country. What they struggle to do, however, is to respond creatively to seismic shifts underway in culture and technology that are impacting education in truly profound ways. The reason why I insist that schools "build the box" is to ensure that what really matters does not get lost. Once a school has decided what is nonnegotiable, however, it must be willing to put everything else on the table for review.

I have a friend who serves as Vice President for Student Life at Grand Canyon University in Phoenix, Arizona. After years of declining enrollment, GCU was taken over by new leadership who decided to follow the model of University of Phoenix and become predominantly an online institution. The plan worked, and GCU's online enrollment soared while the on-campus enrollment continued to decline. Over time, however, the leadership discovered something interesting. The 18–22-year-old portion of the marketplace still wanted to go away to college. They wanted to experience campus life. So the leadership of the school began to ask AND questions. Could they develop a school that had both a strong online presence and a quality residential program? The answer, of course, was yes. Today GCU enrolls tens of thousands of students in its online program, and it has seen its residential enrollment increase tenfold over the last eight years. Liberty University has done much the same thing.

One particular area with which many Christian schools struggle is open or closed enrollment. Some schools describe themselves as discipleship schools and will only enroll students from a family in which at least one parent is a believer. Other schools describe themselves as outreach schools, seeking to use the classroom as a context for evangelism. For some schools the position they take is one of their nonnegotiables. Though I never try to talk a school into or out of either of those positions, I always challenge them to consider looking at the issue through the genius of the AND. It is interesting how difficult it can be for schools to think that way. They just find it impossible to consider that there is a third way regarding enrollment.

If the enrollment issue were a single anomaly this would not be a problem, but it is only one of many similar kinds of issues with which schools struggle. What about these?

- *Technology.* Some schools have a requirement that all work is to be done on a laptop or other device. Some schools give technology scant notice.
- *Finance.* Some schools use a cost-based tuition approach. Other schools cover a large percentage of their costs through fund-raising.
- *Facilities.* For some schools, OK is good enough. Others want to dazzle people.
- *Staffing.* Some schools will hire only state-certified teachers; others will hire anyone with a degree; others are unconcerned about either certification or degrees, the main qualification being people who "love Jesus."
- *Curriculum.* Some schools love the ease, familiarity, and comfort of scripted Christian textbooks; other schools prefer texts that require more critical thinking on the part of teachers and students.

When it comes to strategic planning, the more a school is willing to consider the genius of the AND, the more creative they are likely to be when addressing the initiatives they identify during the process.

Look for the second right answer

Consensus is the enemy of excellence. Consensus is what you reach when you are weary. If you jump on the first answer you uncover as you try to solve a difficult problem or seize an unexpected opportunity, you are likely to miss something truly transformational as a result. As Wilbur Wright observed, "If a man is in too big a hurry to give up an error, he is liable to give up some truth with it, and in accepting the arguments of the other man he is sure to get some errors with it. Honest argument is merely a process of mutually picking the beams and motes out of each other's eyes so both can see more clearly" (Eppler 2003, 55–56).

One way to ensure that you are always looking for the second right answer is to create what are called "excursion teams." This strategy is explored and explained at length in the book *Decisive* by Chip and Dan Heath. Briefly, the Heaths suggest that when looking to solve a particularly difficult problem, you must avoid what they call early lock-in (the first right answer) by surfacing multiple options. To surface those multiple options they suggest that rather than use any of the popular brainstorming techniques, that you create what they call "excursion teams." These teams then set about to independently and simultaneously develop a solution. When each team has completed its work, they then come back together to present their solutions. By doing their work independently, they are likely able to generate more creative solutions simply because there are two, three, or even four teams working on the problem rather than one. It is a great idea that can be used in all kinds of problem-solving and planning scenarios. (2013, 50–56).

Learn to lead with questions

Great questions are like the headlights on your car. They dispel the darkness and shed light on the unseen. Years ago I discovered a book by Dr. Bruce Lockerbie with the intriguing title *Asking Questions* (1980). I often referred to that book when teaching a class. We all know that asking questions is a far better teaching technique than simply dispensing information. Asking questions adds a level of interest and creates a greater level of engagement.

In a planning process asking good questions does something equally important. It forces us to openly consider issues crucial to the problem-solving process that might remain below the surface otherwise. Consider this brief list:

- What are our constraints?
- Why are they constraints?
- What are our possible options?
- What makes them options?
- What are our assumptions?
- What are we trying to achieve?
- Why is that important?
- What is most important now?
- What happens if we fail?
- What happens if we succeed?
- What don't we know that we need to know?
- Who can help us discover what we don't know that we need to know?

I'm sure that with a little thought you could add to that list. Remember this. Questions are better than assertions. Questions create an atmosphere that fuels inquiry and creativity. Assertions create an atmosphere that squelches inquiry and creativity. Which kind of atmosphere to you believe is likely to lead to quality solutions to tough problems?

Track the conversation

We are constantly talking about the importance of seeing the "big picture." Yet we often use methodologies that make it impossible for anyone to see that big picture. Consider our use of technology in the classroom. Remember how we taught math back when we used those primitive teaching tools, chalkboards and chalk?

You can see a great illustration of what I am trying to say if you watch the movie *Good Will Hunting*. In the movie, Will is working as a janitor at Harvard University when he happens upon a math problem that sprawls across several chalkboards in a classroom. It is an unfinished problem awaiting a solution. Because he can track the problem from its beginning, Will (who we discover is something of a math savant) is able to complete the problem, much to the consternation of the professor who has been toiling at the task for months.

That is how we used to teach math back in the chalkboard-and-chalk days. With the introduction of overhead projectors and now computer screens, it has become difficult to do that same kind of tracking. In the strategic planning process I have discovered that using some kind of mapping strategy is essential. Often, for example, when jotting down thoughts about the mission of a school or the school's core values or the challenges faced by the school, I discover that the most insightful comments occur early in the conversation or perhaps are missed during a heated discussion.

When brainstorming you must write everything down. As the old Chinese proverb goes, "A ragged pen is better than a good memory." In so doing you will create a treasure trove of thoughts and ideas that may not bear immediate fruit but may prove of great value down the road.

Science and Art

Strategic planning is equal parts science and art—one of those genius-of-the-AND kind of things. The lines distinguishing between the science and the art aspects can actually get pretty blurred. I don't know if I can even give a percentage. Some people I know who engage in strategic planning tend to lean in the direction of science. They have all kinds of "proven practices" that they impressively employ throughout the process. Their strong suit is research, and as we know, the answer to everything and the solution to every problem can be found in the research (!)—only it can't. As I've heard Simon Jeynes (a brilliant consultant at Independent School Management) say often, "It's data. It is. But it can't tell us why."

I probably lean toward the art side of the equation in strategic planning. Maybe even a bit too much. Perhaps that is why I agree with these observations from Malcolm Gladwell: "The adaptive unconscious does an excellent job of sizing up the world, warning people of danger, setting goals, and initiating action in a sophisticated and efficient manner" (2005, 12).

Whether you lean toward the art or the science, however, I do believe that you will find these "rules for the road" to be helpful as you engage in a strategic planning process. Pay attention to them. Learn more about them. Employ them.

PART TWO

The Process of Strategic Planning

5

Are You Ready for This?

What does it take to hike the Appalachian Trail? That was a question I posed to David Rough, Dean of Academics at Dayton Christian School. I had just started a strategic planning project at DCS when I first met David and in conversation discovered that he was planning to spend the coming summer break trekking the 2,168.1 miles of the trail—from Mount Katahdin, Maine, to Springer Mountain, Georgia. I admire people who would take on such a challenge. I also think they are a bit nuts. Walking to my local Starbucks is as big a test of my endurance as I ever want to experience.

After my conversation with David, I know what you don't do. You don't just wake up one morning and say, "Hey, I think I'll head to Maine and stroll on down the Appalachian Trail." Try that and you'll end up in a hospital—or worse, a morgue. An undertaking of this complexity requires rigorous training and thoughtful planning. David walked five miles every day of the week and up to twenty on Saturdays for months in preparation for his hike. In addition he had all kinds of logistical issues to address. You can only carry so much food and water while traversing rather rugged terrain. So he had to plan on connecting with his wife at various points along the trail to replenish his supplies.

Then there was the matter of footwear. Walking miles on any kind of ground will take a toll on anyone's feet. Buy the wrong boots, however, and a grueling trip can quickly reach a premature conclusion. It takes time to research all the options available and then to make sure that those boots are broken in prior to starting the trip.

David Rough did his homework and properly prepared himself physically for what would be a grueling but hugely satisfying experience. As a result he is one of the few who have actually started and finished the journey. No amount of preparation can guarantee success in every situation. There are simply too many variables, too many opportunities to slip and fracture a bone or tear a ligament. Fail to properly prepare, however, and your likelihood of success will hover somewhere around zero.

The same thing is true of the strategic planning process. While not nearly as arduous as a journey down the Appalachian Trail, a sound strategic planning process will stress even a healthy organization. Start the process from a position of weakness, and success is unlikely. In this chapter, therefore, my goal is to help you think through the issues, attitudes, and realities that could doom or derail your planning efforts; I will also provide some practical ideas for how to lay a sturdy foundation for your endeavors. I'm going to begin this conversation with a look at a pretty overworked word.

Prevailing Paradigms

I have a little test in which I'd like you to engage. Grab a pen and paper (yes, I know that pens and paper are rather low-tech tools and out of vogue in many circles, but humor me) and write a formal definition for the word *paradigm*. It might prove to be a more challenging task than you imagine. *Paradigm* is one of those words that has been used so much that it has lost much of its meaning.

The first time I encountered the word was in Thomas Kuhn's book *The Structure of Scientific Revolutions*. Kuhn was interested in how what he called paradigms impacted the process of scientific inquiry. He described paradigms as "accepted examples of actual scientific practice ... that provide models from which spring particular coherent traditions of scientific research" (cited in Barker 1993, 31).

I am certainly not a scientist or social scientist, but I can see how conversations regarding topics like climate change and racial disparity could easily fall prey to paradigms that emerge as "the truth of the matter" that over time influence how a person might evaluate particular information or shape responses to certain circumstances. Indeed, I suspect all of us are guilty of that kind of manipulation.

In his book *Paradigms: The Business of Discovering the Future*, Joel Barker provides what I believe to be a good definition of *paradigm*: "A paradigm is a set of rules and regulations (written or unwritten) that does two things: establishes or defines boundaries and tells people how to behave inside those boundaries in order to be successful" (1993, 32).

For example, I began my teaching career in a very authoritarian, hierarchical kind of organization. You were entitled to your opinion as long as it supported the status quo or remained unexpressed. The chain of command was rigidly enforced, and failure to adhere to that chain was quickly and painfully punished. It was possible to influence change, but it required a high level of patience and deft political maneuvering. I was good at neither. My approach was more direct, more incendiary, and thus less effective.

We're all familiar with the phrase "sacred cows make the best hamburger." Here is reality, however: unless and until we can identify the paradigms that actually do shape why and how we do what we do, it will be difficult for us to think and act creatively. Bottled up by our paradigms, we are likely to become increasingly irrelevant.

Paradigms are not biblical principles. They are not theological certainties. They are not even, for the most part, supported by research. Rather they are generally ideas that have gained currency over the years for less-than-rational reasons. And even when a foundational principle is advanced as a basis for a paradigm, it is usually the application of a principle, not the principle itself.

Nothing, for example, has had a stronger grip on how we structure schools than the concept of hierarchical organizations. Just take a look at the typical school org chart or read organizational literature from the 40s, 50s, and 60s and you will see what I mean. When the idea of hierarchical structure began to be questioned in recent years, the resistance to change was initially strongest in Christian organizations, and indeed continues to remain strong in many schools.

My purpose here is not to make a case that flatter organizations are inherently superior to hierarchical organizations, though I think they are. Rather, it is to observe the power of ideas that become institutionalized and harden into paradigms. Those paradigms then not only shape the day-to-day operations of a school but will likely influence the planning process. Some of those paradigms are relatively harmless. Others, however, can have a disabling effect on the planning process.

Here is a short list of disabling paradigms that I have observed in Christian schools.
• *Ministry mentality.* I want to make a very clear distinction between a genuine ministry heart and a kind of flawed thinking that dresses itself up in theological or spiritual language. Sadly, this paradigm reveals itself in a number of attitudes and beliefs.

- *Professional practices.* These are the things we do every day at our schools without ever asking, Why do we do this, whatever this is, this way?
- *Organizational silos.* Much has been written on this topic. Little has been done in the typical school. Silos are the enemy of an integrated, focused approach to problem solving.
- *Organizational inertia.* This is the "if it ain't broke, don't fix it" mentality that dooms so many organizations to continuing mediocrity. Few paradigms are more subtle or more powerful.

Ministry mentality

Here are some of the attitudes and ideas that taken together form this disabling paradigm:

- **People are more valuable than competence.** This is the idea that what we honor in our staff most are things like loyalty, love for kids, love for Christ, hard work, and sacrifice. Who can argue with that? Of course we want our staff to possess all of those qualities. All of those qualities, however, will not make up for poor performance in the classroom or office.

  Parents absolutely want teachers who care deeply for their students. They also, however, want teachers who perform with excellence in the classroom, teachers who are continuously growing in their professional performance. One without the other is a bit like food without water. Eliminate either and sooner or later you die.

  Far too many schools set themselves on the path to mediocrity because the leaders of those schools are unwilling to make the tough decisions when it comes to faculty and staff. This is one of those places where the "genius of the AND" makes sense. You need teachers and staff who perform with exceptional skill at the task for which they have been hired AND who also love kids. Both-and, not either-or.

- **Serviceable is enough.** This is the paradigm that shapes so many decisions about the facilities we build and the programs we equip. Extravagance is just that, an extravagance. Money alone solves nothing. However, beauty is not an extravagance. Curb appeal is not simply a way to attract the attention of people. Rather, as I noted in chapter 3, it is an expression of our obligation to reflect the true nature of God before a watching world—a world that includes your students and their parents. As someone once observed, "God don't make no junk." Poor grammar, perhaps, but good theology.

There is more at stake here, however. Things like well-equipped science labs, quality music and arts space, and superior, continuously improving technological infrastructure tell people that you are serious about providing a quality education for your students. You may never be able to fully reproduce the facilities of the public school down the street, but you absolutely must ensure that you don't skimp on the essentials.

- **Difficulty in linking excellence with success.** This attitude is similar in nature to the previous point, with a key twist. We somehow think that all that matters is how hard we work or how much we love our job. Thinking that way will keep you mired in mediocrity. Hard work and good intentions are essential. They are just not enough. You've actually got to deliver what you do with unmistakable excellence.

Now excellence, as I've often remarked, is a difficult idea to quantify. People often mistake excellence for the facades of beauty that we can erect with relative ease. Beauty attracts our attention. It grabs us and will not let us go. Unfortunately, it can also mask poor quality. Think of that visually appealing restaurant where you received a not-so-good meal. Beauty is not a substitute for excellence. Nor is a lack of resources an excuse for failing to pursue and achieve excellence.

Do what God has called you to do with obvious excellence, and people will line up at your door. If you struggle with your enrollment, look first at the quality of your staff and their performance, not at your marketing strategies. Excellence is the foundation for marketing success.

- **A failure to understand the difference between cost and investment.** If the prime factor in student retention is faculty culture, why are we so reluctant to invest in our faculty? I promise you that parents, even those with limited resources, will be most hesitant to withdraw their children from a school where they are receiving an exceptional education. Thus, providing reasonable compensation and quality professional development opportunities to your faculty is not simply a cost. It is most fully an investment that will provide a good return. The same could be said for improving your facilities.

Your budget is not a static thing (money in, money out). Rather it is a dynamic document reflecting your commitment to excellence or manifesting your fear of financial failure. Solomon reminds us, "hope deferred makes the heart sick"

(Proverbs 13:12). Withhold adequate compensation from your faculty and staff or create a budget with no capacity to address critical facility and programmatic needs, and you start a downward spiral that will become increasingly difficult to arrest.

It isn't just a matter of "spending money to make money." Indiscriminately spending money solves nothing. Our current system of publicly funded education illustrates that. In one sense the whole point of strategic planning is to provide a blueprint for how to better invest the resources God makes available to you.

• **"God will take care of us."** How often have you heard someone say, "We just need more faith"? Remember our earlier discussion of God's sovereignty? Finding the exact place where God's sovereign work and our human obligation meet is never easy. There is no exact formula of which I am aware.

What I do believe, with a high degree of certainty, is that God never promises to ride in and rescue us from the consequences of our faulty thinking, flawed decision making, or less-than-stellar performance. Make enough bad decisions or perform poorly enough over a long enough period of time, and you are going out of business. As someone once noted, "Stupid should hurt." Believe me, it does.

The problem isn't typically faith or lack of faith, trust or lack of trust, belief or lack of belief. Typically it is a continuous pattern—and here we go again—of faulty thinking, flawed decision making, and poor performance. Sometimes we do find ourselves in situations beyond our control, situations we did not create but to which we must respond. If the biggest employer in your community is the local military base and Congress closes it, you are likely to suffer a powerful fiscal blow. Will faith reopen that base? Not likely. Prayer for wisdom, however, makes a lot of sense. Making equal sense might be contacting the person responsible for economic development in your area and offering your help.

Professional practices

Pull out your daily schedule. Does it look something like this? A series of five, six, or seven 50-minute blocks of time during which students attend class. A student may attend some kind of science class, followed by some kind of math class, then a history class, a foreign language class, a literature class, PE, and a Bible class. A bell or buzzer announces start and end times. Students may be given five minutes to transition from one class to another. At the beginning of the day there may be a homeroom period, with lunch around the middle of the day.

Sound familiar? Probably. So here's my question: Why do we do it that way? When I pose the question, which I frequently do during a workshop, the answer I receive most is, "That's the way we've always done it." I've never had someone say, "We do it that way because in our study of the research on student performance we have found that 50-minute blocks of time are the best way to engage in teaching and learning."

There is a reason no one has ever given me that response. There is no research suggesting that a series of 50-minute periods is the best way to deliver education. In fact, I would suspect that many of you reading this book have experienced times when a 50-minute class has proved both limiting and frustrating. So why do we keep structuring our school days around those 50-minute periods?

The answer, of course, is simple. It is the way we've always done it, and it illustrates just how powerful and limiting professional practices can become in shaping how we do what we do. As Mark Eppler notes, "People have a tendency to fall in love with their tools. Those 'tools' may be a favorite hammer, preferred piece of software, or a long-established way of doing things. We return to them time and again, preferring their familiarity to the uncertainty of 'things different.' Our love affair with our tools often skews how we define a problem" (Eppler 2003, 102).

Changing our practices for the sake of novelty is most certainly unwise. Equally unwise, however, is blind allegiance to that long-established way of doing things. A strategic planning process done well may call for changes—in some cases significant changes—in how we deliver our mission. This will require a willingness to reexamine all of our professional practices.

Organizational silos

Does your elementary principal have regular conversations with your high school principal? What about your athletic director? Does he or she ever sit down for extended periods of dialogue with your director of fine arts? Is there much dialogue between the head of your science department and your advancement director? If not it is probably because your school, like most organizations, finds itself living in clearly defined and isolated silos. Such silos are hazardous to your school's health.

Take the budgeting process as an example. How often do all of the key department heads sit down together to discuss both development and oversight of the budget? Has that ever happened at your school? If not, it should. Silos make it difficult to develop and deepen understanding about the holistic, integrated nature of a school. Only when people learn to see things from a variety of perspectives can they make decisions that truly advance the mission of the whole school as opposed to their portion of the school—their silo.

An athletic program is no more a school than an arm or a leg is a whole body. Like the brain to the body, the academic program at a school is essential. But without a nose there is no sense of smell, without the eyes there is no sight, without ears no ability to hear. Only when all aspects of the body function in concert with one another can the body function at 100 percent. As the apostle Paul notes, "The eye cannot say to the hand, 'I have no need of you'" (1 Corinthians 12:21).

The planning process that ignores entrenched silos is likely to founder. That is one of the reasons why so many top-down planning efforts fail. So before you choose to engage in a strategic planning process, you need to take a look across your organization to determine whether your efforts are characterized by a high degree of cooperation between departments or whether there is a tendency toward kingdom building among those departments. If kingdom building is your default mode, it would be wise to take your team leaders away to explore how best to build a team that cooperates toward a common end before initiating a strategic planning process.

It is not only prevailing paradigms that can derail your planning efforts. There are a number of other internal flaws that can make it difficult for you to think much beyond the ringing of your afternoon dismissal bell. Let's take a brief look at some other problems that planning can't solve.

A culture of crisis

It is not only prevailing paradigms that can derail your planning efforts; it can well be the very culture of your organization. Remember the story of Dave Rough. Dave was not a young guy when he resolved to undertake his trek down the Appalachian Trail; he was well into midlife. He was, however, a lean, mean, walking machine prior to that decision. He maintained a healthy lifestyle that included good eating habits and regular exercise. To successfully accomplish such a challenging goal he had to step things up a bit, but he didn't start from a position of weakness.

That isn't to suggest that traversing the Appalachian Trail is something beyond the reach of a person who has suffered an injury, survived a serious illness like cancer, or who has not lived as disciplined a lifestyle. It is to say, however, that when you start with those kinds of deficits your preparation will require a bit more from you, and you may need to focus on addressing a specific issue prior to engaging in your overall preparation efforts.

Much the same is true as you consider any strategic planning process. Prevailing paradigms can be a problem. A culture characterized by continuous crisis is an even greater hindrance. Below are some of the things I look for when trying to determine whether a school is healthy enough to engage in rigorous strategic planning process or not.

Weak, fractured, or incompetent leadership

This is true at either or both the building level or the board level. As John Kotter notes, "While I would agree in general that many elements contribute to an organization's results, most of these factors can be influenced by good or bad leadership" (1999, 2).

That has certainly been my experience in working with schools. I've yet to find a process or formula that is able to overcome the impact of poor leadership. In battle, soldiers die when inept leaders are in charge. In business, companies fail when incompetent leaders are in charge. In politics, countries flounder when ineffectual leaders are in charge. Schools are no different. Sadly, ineptness, incompetence, and ineffectiveness are far more common than excellence.

Exceptional leaders, however, cannot and will not tolerate inept, incompetent, or ineffective performance from themselves or from those who serve with them. They will inspire, push, cajole, and encourage their teams to greatness. They will do so because they possess a dynamic combination of character and giftedness that won't permit them to do otherwise.

Remember: leaders matter. A lot.

Organizational inertia

"We're good. All steam ahead." The captain of the Titanic said something like that just before the big ship hit the iceberg that sank the unsinkable. It's what a lot of otherwise capable leaders have said about their organizations just before sliding into obscurity. As Jim Collins notes, "When the rhetoric of success ('We're successful because we do these specific things') replaces penetrating understanding and insight ('We're successful because we understand why we do these specific things and under what conditions they would no longer work'), decline will very likely follow.... Those who ... overestimate their own merit and capabilities—have succumbed to hubris" (2009, 21).

Self-satisfaction is a debilitating disease. Unfortunately, it afflicts a lot of schools that from a distance look healthy. Here is what I look for in determining whether a school has slipped into a period of organizational inertia.

- Happy talk from senior leadership that contrasts with what I hear when talking with faculty, staff, and students.
- A lack of sufficient feedback from external sources such as parents, local church leaders, donors, and alumni. Customer research is a must.
- A shoot-the-messenger-of-bad-news, low-candor, low-confrontation culture. It doesn't take many interviews with faculty and staff to discover if this is true at a school. Shoot a couple of such messengers and your stream of helpful information is guaranteed to dry up.
- Overall low performance standards. It isn't difficult to live up to low standards. If I'm not hearing about specific efforts to evaluate and elevate academic performance, I become suspicious that perhaps the school is coasting along. Schools unaccustomed to rigorous self-assessment will find strategic planning difficult.
- Sometimes too much past success and too many resources can make it easier to assume that all is well at a school. Good schools, like good athletes, can live off past performances until they wake up one day and discover that they are no longer good. Better to stay hungry, to keep pushing toward ever-greater levels of performance.
- Sometimes it is the absence of crisis that allows for inertia to set in. Failure can be fertile soil from which to grow a healthy school. Failure certainly forces leadership to look with care at what put the school at risk and to consider other options for moving ahead.

Inertia is easy to manage. It is much like dropping a marble into a bowl. After a bit of rolling around it finds its place at the bottom of the bowl. Once there, it requires no energy to maintain what is called static equilibrium. Flip the bowl over and try to balance that same marble on the outside of the bowl, however, and the task becomes much more difficult. It requires constant adjustments, or the marble will simply roll off the bowl onto the table or floor. Inertia is easy. No effort is necessary. Managing a dynamic organization, on the other hand, requires much effort. The rewards, however, are worth the effort.

Lack of trust "Trust," as Patrick Lencioni observes, "lies at the heart of a functioning, cohesive team. Without it, teamwork is all but impossible" (2002, 195). The research supporting that assertion is pretty extensive. I would highly recommend reading Lencioni's book *The Five Dysfunctions of a Team* and utilizing the brief questionnaire at the end of that book. It will give you a good sense of the level of trust among the members of your leadership team and faculty.

Trust is fragile, difficult to maintain, easy to lose. Fail to honor promises, both the explicit and the implied ones, and you will lose the trust of your team. Fail to keep confidences or to speak truthfully in every situation, and trust vanishes. Make too many poor decisions or continually ignore wise advice, and no one will trust you. Prove to be a person worthy of trust, however, and people will follow you almost anywhere. Hopefully you see the connection to the strategic planning process. If people don't trust you, why would they be excited about something so challenging?

Fear

Have you ever been frozen by fear? I have. It's an ugly feeling. You know that your failure to act can only lead to a bad conclusion, but you just can't seem to move, to respond appropriately. Unfortunately, fear is the normal human response to threatening situations. Courage is not.

Courage is not really the opposite of fear. Courage is the decision to act in the face of fear. It is what soldiers do when heading into battle. It's what firefighters do when running into a burning building. It's what a congressman does when deciding to cast an unpopular vote on the basis of conscience, knowing that the vote may cost the next election. It's what we do when we suppress the urge to run away and choose rather to stand.

Fear paralyzes us. It can also paralyze an organization. There is a great illustration of this in the Old Testament book of Nehemiah. Nehemiah had arrived in Jerusalem with permission from Artaxerxes, emperor of Persia, to rebuild the walls of the city. Lots of powerful people, however, were opposed to the project. These people benefited from the status quo. They stood to lose a lot of money and control if construction of the wall proceeded to a successful conclusion.

About halfway through the construction process, the opposition organized itself, predicting disaster and threatening harm to both Nehemiah and the people involved in the project. You know the story. You've probably lived this story. The threats and intimidation began to take their toll. Fortunately Nehemiah did not give in to the fear that seemed to be gripping the hearts of the people. Rather he stood before the people and declared, "Do not be afraid of them. Remember the Lord, who is great and awesome, and fight for your brothers, your sons, your daughters, your wives, and your homes" (Nehemiah 4:14).

The antidote to fear is not courage. It is confidence. Courage flows from confidence. For soldiers and firefighters it is confidence in their training, in the wisdom of their leadership, and in the rightness of their cause. The same is true for the people at your school. When they see leaders making wise decisions based on sound planning and when they realize that what drives those leaders is a passion to fulfill, with excellence, the purpose given them by an "awesome" God, then fear tends to dissipate like fog on a sunny day.

Other Symptoms of Poor Organizational Health

Here is a checklist I use when deciding whether a school is ready to engage in a rigorous strategic planning process.

• Frequent leadership or staff turnover. The average tenure of a head of school is around three years. That happens because boards don't have a good means for choosing a new head of school or for effectively evaluating the performance of the head of school. Turnover is a symptom of this poor process.

• Poor staff morale. According to research by Independent School Management, the primary factor in low retention numbers is poor faculty culture.

• Disengaged or inappropriately engaged boards. Far too many boards of Christian schools come to their tasks ill equipped and perform consistently with that reality. Board development is absolutely essential to organizational health.

• Disengaged parents. The tendency for most parents is to adopt a fee-for-service relationship with the school. They write the check, you perform your duty. Sadly, most schools are happy with that arrangement—happy, that is, until the need arises for a capital fund-raising campaign. Then they want everyone on board. You've got to work at engaging your families, and the best way to do that is through constant, consistent communication and by connecting your parents' gifts with needs at your school. People will almost always invest time in something that interests them.

- Weak retention numbers. If you are losing significant numbers of students from year to year it is not because your tuition is too high. It is because your performance and faculty morale are too low.
- Too much debt. I don't know how to say it any more clearly: Never burden your operational budget with capital debt. "The borrower is the slave of the lender" (Proverbs 22:7). Schools, like households, that can't manage their budgets are heading toward fiscal disaster.
- Overdependence on fund-raising. Every school needs to raise money to fund worthwhile capital projects. With rare exceptions, such as schools in difficult urban environments, schools that must raise money to cover operational costs put themselves at risk. Donors hate giving money to turn on your lights or to cover the salaries of your teachers. You've got to make wise fiscal decisions if you want to remain a healthy school.
- Reduction or elimination of funding for basic maintenance, marketing, resource development efforts, professional development, or program enhancement. There will be times when you must take extraordinaty measures to manage your budget. When those brief periods turn into typical behavior, however, you are putting your organization at risk.

Downloadd documents 5.1, 5.2, and 5.3 at https://www.acsi.org/tradebooks/psr/6518. They can help your leadership team discover and analyze the organizational health of your school.

Concluding Thoughts

I've never, not for even a minute, considered taking on the Appalachian Trail. I'm happy for people like Dave Rough. He's a great guy with lots of fascinating stories to tell of his adventure, but I am unwilling to take on the task of getting ready for such a journey. I do want, however, to be part of making a difference in the lives of kids. To do that well requires the same kind of commitment to doing the right things well.

School leadership is not for the faint of heart, for the lazy, for the uncommitted, or for the indecisive. School leadership is hard work. It is about continuously making good decisions about perplexing problems and unexpected opportunities. It is about building strong teams and learning to unleash them in pursuit of a common purpose. It is about focusing both on current needs and on what lies beyond the horizon. It is about winning the hearts and minds of parents, students, pastors, donors, and community leaders. Did I say something about hard work?

You can't do that as a person or as an organization if you are not healthy. So get healthy. Take whatever medicine and do whatever exercise is necessary to get and stay healthy. If you do, then you will be ready to take on the rigors of a quality planning process.

6

Choosing Your Task Force

As the early church was experiencing explosive growth, Satan unleashed attack after attack—desperate attempts to thwart the plan of God for the redemption of humankind. In Acts 6, Satan used a simple strategy: divide and conquer. "Now in these days when the disciples were increasing in number, a complaint by the Hellenists arose against the Hebrews because their widows were being neglected in the daily distribution" (6:1).

Sound familiar? At your school that complaint may come in the form of an unhappy director of fine arts who resents that so many resources are being lavished on the athletic program, or from the elementary principal who feels left behind by the investment being made in the new high school biology lab. There never seems to be enough money for all the things everyone wants to achieve. Making it worse are the subtle suggestions that favoritism is a driving force behind how resources are invested. It's the "Mom always liked you best" phenomenon.

The situation in Acts 6 created a real possibility for fracture in the early church. On one side were a group of widows whose ethnic and national background was Jewish and Palestinian. On the other side were widows whose ethnic and national background was Gentile and Greco-Roman. Both groups had come to embrace Jesus as Messiah. As a consequence, both groups had been excluded from the welfare provided by the various Jewish synagogues in Jerusalem. They now had to rely on the generosity of other followers of Jesus.

The one group was local with strong ties to the community. The other group was "different," not from around there, possibly among the large group of pilgrims in Jerusalem who had heard and responded to the sermon Peter preached on Pentecost.

Many of those pilgrims, rather than returning to their homes, had apparently remained in Jerusalem long after the normal time of departure. By this time their resources would be running low. Widows, without the means to produce income, would be most at risk.

There is even a whiff of racism at work here—not surprising, since racism has plagued humanity since the Fall. All of us are susceptible to racism because all of us are susceptible to the impact of sin. Redemption, however, sets us free from the power of sin and enables us to act in a manner that reflects the very nature of our Creator, in whose image we are made. In that image "there is not Greek and Jew, circumcised and uncircumcised, barbarian, Scythian, slave, free; but Christ is all and in all" (Colossians 3:11).

Sometimes, however, old patterns drive our behavior in spite of our best intentions. That was apparently what was happening in Acts 6. Those old patterns can be so subtle and thus so powerful that we are unaware of what is at work in our decisions and behavior. That in and of itself is a great lesson for all of us. The response of the apostles to this problem, however, was pure genius and should be a model for problem solving in both our personal lives and in the organizations we lead. Consider with me how they responded to this crisis.

Note first of all that the apostles did not initiate the conversation. The problem was identified by the Hellenistic Jews. Second, note that they didn't attempt to solve the problem on their own. The disciples did create a framework for solving the problem, but they included the Hellenists in the process. In the end the apostles bore the responsibility for ensuring that the issues were resolved, but they did not attempt to do it on their own. And note who actually implemented the solution. It wasn't the apostles but the Hellenists who chose seven of their own company to actually implement the decision all agreed made sense in this situation.

Let me break this down a bit. In doing so I want to give appropriate credit to my dear friend Bud McCord, a long-time missionary to Brazil. Bud shared these ideas with me many years ago. They make so much sense in the context of decision making in the family or in an organization.

First of all, in any decision-making process, whether in a family or organization, anyone one who is part of that family or organization should be given the freedom to bring an issue—for example, a problem that needs to be solved or an opportunity that has arisen—to the attention of those in leadership. We can call this person an Initiator. In a family this could be a child or a parent. In a school it could be a janitor or a teacher or a coach. When it comes to initiating a discussion, position in the family or organization should never be a limiting factor.

Second, when a decision must be made, there is typically a shaping process. This is true even in most emergency situations. It is simply wise to get input from a wide range of people if at all possible. Among those whose input you should seek are those who will be responsible for implementing the final decision and those who will be most affected by the decision. How you select those Shapers is crucial. We will explore that identification process in some detail in this chapter.

Third, someone will bear ultimate responsibility for the outcome that follows the decision. We can call this person the Finalizer. The Finalizer is the person who wears the bull's-eye, so to speak. It is not a position of power; rather, it is a position of responsibility.

Fourth, someone must implement the decision. It seems pretty simple to me that those who will be asked to serve as Implementers should be among those who serve as Shapers. And here is a key point. Anyone in leadership can give away all of the authority needed by those Implementers to get the job done in an appropriate way. What a leader can never do is give away the responsibility. The leader always wears the bull's-eye in public.

This quick—actually way too quick and way too superficial—review of the events recorded in Acts 6 seems to provide a sound pattern for us to follow as we consider how to actually engage in a strategic planning process. There is one additional fact, however, that will be helpful to us as we consider the recruitment and design of a strategic planning task force.

Deacons, Committee, or Task Force?

Each year, from among the congregation of the Baptist church I attended growing up in Miami, Florida, we chose seven men to serve as deacons. As a kid I didn't really pay much attention to this process that was always part of the annual church business meeting. Once I headed off to Bible college, however, my interest in all things "church" increased significantly; so on one visit home I managed to make an appointment to meet with the senior pastor of our church.

I posed these questions to my pastor: What exactly is a deacon? What do they do? And why do we have seven of them? In response to my questions, he took me to Acts 6. From that text he explained that deacons were men who took on tasks at the church that would interfere with a pastor's primary role of preaching and prayer. We had seven deacons because that was the number we were given in the text. That all made sense to me. And after all, no less an authority than C. I. Scofield assured me in his notes on this text that what my pastor was saying was true.

It wasn't until years later that I discovered that perhaps both my pastor and the esteemed Dr. Scofield might have been mistaken. First of all, the idea that the seven men mentioned in Acts 6 were deacons is probably not accurate. Second, that the number of deacons should be limited to seven is also probably not valid. What we do have here in all actuality is probably the formation of the first strategic planning task force in the history of the church. Let me explain.

It is only in retrospect that we see the Church emerging in Jerusalem following the death and resurrection of Jesus. Most of the disciples would have viewed themselves as Jews who had discovered and embraced the true Messiah. This is the substance of the message Peter preached on the day of Pentecost. In that message he identified Jesus first as Jesus of Nazareth and then declared, "Let all the house of Israel therefore know for certain that God made him both Lord and Christ, this Jesus whom you crucified" (Acts 2:36). In other words, Jesus of Nazareth was the long-prophesied Messiah. There was no mention of "the Church." The Messiah, most Jews believed, was to be sent to the nation of Israel, not to something called "the Church."

Why does that matter? It actually matters a lot because it helps explain both the horrific response of the Jewish leaders to the phenomenon unfolding in the city of Jerusalem and the decision-making process of the apostles, who still considered themselves Jewish. Thus they would think and act as Jews would think and act. It was common practice for Jews to form what we would today call a task force in response to a crisis or some other event that was out of the ordinary. The number of participants on that task force was typically set at seven. This explains what the apostles did in response to the emergency involving the Hellenistic widows.

This background is important because I find so much resistance to the idea of a strategic planning task force. Most schools, when engaging in strategic planning, choose to limit the task force to the members of the school board and the head of school, perhaps with a few other administrators thrown in. This group will (hopefully) attempt to gather data from other parts of the constituency such as teachers, staff, students, alumni, donors, parents, and maybe even local church leaders. The actual planning, however, will be done by a small group, typically the board and head of school.

The reasons given for this approach are threefold.
1. If the group gets too big, it becomes unwieldy.
2. Since the board wears the bull's-eye and is given the responsibility to "guard the trust" of the school, they should be the ones who set the direction for the school.
3. The more constituents you add to a task force, the more private agendas you must deal with during the planning process.

All three concerns are legitimate. Larger groups are more difficult to manage. In the end the board does "guard the trust," meaning they are responsible for ensuring that no decision made during a strategic planning process puts the school at risk or moves the school off its mission. Finally, it is true that the more people you include on the task force the more agendas you will be forced to consider. (I addressed that reality in chapter 3.)

It is my belief, however, that none of those concerns outweighs the benefits of a properly constructed and wisely recruited task force. That doesn't mean that I am right. I certainly understand why people are reluctant to assemble a strategic planning task force as I will suggest. I just believe the result will be superior, and equally important I believe that the support for the plan will be greater (more on that in a moment).

Remember this: "In the counsel of many there is wisdom" (Proverbs 11:14). Why do you think that is so? I think it has to do with how we are wired and how our fallenness can affect how we make decision.

The Problem of Blind Spots

All of us have a filter, a characteristic way of responding to the world around us. That filter is a unique blend of our personal and professional experiences, the reading and study we have done, the people with whom we have interacted, our cultural contexts, our theological beliefs, and—very importantly—it is influenced by our basic wiring as human beings. Those influences are powerful but subtle, shaping how we "see" everything from relationships to the work we do to how we set priorities in our personal and professional lives.

Your filter is unique to you. While similar in some ways to how others around you may view the world, it is distinct because your set of circumstances is distinct. Your filter is not a conscious, rational process. As Marcus Buckingham points out, your filter does not "kick in once a week allowing you the luxury of sitting back and weighing up all the alternatives before deciding on the most sensible course of action. Rather your filter is constantly at work sorting, sifting, creating a world in real time" (2001).

As the apostle Paul would put it, some of us are eyes in the body. Others of us are ears, hands, and feet. We tend to think from those perspectives and tend to think that our perspective makes the most sense. The fact of the matter is that we benefit when we engage all of those perspectives to bring clarity to an issue or to solve a problem. Otherwise we enter the decision-making process blind, deaf, or without mobility.

We need lots of different outlooks when engaging in something so crucial to the future of an organization as strategic planning. Thus we can ill afford to begin the process with blinders on.

The Need for Constructive Conflict

We are deathly afraid of conflict, so much so that we will go to almost any length to avoid it. Conflict, however, is not only inevitable in any situation where you include people who bring a broad range of perspectives, it is also essential to any quality decision-making process. If we only invite ears to be part of our team, the solution we create will likely end up looking suspiciously like an ear.

In his account of how the Wright brothers solved the problem of heavier-than-air controlled flight, Mark Eppler makes this observation: "As they challenged each other's positions, their unshaped ideas and opinions were hammered into the form of a potential solution" (2003, 45).

It isn't only the Wright brothers who have successfully practiced constructive conflict. Read accounts of any major scientific accomplishment of the last 100 years and you will likely find that discoveries and results came only after much arguing. Iron does indeed sharpen iron (Proverbs 27:17).

As Solomon reminds us, "An intelligent man acquires knowledge, and the ear of the wise seeks knowledge." Why? Because "If one gives an answer before he hears, it is his folly and shame" (Proverbs 18:13). Wisdom demands that we gather as much quality information as we can before making a decision. Only a fool would believe himself or herself to be in possession of all necessary information.

Remember those blind spots that plague all of us? It isn't just blindness about how we see the world, but also blindness about what we think we know when looking at the world. None of us, and I mean none of us, is in possession of all of the information we need to address the challenges we face or the problems we must solve. We need, therefore, not only the perspectives of others, but their knowledge as well. That is why "The heart of him who has understanding seeks knowledge" (Proverbs 15:14), and it is why "without counsel plans fail" (Proverbs 15:22).

It is not my intent in this brief space to describe a model for constructive conflict. Rather, it is my intent to emphasize that solving truly difficult problems or forging a sound strategic plan is unlikely to happen without that conflict, without the bringing together of a variety of viewpoints and pools of knowledge. Conflict will be the inevitable result of those colliding viewpoints and pools of knowledge. Making that conflict constructive is your goal. In the bibliography at the end of this book you will find a number of resources that will help you achieve that goal.

The Power of Ownership

What people do not understand they cannot own. What they do not own they will not support. Engage in enough autopsies of failed capital campaigns and you will discover the truth of that statement.

I have a dear friend who was approached by his pastor and asked to give a lead gift to a capital campaign focused on providing the resources to build a new sanctuary at the church. This friend is a successful business owner who has generated significant wealth during his lifetime. He is also a very wise man who understands his stewardship responsibility. Thus he asked his pastor this question: "Why do we need to build a new sanctuary?" The pastor's response was brief and to the point. "We need more space to accommodate the growth in our church."

That reply led to a second question from my friend. "What are you planning to do with all of these new people?" At that question the pastor stumbled. He had no answer to that question. In the planning process that question had apparently never been considered. My friend, who was never asked to serve on the task force, was asking what to him was the key question. Is this project about investing in a building or in people? He simply could not understand the rationale for the project. And because he could not do so he could not own or support the project—a project, by the way, that ended up putting this church several million dollars in debt.

It is certainly true that not everyone in an organization can be part of the planning task force. What is true, however, is that support for a project—and virtually every strategic planning process—will increase to the extent that the task force involves not only the leaders of the school but those whose gifts will be required to fund the project.

I love this quote by Tom Peters: "People who are part of the team, who 'own' the company and 'own' their job, regularly perform a thousand times better than the rest" (2016). Imagine what would happen at your school if your parents were invited to be part of making decisions for which they will be asked to pay. Identify the right people, and the impact will be significant. Each of those parents can become a positive force in influencing how dozens of other parents view the leadership of their school, how those leaders make decisions, and how those decisions have the potential for improving the educational opportunities for students at the school.

There is one additional—and, I believe, major—benefit that accrues from involving parents, alumni, and donors in your strategic planning efforts. In so doing you will give yourself the opportunity to observe those individuals as they work together toward a common purpose. Two things will often happen. First of all, you are likely to discover potential new board members. Second, you will have the opportunity to ignite and fuel a deeper passion for the purpose, mission, and vision of your school among some key people. Those are likely to be among the most positive outcomes of your strategic planning efforts.

Who Should Be on the Team?

No one has said it better than Jim Collins: "The executives who ignited the transformations from good to great did not first figure out where to drive the bus and then get people to take it there. No, they first got the right people on the bus (and the wrong people off the bus) and then figured out where to drive it" (2001, 41). The same rule applies whether you are staffing a school or forming a strategic planning task force. Quality produces quality. Identify and recruit quality people, engage in a quality process, and the likely outcome will be quality work. It really is that simple.

So what qualities should you be looking for when recruiting your task force?

• **Character.** Every task force member must be a person of unimpeachable character. It is the first qualification Paul mentions when speaking about choosing elders in the church: "Therefore an overseer must be above reproach" (1 Timothy 3:2). Character first—always first.

• **Commitment.** Ask this question regarding every candidate: Has this person historically been supportive of our school? Here are some other questions that can help flesh out the meaning of *supportive*. Has this person given financially to the school? Is this person a positive spokesperson for the school? Has this person been involved in projects at the school? In other words, does this person "have skin in the game," or only been on the sidelines? There will be a place later in the process when you can reach out to specific people with specific gifts, knowledge, or influence. For the initial task force, however, you must look for people who already passionately "own" the mission of your school.

• **Competence.** You are not assembling a team to construct a new delivery system to transport people and material to the space station, so technical expertise is not at issue here. What you are looking for, however, are people who are gifted thinkers, who have a proven track record in their chosen profession (including the profession of homemaker), who are articulate, thoughtful, hardworking, able, and wise. If you don't know a person well enough to know those kinds of things, then he or she shouldn't be serving on your task force.

• **Compatibility.** It is not enough for the person to be committed to the school. The person must also demonstrate a clear understanding of your mission, your core values, and core beliefs. There are many people who love your school because it offers a quality education in a safe environment. They love you for loving their child. That isn't enough. Your task force will be looking deeply into the very heart and core of your school. You want people who understand that heart and core. Think of it this way: Should you ever need open-heart surgery, who do you want performing that surgery—a pediatrician or an experienced heart surgeon?

• **Chemistry.** Solomon warns us of a particular kind of person. "Whosoever isolates himself seeks his own desire; he breaks out against all sound judgment. A fool takes no pleasure in understanding, but only in expressing his own opinions" (Proverbs 18:1–2). Avoid that person. Choose instead people who exemplify these qualities:

- "Whoever is slow to anger has great understanding" (Proverbs 14:29).
- "A tranquil heart gives life to the flesh" (Proverbs 14:30).
- "A soft answer turns away wrath" (Proverbs 15:1).
- "A gentle tongue is a tree of life" (Proverbs 15:4).
- "A glad heart makes a cheerful face" (Proverbs 15:13).
- "The heart of the wise makes his speech judicious and adds persuasiveness to his lips" (Proverbs 16:23).
- "Gracious words are like a honeycomb, sweetness to the soul and health of the body" (Proverbs 16:24).
- "A friend loves at all times, and a brother is born for adversity" (Proverbs 17:17).
- "A joyful heart is good medicine" (Proverbs 17:22).
- "Whoever restrains his words has knowledge, and he who has a cool spirit is a man of understanding" (Proverbs 17:27).

I could add to the list, but I think you get the message. It's what I call the "hang-out factor." Think about this person stranded with you on a desert island, and you will get the picture.

- **Confirmation.** Here is a basic rule: When in doubt, don't. If everyone who is on the nominating team doesn't wholeheartedly agree that a particular person belongs on the task force, then don't choose that person. There must be a 100% vote in favor of the person.

Getting It Done

With all of that important foundational information in place, it is time to actually put together the task force. Here are some practical steps that you should follow to accomplish this important undertaking.

Clarify task force responsibilities

As you set out to identify and recruit your task force, you will need to develop clear job descriptions for task force members. You can be sure that they will be asking you for one. Back in chapter 2, I provided an outline of the planning process. You will want to make that outline available to those you hope to recruit. That outline will tell task force members how long the process will take. In addition, you will want to make sure they understand that task force members will be responsible to do the following:

- *Attend all scheduled meetings.* Your responsibility is to ensure that everyone is informed of each meeting well ahead of time.

- *Complete all assignments to the best of their ability.* There will be research to be done and action plans to construct. For some participants this will be new territory. When I work with a school, I take time to provide necessary instruction for each task.

- *Willingly and enthusiastically engage in the conversation that this process requires.* As a facilitator I have structured a process that makes it easy for everyone to engage, but on occasion a bit of encouragement is helpful.

- *Positively communicate into their sphere of influence.* From the beginning, school leadership will let the school community know that a strategic planning process is underway and why the process is important at this time. It is not the responsibility of the participants to share particulars of the process. In fact, that is unwise. What they need to share is their sense of excitement at being involved in the process, their sense of joy that school leadership has chosen to move ahead with the process, and their sense of satisfaction at how well the process is going.

- *Embrace the reality of a six-month time commitment.* Remember, strategic planning is not an event, not a single weekend conversation. Rather, it is a process—a process that will take time to unfold. The work necessary to identify truly strategic initiatives and then to create workable action plans is the work of months, not a weekend. Task force participants need to understand and embrace this reality.

Create a nominating task force

Notice I didn't say to create a nominating *committee.* Your board may already have a nominating committee that identifies and nominates potential new board members. A committee is a group of people with a specific ongoing responsibility. It is limited in scope and authority but not in time. A task force is also limited in scope and authority but it is also limited in time. This will be a one-time task—at least one time for a period of years.

This task force should consist of three to five people chosen from among the board and senior leadership team of the school. Their job is to identify individuals who meet the above qualifications and to present that list to the board for final approval.

The first task for this group is a simple brainstorming activity. Using a whiteboard or flip chart, they simply begin to write down names. As in any other brainstorming activity, this is not a time to editorialize. If a name is given, write it down. You will want to produce a fairly substantial list.

Use the evaluation grid (document 6.1, downloadable from https://www.acsi.org/tradebooks/psr/6518) to do a first-pass check of possible candidates. Eliminate without hesitation. Quality is more important than numbers. Sometimes it might make sense to do a deeper dive. Remember this: if few people in the room have an adequate knowledge of a particular person, that in and of itself should be cause for hesitation. Remember as well that the board will make the final decision.

I'm often asked two questions at this point: How many? What kind of balance? The answer to the first question is simple. Anywhere between eighteen and thirty is a good number depending on the size of your school. Most people think thirty is way too many members for a task force. Perhaps. I think it depends on how the process is designed and how well the task force is managed.

In my experience too many members is seldom the problem; too few often is. The process will create a lot of work, often more than a few people can handle. This is a good opportunity to see the gifts and abilities of individuals beyond the staff and board as they work together to accomplish the initiatives identified during the planning process. That alone is worth all that it takes to keep the task force moving along.

The answer to the second question is a bit more challenging. Let's begin with this. I don't believe that you should seek to achieve some kind of artificial balance on the task force. You don't need a particular percentage of board members vis-à-vis a particular number of staff or parents or alumni. Always begin with this in mind: get the best possible people to serve.

And do not seek to create some kind of representative group. Addressing personal agendas is challenging enough. Creating competing interest groups makes that challenge more difficult. This is a team, not a representative assembly. Its goal is to discover God's vision for the school, not to craft a vision based on how best to balance competing priorities.

You certainly want a cross-section of the school: board members, administration, staff, faculty, parents, alumni, students, and donors. In some cases individual task force members will be members of more than one category—both faculty and parent, both board member and parent, both donor and alumni. Remember, you are looking for different perspectives, not different agendas.

Recruit your task force

Once you have your list of names, it is time to actually recruit those individuals to serve on the task force. These are busy people. They aren't looking for another way to spend their time; they already have too little time as it is. And they most definitely aren't looking to waste their time on a project that will end its life as a notebook on a shelf somewhere. Unfortunately, many of the people you will approach have had negative experiences with strategic planning or know people who have shared horror stories. So when I say you must recruit them, I mean just that.

This is a task for the head of school and chair of the board. Recruitment must be highly personal and, where appropriate, it must be highly persuasive as well. I'm not talking about twisting arms. I'm talking about making a case for why the work of the task force is crucial to the future of the school. This isn't business as usual. A quality strategic planning process will set the direction of a school and determine allocation of resources. Serving on a strategic planning task force is an incredible opportunity.

With names in hand, the head of school and chair of the board should decide who should contact whom. Sometimes a personal relationship will guide that decision. Sometimes it's a matter of flipping a coin. What matters is that the initial contact should be personal. That first conversation should focus on two items: why a strategic planning process at this time, and why you need this person to serve.

Don't look for a yes at this time. Let them know that you will be sending a letter explaining in more detail the process and their role in the process. You will be back in contact after they have received the letter to answer any questions and to see if they are interested in serving. Document 6.2 (downloadable at https://www.acsi. org/tradebooks/psr/6518) is a sample invitation letter.

If they agree to serve, great, but your work is not done. It will be important that you stay in contact with the task force members to update them as the time approaches for the initial strategic planning retreat. You will then want to keep them informed about each subsequent meeting in which they will be involved. Never let them wonder about what's happening or about their role in what's happening. Keep them in the loop. People dislike uncertainty. Quality communication dispels that uncertainty.

What if you don't get enough positive responses to your invitation? If that happens, you will want to regather your nominating task force and see if you can identify other names. It seems unlikely to me, however, that you simply overlooked quality candidates. So it might make sense to step back and ask this uncomfortable question: Why can't we find enough quality people who are willing to serve in such an important task? You may find yourself deciding to postpone the planning process in order to do the work of improving communication with your constituents.

Passion Beats Perfection

One final thought. There are no perfect people. Surprised? Of course not. You wake up every day and live the reality of life in a fallen world, rubbing shoulders with fallen people, who are rubbing shoulders with you, another fallen person. Obviously you want to find mature people who exemplify the qualities identified above. Like leadership, maturity matters. Avoid the immature the way you would avoid the plague.

Beyond maturity, however, nothing matters more than passion. Passion is unmistakable. People know when you are passionate about something. Let's end this chapter with another quotation from Jim Collins: "It may seem odd to talk about something so soft and fuzzy as 'passion' as an integral part of a strategic framework. But throughout the good-to-great companies, passion became a key part" of what they were doing. It is important to remember, however, that, "You can't manufacture passion or 'motivate' people to feel passionate. You can only discover what ignites your passion and the passions of those around you" (2001, 109).

Find those people, unleash them through a great process, and the results will amaze you.

What Is Nonnegotiable?

My all-time favorite movie is *Chariots of Fire*. I've probably watched it thirty times since it premiered some thirty years ago. Aside from the obvious talent of the filmmaker, and a score for the ages, what so captures me is its powerful contrast of two men: Harold Abrams, driven to prove himself worthy in a world not so hospitable to people of Jewish descent, and Eric Liddell, a son of missionaries who is driven by his passion for God.

What makes the story so fascinating to me is that both men use the same vehicle—running track—to achieve their very dissimilar ends. Both men are gifted. Both men are disciplined. Both men are able to balance the competing demands of pursuing a university education and the quest for Olympic gold. Yet in nearly every other way they see life through completely different lenses.

Perhaps my favorite scene in the movie, and the one that captures for me the essence of the story, occurs on a hillside overlooking the city of Edinburgh. Let me set the stage for those who may be unfamiliar with the story. Because of the time necessary to pursue both his studies and his training regimen, Eric shows up late once again for the Bible study that he, his sister, and his sister's husband have been leading. As the final student heads toward the exit, Eric makes a hurried entrance. His sister casts a glance of disapproval in his direction.

Recognizing that he has once again disappointed her, Eric convinces her to follow him out of the room in which they have been meeting and out onto a hillside. Once there, he delivers a message that he knows will grab her heart. He tells her that he has been accepted to return as a missionary to China, where his parents have served for many years. With that message a look of joy is clearly present on his sister's face. A look, however, destined to disappear quickly.

He then proceeds to tell her that before he heads back to China he intends to run in the Olympics. It is then, as his sister's face once again projects a message of disappointment, that Eric utters the words that lie at the heart of this story and that reveal his deepest motivation: "God made me for China. But He also made me fast. And when I run I feel His pleasure. To not run would be to hold Him in contempt."

Grasp the significance of that statement, and all that I say in this chapter will make sense. God made all of us in His image and gave to each of us a driving purpose. In his book *The Purpose Driven Life*, Rick Warren (2002) makes this observation: "You were made by God and for God, and until you understand that, life will never make sense."

It is not only individuals who have been made for a purpose, but organizations as well. In some senses every church and every school pursues a similar purpose and seeks to achieve a similar mission. In other ways, however, our callings are unique.

As I've often noted, God is not the great Xerox machine in the sky rolling out endless copies of the same person or the same organization. All of us, persons and organizations, occupy different places, exist in different cultures, are surrounded by different communities, and are driven by different passions. During the strategic planning process it must be your first goal to clearly identify a number of key realities about yourself—realities such as who you are, why you exist, and what you hope to accomplish. In so doing, you distinguish yourself from everyone around you and decide what must never change.

You will do so because you need a clear blueprint to build a strong organization, a blueprint that will
- focus personal and organizational energies toward powerful ends;
- prevent you from becoming distracted and sidetracked while in pursuit of those ends;
- keep you from spending time, money, and effort unwisely on things that don't make a difference and aren't related to your purpose and mission;
- provide a sound framework for thinking, deciding, governing, and evaluating your efforts;
- remind you why what you do really matters; and
- help you communicate what is really important to everyone connected with your school.

You will also do so because as you journey forward in a turbulent world, you will always need a compass to guide you toward your organizational North Star.

Why Now?

When I share an overview of my planning process with school leaders, they often make the following observation and pose the following question. "Dr. Pue, we already have a mission statement. We created it years ago. We have already identified our core values. We did that years ago as well. We really have no intention of changing anything. Why, then, would we spend time during the strategic planning process going back over questions we long ago answered to our satisfaction?" Those are fair questions. Let me see if I can provide satisfactory answers.

I don't remember when I first saw this quote from T.S. Eliot (1943, 39). What I do remember is how powerfully it grabbed my attention. Take your time to read and ponder these lines:

> We shall not cease from exploration
>
> And the end of all our exploring
>
> Will be to arrive where we started
>
> And know the place for the first time.

As educators we like to remind ourselves that we are to be "lifelong learners." I sometimes think that what we mean by that is that we are to be enrolled in some kind of course, workshop, or professional development program at all times. None of those things are bad. I suspect that a lot of what drives us is less the pure joy of learning something new, but more a rather pragmatic motivation related to continued professional certification and increases in pay.

Eliot actually echoes similar language to that found in one of the apostle Peter's letters to the churches. Read the brief passage and see if you can spot the similarities of thought.

Therefore I intend always to remind you of these qualities, though you know them and are established in the truth that you have. I think it is right, as long as I am in this body, to stir you up by way of reminder (2 Peter 1:12–13).

If both the great apostle and the great poet are right—and I believe they are—there are many reasons why you need to periodically revisit, review, and possibly even revise the statements that you have created that define and direct your school. One of the primary reasons is the simple need to refresh your thinking—to remind yourself of what is most important and why it is most important. Let's be honest:

it is just too easy to forget what matters most. Life is like a whirlwind driving us relentlessly along. Some days it is all we can do just to hold it together, to keep everything from blowing apart.

At times like that (which is much of the time) your thoughts are seldom drawn to your mission statement, a statement that is often long on concepts but short on elegant passion—one that in all reality may look pretty much like every other Christian school mission statement out there.

Not only do we live in a whirlwind, but also the words we use are often obscure in their meaning. That is especially the case when we employ jargon that means so many different things to different people. Consider concepts such as these:
• Biblical worldview
• Partnership with parents
• Pursuit of excellence
• Christ-centered environment
• Integrating faith and learning
• Loving and caring environment
• Developing the whole person
• To glorify God

Does any of that sound familiar to you? I suspect so. I'm not suggesting that any of that language is inappropriate or wrong. It isn't. What it can quickly become, however, is background noise. Language like that only has power when we constantly remind people what it means and when how we define ourselves is carefully and consistently aligned with our everyday practice. Whatever the case, we will always benefit from taking a new look at who we say we are.

The Key Questions You Must Answer While Deciding What Is Nonnegotiable

Just what is the difference between mission and vision? What is the difference between purpose and mission? What are values, and why do they matter? Are there things that can change over time? Are there things that must never change? Those are all questions that I will address in this chapter. I'll begin by simply listing a series of questions that you will need to answer about your school during this process if you hope to have clarity about who you are and what you hope to achieve.

- *Why do we exist?* Answering that question tells you your purpose.
- *What do we exist to do?* Answering that question tells you your mission. Mission is what you do in response to your purpose.
- *What shapes our every action?* Answering that tells you what you value. As we will see, there are three kinds of values: permission-to-play values, aspirational values, and core values.
- *What sets us apart?* Answering that question tells you what makes you distinctive in the marketplace.
- *What is our desired impact?* Answering that question tells you what difference you hope to make in the lives of your students.
- *How do we plan to make that impact?* Answering that question describes the means you will employ in trying to make that difference.
- *Whom are we trying to impact?* Answering that question tells you who your customer is.
- *What do we believe to be true?* Answering that question tells you what is absolutely nonnegotiable.

Let's take a look at each of those questions in turn.

Why do we exist? What is our purpose?

Simon Sinek (2009) makes a powerful case that the companies and organizations that truly excel are ones able to identify their singular purpose for existence. He argues that most companies and organizations can quickly describe *what* they do. He then continues by observing that some companies and organizations, ones able to separate themselves from their competitors in the marketplace, are able to express clearly the *how* of their company—the means they employ in delivering their what. What sets the great companies apart from the good companies, however, is the clarity they bring to the question of *why*. Why do we exist to do what we do? This is the purpose question.

The adjoining figure provides a graphic illustration of what Sinek is saying in his Golden Circle presentation. I've added one additional piece as a result of a conversation with a group of Christian school leaders. During that conversation Stephen Reel, former head of school at Southside Christian in Greenville, South Carolina, made the observation that what is missing from Sinek's model is the real

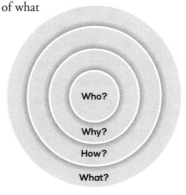

heart of any Christian school—the person of Christ. He is right in that observation. It is what I think people mean when they say, "We are a Christ-centered school." Therefore, I added "Who" at the center of the illustration.

There is a reason, however, for what Sinek observes in great companies like Apple and Southwest Airlines. People are not motivated by jargon. They are motivated by passion, and as Jim Collins notes, "You can't manufacture passion or motivate people to feel passionate. You can only discover what ignites your passion and the passion of people around you" (2001, 109). Every believer, regardless of his or her particular calling, should be motivated by a passion for the person of Christ. But there are reasons why some Christian schools seem to flourish while others flounder. One of those reasons revolves around this idea of purpose. Schools that flourish are schools that have discovered the why behind their what. Others—those that seem to struggle—have not.

Ask yourself these questions: Why do I get up every morning and do what I do? What motivates me to do what I do? What would happen in my heart if I suddenly couldn't do what I do anymore? What would be lost if what I do couldn't be done anymore? How would the world be diminished?

In answering those questions, you will begin to find your purpose in life. In answering those questions as a school, you will begin to find your school's purpose in the world. And if after answering those questions your heart doesn't ignite with passion, then you need to find something else to do with your life. First of all, if you don't, you will be miserable. Second, your school will likely fail because people will sense your lack of passion. Listen carefully to Harry Beckwith: "Clients" (and your parents are clients) "love passionate people and passionate businesses because passion stimulates them— they feel it and feel better too—and because they know that passion produces better work. *Passion inflamed by belief and purpose wins*" (2003, 258; emphasis in original).

So, why do you exist? What is your purpose? Why do you do what you do? Don't just tell me *what* you do. Don't tell me that you teach from a biblical worldview. Don't tell me that you seek to cultivate in your students Christian character. And please don't tell me that you provide a holistic education. Don't tell me any of that until you can tell me *why* any of that matters. Even if I don't agree with your why, I need to know that you are driven by something that so captures your very being that you can't imagine doing anything else.

Before anything else, answer the why question.

What do we exist to do? What is our mission?

Rollin King, the founder of Southwest Airlines, when asked in 1972 why, in the face of incredible competition and stifling government control, he would want to start a new airline, answered with a statement like this: "We're the champion for the common man" (Sinek 2009, 70–71). Most people could not afford to fly. He wasn't concerned about competition with other airlines such as Pan American, Eastern, TWA, or Braniff International (all of which, by the way, no longer exist while Southwest flourishes). His plan was to compete against the family automobile!

To do that, he had to figure out how to make flying less expensive. His mission was, therefore, in one sense obvious. Southwest had to become the "low-cost airline." How Howard Putnam, CEO of Southwest Airlines, did that is described in the book *Great by Choice* (Collins and Hansen 2011). The point here is this: Mission is what you do in response to your purpose. It is a direct response. If my purpose is to be a champion for the common man, then it makes sense to find a way to making flying less expensive for the average American and thus more appealing. If it is cheaper to fly to my destination than it is to drive to my destination, then I'll likely consider purchasing a ticket. Mission always follows purpose.

Consider your school, for example. Let's say your purpose is this: "To ensure that children thrive in the world as followers of Jesus Christ despite the powerful influences of culture, media, and secularism." What would you do in response to that purpose? This is where you might talk about the importance of developing a biblical view of the world or the importance of discernment or learning how to appropriately and effectively engage a world awash in cynicism, skepticism, and secularism. Mission statements don't have to be brief. Purpose statements do. Wordiness is not a virtue, but neither is a truncated, superficial explanation of what you do.

One of the best purpose statements I have ever heard was developed by a school in south Florida. It had all the elements of any powerful purpose statement: brevity, memorable language, clarity, and most of all it generated the best response possible to a purpose statement. It first captured people's attention and then prompted people to respond with, "Could you tell me more?" No one's eyes glazed over. No one yawned. No one said, "Well, I've heard that a dozen times."

That statement, which took over a year to develop, went like this: "XYZ Christian school exists to give students roots, dreams, and wings." Like I said, no jargon, just powerful imagery. When I first heard the pastor, who served as president of the school, utter that statement I thought, "Wow!" Then I asked this question: "Tell me what you mean by that." He then immediately took all of us in the room to three biblical texts and used them to give one of the best explanations of Christian schooling I have heard, and it took him less than three minutes to do so. In giving his response to my question he explained—again in brief, memorable language—the mission of the school. I'll leave it to you to figure out the texts he used.

Remember: mission is what you do in response to your purpose.

What shapes our every action? What are our values?

Ever been to an Indian or Korean restaurant? How about an Italian ristorante or a French bistro? How about a barbecue pit or a Mexican restaurant? In any of those places, one of the first things you notice is the aroma hanging in the air and clinging to every surface. Indian means curry. Korean is an interesting mixture of garlic and red pepper. Italian is garlic and mozzarella. French is a bit more subtle, a mixture of many herbs and spices. Barbecue is wood smoke. Mexican means a unique collection of spices. In every case, however, there will be a distinct aroma that will tell you what type of eating establishment it is.

Think of values in that way. They are the marinade that flavors everything you do at your school. Don't believe me? Here's a simple experiment. Visit a Montessori school, a classical school, a high-end college prep school, and a fundamentalist Baptist school. I guarantee you that within half a day, without knowing the name of the school, you will be able to discern the differences and come close to guessing the kind of school you are visiting. Core values, as Patrick Lencioni calls them, are that noticeable (2012, 91–104).

So what is the aroma I would most notice if I came and visited your school? And would the scent I read about in your handbook match the one I would encounter during my visit? The challenge for most of us is that what we often identify as a value is really what Patrick Lencioni identifies as an aspirational value. It isn't what we really are; rather it is what we aspire to be, what we hope to be, what we wish were true about us.

One school I worked with talked about its "relentless pursuit of perfection," borrowing from a marketing line for the Lexus brand of automobiles. As I walked around the campus, I got a more Chevy kind of feel—solid, but not spectacular, and certainly no sense of any kind of pursuit. It was actually a pretty static environment. The school was providing a good education, but not a great one, and I saw no evidence that they were really working with any level of urgency to raise the level of performance among their faculty. Beyond a periodic workshop, it was every person for himself or herself. The idea of a learning community with a common goal of developing a truly innovative academic program was nowhere to be found.

Your values, to be what Lencioni calls core values, must be what is actually true of you, not what you wish to be true. Here are some questions Lencioni (2012, 94–103) suggests an organization ask itself to determine if something is truly a core value:
• Is this trait inherent and natural for us?
• Has it been apparent in the organization for a long time?
• Is it something we have to work hard to cultivate?
• Do we use these values in every hiring decision?
• Are we willing to be punished for living those values?

What are you willing to be punished for? What will and must absolutely, unmistakably characterize your school in its pursuit of providing an education that is truly Christian? To get to that kind of value, I use a simple brainstorming activity.

I ask two open-ended questions:
• XYZ Christian school is ...
• XYZ Christian school does …

As in any brainstorming activity there are no right answers and no wrong answers, and no editorializing is allowed. I use a large sticky-edged flipchart to record all of the answers, which allows me to continually display all the responses on the wall. When the group has run out of useful things to say, I next have them break into small groups to categorize the responses. One of those categories is for those statements that people view as representative of the values they believe characterize the school.

I then have them engage in another exercise (document 7.1, downloadable from https://www.acsi.org/tradebooks/psr/6518), during which they will separate the value into one of Lencioni's categories:
• Permission-to-play values
• Aspirational values
• Core values

Deciding what is truly a core value as opposed to an aspirational value will almost always prompt a bit of intense discussion—which, by the way, is one of the key reasons I use the exercise. If you think you are an Italian restaurant but all of your ingredients fit better into a recipe for curried lamb, you may have to rethink some of your basic assumptions. Document 7.2 (downloadable from https://www.acsi.org/tradebooks/psr/6518) can help you distinguish core values from aspirational values.

What sets us apart in the marketplace? What makes us distinctive?

Here's a hint. Unless you are the only Christian school within a fifty-mile radius, it isn't your Christian philosophy of education. As VP for Advancement at The Master's College in Santa Clarita, California, I had to deal with the fact that there were seventeen evangelical Christian colleges in southern California, and most of them were our direct competitors.

I know that we don't like to think that way, but when you are trying to grow your enrollment, competition is a reality. Virtually every student who visited our campus or filled out an application also did so at Westmont, Biola, or Asuza Pacific, to name just a few. I had to give them a good reason for choosing TMC over those other excellent schools. If I couldn't articulate what made TMC distinctive and why those distinctions mattered to a particular student, then I put the future of TMC at risk.

So, what does set you apart? What is your Purple Cow? "The essence of the Purple Cow is that it must be remarkable" (Godin 2009, 2). Remember this, however: the Cow is rare and it's rare because people are afraid. As Seth Godin observes, "If you're remarkable, it's likely that some people won't like you. That's part of the definition of remarkable. Nobody gets unanimous praise—ever.... Criticism comes to those who stand out" (45).

There are many possibilities you could identify:
• Location
• Facilities
• Your philosophy of education
• A particular program (e.g., science, music, athletics, off-campus internships)
• Your historical reputation
• Your affiliation with a church or denominational group
• Your lack of affiliation with a church or denominational group
• Your theological distinctives

- Your lifestyle distinctives
- Your history of college placements
- A particular approach to curriculum or instruction
- Class size
- Faculty quality

Different things will resonate with different people. If you are just another Christian school somewhere in the middling middle, then you must understand that marketing will continue to be a challenge for you. If nothing sets you apart or if what sets you apart doesn't matter to most people, then you will probably continue to struggle to build and maintain a consistently strong enrollment.

Here is a helpful exercise. Invite your parents to participate in a series of focus groups. Look for a cross-section of parents from your elementary, middle, and high schools—parents who are new to your school and parents who have been around for a while. Plan on an hour with each group. Ask each group the following questions:
- What first attracted you to this school? Make them be specific.
- What was the primary characteristic of this school that most motivated you to enroll your child here?
- What have you discovered since you enrolled your child at this school that helps keep you here?
- What have you discovered since you enrolled your child at this school that most frustrates you?
- When you talk to your friends and neighbors, what do you tell them about why you continue to enroll your child at this school?
- When you talk with your friends and neighbors, what do they say about this school?
- What descriptors do you use in explaining this school to them?

You'll learn a lot about what people perceive to be your distinctives. Those perceptions may or may not match your own. Where there is agreement between what you think and what your parents observe, then you may have a legitimate distinctive. Where you have disagreement, you have dissonance and need to reexamine your assumptions. With this kind of real-world information in hand, you are in a position to focus on the distinctives that positively set you apart in the marketplace and to address negative distinctives that harm your reputation in the marketplace.

What is our desired impact? What difference are we trying to make in the lives of our students?

The early Greek philosophers wrestled with the question of *telos*. Is there an "end," a point, a purpose to the movements and actions in reality? It's an important issue for us, too. Is there a point to all of the activity involved in the thing we call education? It is an important question—one every parent is asking, even if the question is never asked directly. In fact, I believe that your parents are more concerned about what will happen in the life of their child than they are about what their child will do at your school. There is an old proverb that captures this concern: "The proof of the pudding is in the eating."

"True education," as Steven Garber observes, "is always about learning to connect knowing with doing, belief with behavior" (2007, 43). If that observation is accurate, then any school, your school, must imagine that end in the life of every one of your students and then develop strategies that you believe will be likely to achieve that end. Then you must develop a means for discerning whether the strategies you are employing actually lead to the end you desire. It is never enough to presume your efforts are producing the desired results. You must engage in a bit of real-world examination.

One school I worked with did this well. It all began with an intentional strategy to have each faculty member at the school build a mentoring relationship with his or her students. Teachers took the time to learn how to nurture that mentoring relationship, and as a result the students learned as much from their teachers beyond the classroom as they did in the classroom.

So it wasn't at all unusual for those teachers to stay in contact with their students after graduation (which, by the way, helps build a strong alumni program). And thus it wasn't out of the norm when those same teachers made plans to meet with those students during the Christmas break after the students' first semester away at college. Those meetings took place at a local coffee shop or pizza place and usually involved several students at one time. And while there was a lot of general banter about life away at college, there was a very specific purpose to that meeting. After catching up a bit, the teacher would ask two questions:

• Where did we fail in properly preparing you for your first semester at college?

• What did we do that was most helpful?

What Is Nonnegotiable?

The answers to those questions provided those teachers and that school with ideas and insights into how better to do what they believed was their primary purpose as a school: preparing students for the world they would be facing upon graduation. It helped them further refine what they called "The Portrait of a Graduate." They understood that not every portrait would be a masterpiece—that some students, for a variety of reasons, would resist or ignore or simply misunderstand the efforts of their teachers. They also understood that they were planting seed that might not take root until years into the future.

So they continuously worked together to better understand the end, the *telos*, toward which they were guiding their students. They understood that life is a journey toward something, and that every event and every activity and every class should be viewed as a means of moving their students toward that goal.

The planning process must never be viewed as a means to a better facility or a new program. It must always be seen as a means of finding ways to better pursue a God-given purpose, of achieving a God-given mission, and of reaching a God-designed end in the lives of students.

To help guide you to development of a portrait of a graduate, see document 7.3 (downloadable from https://www.acsi.org/tradebooks/psr/6518). On that worksheet I pose two open-ended statements for you to complete:
• A graduate of XYZ Christian school is … (These are the qualities that you hope will be observable in the lives of your graduates.)
• A graduate of XYZ Christian school can … (These are the life skills that you hope all of your students will possess when they graduate.)

What you eventually create will certainly be a bit aspirational in nature. Even the most mature of your graduates have a lifetime of maturing ahead of them. However, students need to be stretched. We are often too willing to accept a cynical view of our young people, but they are unlikely to reach expectations that have never been set for them. As the philosopher Alfred North Whitehead argued, "Moral education is impossible without the habitual vision of greatness" (cited in Brooks 2015, 107).

In his wonderful book *The Fabric of Faithfulness*, Steven Garber makes a similar observation. He writes, "You cannot have hopeful and responsible action without some vision of a possible future. To put it another way, if there is no point in the story as a whole, there is no point in my own action" (2007, 61). Your job is to provide your students with both a "habitual vision of greatness" and an ultimate point to the story. There will be many similar elements in the portrait you paint of each student. Each, however, will have nuances that will make him or her uniquely what God desires.

Here are some questions to ask about your school:
• How do we define results for our school?
• What are our criteria for success?
• How do we stay in touch with our graduates?
• Do we even have a means for staying in touch?
• What are we learning from our graduates?
• What is our overall relationship with our alumni?

How do we plan to make that impact? What strategies will we employ in pursuit of our purpose?

We all employ particular means to achieve particular ends. We choose, for example, a specific curriculum because we believe that by choosing that curriculum we will help our students better learn the content of a particular course and then perform at a high level on a standardized test. We make similar kinds of decisions when it comes to identifying the instructional strategies we will employ in service to our curriculum. As professional educators we are aware that the teaching-learning process requires continued assessment and revision.

Yet, I am often amazed that when it comes to the character and spiritual formation aspect of our mission, we seem willing to make assumptions about the best means to employ in pursuit of that crucial end. This is where we tend to get caught in our professional paradigms. If chapel is a good idea, then perhaps a better idea is increasing the number of chapels or giving students the opportunity for greater involvement in planning chapels, or longer chapels or shorter chapels. But perhaps what we need to actually consider is the value of chapel itself.

Do we, for example, have any evidence that chapel makes a difference in the lives of our students? Have we considered the fact that most of our students attend church on a weekly basis? And after all, what is chapel but a church service by another name? Have we ever considered the possibility of chapel/church overload? Years ago (I'm talking sometime in the early-to-mid 1980s) I read an article by Irving Jensen, who at the time was head of the Bible department at Bryan College in Dayton, Tennessee.

What Is Nonnegotiable?

The title just grabbed my attention: "Are We Fattening Geese or Training Athletes?" In that article he argued that we seem to be intent on stuffing our students with more and more content, when we need to be finding more and more ways to help our students take what they are learning "into the field," so to speak.

Because fieldwork is not so much a part of how we do education (it's hard to do much fieldwork when our professional paradigm is a set number of 50-minute on-campus classes a day), we really don't think much about how to put what our students are learning into a real-world context. Thus, our typical approach to improving our instructional strategies is to work toward improving the delivery of ever-better content.

The strategic planning process gives you the opportunity to rethink not only the ends you hope to achieve but also the means to achieving those ends. In a letter to one of his former students, Augustine pointed us in the right direction as we consider this aspect of the planning process. To that former student he wrote, "For boys do not need the art of grammar which teaches correct speech if they have the opportunity to grow up and live among men who speak correctly" (cited in Garber 2007, 136).

I love this question, posed by John Roth in his book *Teaching that Transforms* (2011, 77): "At the heart of all theological reflection is a question that humans have pondered since the beginning of time: How do heaven and earth meet? How does the transcendent world of the Spirit intersect with the ordinary material world of time and space?" It is your task during this planning process to not only identify important strategic initiatives, but to also to ask and answer that question.

Here are some questions that you might use to initiate your discussion:
• Is there anything we do that is ineffective at helping us achieve our purpose?
• If so, why do we continue to do those things?
• How do we evaluate the effectiveness of our current strategies?
• What are we learning as we engage in that evaluation?
• Can we make the case that the effectiveness of what we do is greatly affected by how we do it?
• What can we do differently?
• Are there other schools from which we can learn something helpful?

Whom are we trying to impact? Who is our customer?

Peter Drucker (n.d.) makes an interesting observation that every Christian school leader must consider: "The organization that starts from the inside and then tries to find places to put its resources to work is going to fritter itself away." Read that thought several times, and carefully consider what Drucker might be saying that applies directly to you and your school.

In far too many situations, school leaders simply assume that there is a market for their mission. I wish that were true. I wish that Christian parents of school-aged children were eager to enroll their children in a local Christian school. I long for a reality in which pastors of evangelical churches express their support for the idea of genuinely Christian schooling. Unfortunately, neither of those things is a reality. Christian parents in overwhelming numbers see no problem with enrolling their children in the local public school; and pastors, for the most part, aren't interested in getting involved in any discussion on schooling.

If your target audience is children from the homes of believing parents who fully understand and support your philosophy of education, then you are fishing in a pretty depleted pond. Most parents are looking for a safe environment and a quality education. The spiritual aspect is a nice, but not necessary, component in their decision-making grid. Many Christian parents reason that the spiritual dimension can be addressed at church and in the home—which is why when the local public charter school can deliver safety and excellence for free, the local Christian school suffers.

The customer question is one of the most difficult facing Christian school leaders. Unfortunately, we have made it even more challenging by reducing the conversation to whether we will open our enrollment to nonbelievers and thus become an "evangelistic" school or whether we will limit our enrollment to children from the homes of believers and thus become a "discipleship" school. In my opinion, those are false choices.

My opinion, however, is not what matters when you engage in a process of asking what is nonnegotiable. You are free to limit or expand your understanding of "Who is my customer?" What you must do, however, is to wrestle with and understand the implications of the decision you make. If you choose, for example, to limit your customer base to children from the homes of believers, you need to understand the impact that decision will have on how you market your school.

If you choose to open your school to children from nonbelieving families but intend to fully integrate faith and learning, you will need to wrestle with the implications regarding the kinds of teachers you will hire. Some Christian schoolteachers are simply not up to the challenge of working with nonbelieving students.

The question can get even more complicated when you begin addressing issues such as students with specific learning challenges or when seeking to create a more ethnically diverse student body or when considering students who are fully capable of performing well in the classroom but who really aren't interested in attending a four-year college. Are you prepared, for example, for the impact on your percentage-of-graduates-who-attend-college rates?

If it is true that no school can be all things to all people, then the "Who is my customer?" question is one of the most important and challenging that you will need to answer. Documents 7.4 and 7.5 (downloadable from https://www.acsi.org/tradebooks/psr/6518) can help guide you through this process.

Your North Star

If what I said earlier is true—that strategic planning is not a one-time event but a dynamic process—then nothing is of greater importance in the process than determining what is nonnegotiable. In answering that question you are creating a fixed point of reference that can keep you on track throughout your journey.

Think of it this way. Your strategic plan is a compass—a guide to a place you have never been. But a compass only works when it has a fixed point of reference: a North Star. Get this part of the planning process wrong, and you could easily end up wandering into dangerous territory. Get it right, and you can do what the early explorers were able to do: head off into the unknown with full confidence that you will not get lost on the way, that you will arrive at your destination safely.

Whatever you do, don't leave port until you have clearly identified your North Star. Make certain you have identified your nonnegotiables, no matter how long it takes. Once you have made those decisions, however, it is time to step out, to explore, to go where you've never gone before. This is the part of the strategic planning process we will investigate next.

8

What Is Our Current Reality?

On October 17, 1777, English general Gentlemen Johnny Burgoyne surrendered an entire British army to Horatio Gates, commander of the American forces, at Saratoga, New York. If the battle of Lexington produced the "shot heard round the world" then Burgoyne's surrender at Saratoga produced the "shock heard round the world."

Many historians have identified the Battle of Saratoga as the turning point in America's war for independence. The victory heartened the sagging morale of the American forces and helped encourage the French to enter into a military alliance with the fledgling nation. This alliance proved invaluable to the American cause. In October of 1781 the French fleet played a key role in forcing the British army to surrender at Yorktown, thus bringing the American war for independence to a successful conclusion.

At Saratoga the unthinkable happened. A well-equipped, well-trained, professional army sent by the most powerful empire on earth was utterly defeated by a novice army composed largely of farmers and craftsmen and led by men with virtually no military training. Simply put, the world was turned on its head, and the balance of power in the world began to shift from Europe to the new world.

Burgoyne's plan was to end the war by splitting the rebellious colonies in two. This was to be accomplished by driving down from Canada to Lake Champlain, Lake George, and the Hudson River, thus splitting New England off from the middle and southern colonies. The idea was to join Burgoyne's army to one led from the south by General Howe and to do so with all possible expedition.

That, of course, never happened. The plan, initially developed in London, was based on poor topographical maps, and thus unfortunately failed to adequately account for the kind of terrain Burgoyne's army would be forced to traverse. It was countryside with so many trees and other natural obstacles that over one twenty-four-day period Burgoyne was only able to advance his army a mere twenty-three miles. So much for expediency. On paper it was brilliant. In the light of reality it was a disaster.

Adding to the problem was King George III's involvement in the planning process. While the initial idea was not his, the king soon enthusiastically adopted it. Once that happened, serious discussion essentially ended. Anyone who had any misgivings kept silent in the face of the king's endorsement.

If this were a rare occurrence it would not merit our attention. Unfortunately, many plans are created through a process that does not adequately provide for thorough, objective assessment of current realities. This is often true of the planning activities in churches and schools, in which a relatively small number of people participate. Even when a large number of people are involved, objectivity can—and often does—suffer, and objectivity is the lifeblood of any planning process.

The reason for that lack of objectivity is simple. None of us is truly objective. Leaders are not objective. Neither are staff members, students, parents, or supporters. We are all shaped by our personal experiences and private agendas. So unless you are willing to do the hard work of investigating your current context, both the internal and the external context, you are likely to founder at this stage of the planning process.

My goal in this chapter, therefore, is to provide you with tools that will help increase the level of objectivity as you engage in your planning efforts. I love how Jim Collins puts it: "You absolutely cannot make good decisions without first confronting the brutal facts. Leadership is about vision. It is also about reality. Failure to understand that can have devastating consequences" (2001, 70). To help you identify and confront your own set of brutal facts, I am going to ask you to do three things:
1. Ask yourself tough question about your internal realities.
2. Perform an environmental scan to identify and clarify your external realities.
3. Ensure that you are thorough and honest by inviting an objective voice to the process.

(Documents 8.1, 8.2, 8.3, 8.4, and 8.5, downloadable from https://www.acsi.org/tradebooks/psr/6518, can be helpful in stimulating the thinking of the participants.)

What Is Our Internal Reality?

One helpful tool for getting at your internal realities is what is known as a SWOT analysis. In using a SWOT analysis, you will ask the following questions:
• What do we do really well? Those are your strengths (S).
• What needs improvement? Those are your weaknesses (W).
• What additional could we do? Those are your opportunities (O).
• What could do us grievous harm? Those are your threats (T).

Some people suggest that strengths and weaknesses are internal issues while opportunities and threats are external issues. I don't necessarily agree with that thinking. It is certainly true that strengths and weaknesses are internal, but often so are opportunities and threats. Let me illustrate.

Many years ago I helped lead The Master's College through a strategic planning process. When it came time to engage in a SWOT analysis, it was interesting that the participants identified the number-one strength of TMC as its president, Dr. John McArthur. Dr. McArthur was also identified as TMC's number-one weakness, its number-one opportunity, and its number-one threat. Nothing is more internal than the head of an organization; yet in response to all four questions, Dr. McArthur was the first answer.

How was that possible? Here was the logic. Dr. McArthur was the primary marketing focus of the college. Most of the students at TMC came from churches where the pastor had a particular affinity for the theological positions espoused by Dr. McArthur. Thus, as the primary face of the college, he was a marketing strength. He was also considered the greatest weakness because he was largely an absentee president that created some genuine tensions at the college. He was the number-one opportunity because his actual involvement in marketing the college was minimal at the time. And he was the number-one threat because if anything happened to him or he did anything truly egregious it could lead to the collapse of the college.

Strength, weakness, opportunity, and threat—all internal, all wrapped up in a single individual. While that same scenario is unlikely to be true of your school, it is quite possible for all four elements to be internal. We will look at the process for an external scan later in this chapter. But for now, let's begin by looking at how best to engage in a SWOT analysis.

SWOT strategy 1: A large-group brainstorming activity

This is a process I often employ when working with a large task force and when there is limited time. The rules I employ are simple:

1. No editorializing is allowed.
2. No negative personal comments are allowed.
3. All comments must be recorded and visibly displayed.
4. You need a room of sufficient size to allow for all comments to be posted on the wall and easily viewed by all participants.
5. There must be some kind of rating system employed to allow each participant to "vote" for his or her priorities.
6. The goal is to create a preliminary list of possible initiatives.
7. It is best to use an objective, experienced facilitator to lead this process.
8. Always have a "secretary" to record the comments.

Let me take a moment to explain my rationale for each of those rules.

1. No editorializing is allowed.

This is a rule that should be employed in any brainstorming activity. Nothing will kill thoughtful, creative, heartfelt thinking faster than allowing people to continually make editorial comments during a brainstorming activity. It is distracting and can become contentious at a time when people need to be able to express themselves freely.

At this point in the process it doesn't matter if the statements people make are accurate. What matters is the fact that they believe their comments to be accurate. The goal, as my friend Mickey Bowden would say, is to allow people to run their thoughts up the flagpole. Later in the process they will get to see if anyone "salutes," so to speak. At this time it is important to let people say what they want to say without any response.

2. No negative personal comments are allowed.

The goal of this exercise is to focus on specific issues rather than specific people. Another dear friend of mine, Ron Hayden, often observed that 90 percent of all the problems in organizations could be traced to systems, structure, or implementation efforts rather than to individual people. I tend to agree with that observation. Once we allow personalities to enter into the conversation we tend to get sidetracked—or worse, create an unhealthy "this person or group of persons versus that person or group of persons" situation.

That is not to say that we should ignore real problems with real people. If you are to confront the brutal realities, you may indeed have to do that. It is to say, however, that the initial SWOT brainstorming session is not the time to do so.

3. All comments must be recorded and visibly displayed.

In chapter 4, I introduced this ancient Chinese proverb: *A ragged pen is better than a good memory.* That is but one of many reasons why what is said during this brainstorming activity must be recorded. A second reason relates to the initial prioritization process that will follow the brainstorming activity. A third reason is that in recording the comments you preserve them for later scrutiny. Sometimes a good thought gets lost in the moment but upon later reflection is seen as important.

4. You must have a large enough room.

I use a stand or easel and sticky-edged flipchart sheets to capture all of the comments. Since it is not unusual to fill ten to twelve of these large sheets, it follows that you will need sufficient clear wall space on which to post that many sheets. Unfortunately there are surprisingly few rooms in a school where that is possible. Ensuring that all of these comments can be seen and considered is, however, crucial to this activity.

5. You must employ an objective prioritization tool.

It is not at all unusual for a group engaged in this process to identify 100 different issues that must be considered. Reducing that large number to no more than three or four strategic initiatives can be a daunting challenge, one we will explore in greater detail in chapter 9. At this point, however, it is important to take first steps toward prioritization.

To accomplish this task I use a simple strategy. I "give" each person $500 to spend. They can spend that amount in the following way. They can invest their money on any of the issues using the following denominations: $100, $50, and $20. They can, for example, invest five $100 bills on five issues, or ten $50 bills on ten issues, or twenty-five $20 bills on twenty-five issues, or any combination of those bills as long as they do not spend more than a total of $500 across all four categories.

This simple exercise is an effective tool at forcing people to identify what is truly important to them. It also narrows the focus of what is truly important to the entire task force. At this point you will not have the final set of initiatives, but you will have taken a big step in that direction.

6. The goal is to create a preliminary list of possible initiatives.

We will explore this prioritization process in greater detail in chapter 9.

7. It is helpful to use an experienced, objective facilitator to lead this process.

I am always a bit reluctant to make this point because it can seem to be a bit of a conflict of interest. After all, I am a consultant who works with Christian schools, and it could appear that I am just looking for work. That doesn't change the fact, however, that as noted earlier in this chapter, objectivity is the lifeblood of any planning process. Nor does it change the fact that unless you have a lot of experience in leading a brainstorming activity of this kind, it can quickly get out of hand. Even if you are engaged in an internal planning process it makes sense at certain steps along the way to find someone who can serve as an objective facilitator. Usually it is best to utilize the services of someone not connected to the school.

8. Always have a "secretary" to record the comments.

I do this for two reasons. First, having someone else record comments allows me to focus my attention on the members of the task force. It is pretty easy to lose control of a group of 25–35 people in this kind of exercise. If you've ever viewed a western, you know how easy it is to spook a herd of cattle. People are certainly not cattle, but they are still easy to distract. It is the job of the facilitator to keep the process moving along toward a successful conclusion. It is hard to do that while you are trying to write what you hear people saying. It just takes your attention off the group and puts it onto a piece of paper.

The second reason is simple: I have truly terrible penmanship skills. My handwriting is nearly illegible. When it comes time for people to review what has been recorded, it helps if they can actually read the comments.

SWOT Strategy 2: A small-group brainstorming exercise

When I have the time, I will often break a large group into smaller groups of eight to ten people and allow each small group to develop its own list of issues for each of the categories. It will be necessary to identify both a facilitator and a recorder for each group.

To make it possible for both the recorders and the facilitators to engage in the process, I provide each participant with worksheets for each of the SWOT questions. The participants are then given five minutes to jot down their responses to the first question: *What do we do really well?* At the end of the five minutes, each person is asked to call out his or her responses. Many times the responses from the participants are similar, so a decision can be made by the group to include or exclude any comments. This process is repeated for all four questions. No effort is made to prioritize. Prioritization will be done later by the larger group.

The key to success when using this strategy is to create groups that are representative of the larger group. Since the task force is made up of faculty, staff, board, parents, alumni, and possibly students and supporters, you will want to make sure that the smaller groups are composed in a similar way. I have found that simply having the group count off (1, 2, 3, 4) usually works. I just always check the composition of the groups before sending them off to accomplish this task. Sometimes I have to switch a few people around, but by and large that process works.

When the small teams have completed their tasks, I bring everyone back into the main room and have each team put its work on the wall. The large group can then see where there are similarities and differences, and there always are. In fact, I've found it interesting over the years how these small groups can produce some interestingly dissimilar results. There is just something about group dynamics that seems to be at work in those situations.

Once all the small groups have presented their work and the large group has eliminated any truly identical comments, it is time to engage in the initial prioritization step. During this process the group will consolidate and create 5–6 categories from which the final initiatives will be chosen. We will explore the process for choosing the final initiatives in chapter 9. Now it is time to move on to the next phase of this process: the external scan.

The External Scan

Ian Wilson has observed, "However good our futures research may be, we shall never escape from the ultimate dilemma that *all of our knowledge is about the past, and all our decisions are about the future*" (n.d., emphasis in original). For many people in Christian school leadership, the simple answer to that dilemma is prayer. I can't tell you how often I've heard good, well-meaning people say something like the following: "This is God's ministry. When it comes to making decisions, we need to remember that He knows the future and He will guide us into that future if we just humble ourselves and pray for His guidance."

How does someone argue with that? In fact, it is remarkably difficult to do so. As I pointed out in chapter 3, prayer is crucial to the planning process. We are told that if we "lack wisdom" we can "ask God who gives generously to all without reproach." We must, however, ask in faith, without doubting because to do so will leave us tossed "to and fro like the waves of the sea" (James 1:5–6). In the minds of some people what I am about to ask you to do is the very definition of a lack of faith.

While I fully agree with the importance of prayer, I also believe in the importance of getting your facts straight. A very wise man once observed, "The prudent sees danger and hides himself, but the simple go on and suffer for it" (Proverbs 22:3). As Derek Kidner notes about this text, "Scripture gives blind optimism its right name: not faith, but folly" (1964, 147).

Consider these further bits of wisdom from Solomon:

"In everything the prudent acts with knowledge,
but a fool flaunts his folly."
Proverbs 13:16

"The wisdom of the prudent is to discern his way,
but the folly of fools is deceiving."
Proverbs 14:8

"The simple believes everything,
but the prudent gives thought to his steps."
Proverbs 14:15

"The heart of him who has understanding seeks knowledge,
but the mouths of fools feed on folly."
Proverbs 15:14

"How much better to get wisdom than gold!
To get understanding is to be chosen rather than silver."
Proverbs 16:16

"If one gives an answer before he hears,
it is his folly and shame."
Proverbs 18:13

"Apply your heart to instruction
and your ear to words of knowledge."
Proverbs 23:12

"My son, eat honey, for it is good.
and the drippings of the honeycomb are sweet to your taste.
Know that wisdom is such to your soul;
if you find it, there will be a future,
and your hope will not be cut off."
Proverbs 24:13–14

"My son ... if you call out for insight
and raise your voice for understanding,
if you seek it like silver
and search for it as for hidden treasures,
then you will understand the fear of the Lord
and find the knowledge of God."
Proverbs 2:1–5

Do you see any patterns in that brief list of observations? I do. In every one of those passages, prudence is associated with acquiring wisdom—the wisdom that is necessary for making good decisions. Also in every case, wisdom is something we must actively pursue; it doesn't just show up. We've got to expend effort, the kind of effort we would expend to find a hidden treasure. On occasion you might stumble across a gold doubloon that has washed ashore during a storm, but if you want to find the real treasure you are going to have to make a big investment of time, energy, and money. Thus it is when it comes to finding the wisdom we need to make truly good decisions about how best to fulfill God's call in our lives.

Again I will quote Derek Kidner, who captures the essence of what Solomon is saying to you and me here in the 21st century: "... the power of forming plans so often [degenerates] into scheming that it can be used by itself in a bad sense more often than in a good. But these qualities need not be corrupt, and the book [Proverbs] is largely concerned to show that the godly man is in the best sense a man of affairs, who *takes the trouble to know his way about, and plan his course realistically*" (1964, 30; emphasis added).

Here's a question that for years has plagued me: How is it that otherwise good people can make so many bad decisions, decisions that do great harm to the schools they lead—and worse, decisions that make providing a quality education to the students entrusted to their care difficult if not impossible? It isn't that these people are lazy or that they lack passion for their mission. Rather, the missing element I observe is either the ability or willingness to do the hard and sometimes frustrating work of gathering the information necessary to make wise decisions based on solid research of current realities and future possibilities.

None of us possesses the proverbial crystal ball that allows us peeks into the future. What we can and must do, however, is a better job of linking our planning efforts to what is happening or likely to happen in the external environment. That requires, as Solomon suggests, a willingness to "seek knowledge," to "discern our way," to "find knowledge"—and in every case it requires of us persistent effort, hard work, and a healthy awareness of the world around us.

Once we have the necessary information in hand, we have another (equally challenging) task. We must ensure that our research and planning do not create any misalignment between who we say we are and what we decide to do. That is why answering the question "Who are we?" at the beginning of any planning process is critical.

With that as foundation, let's jump into a strategy for performing a thorough environmental scan.

Key External Factors to Consider

Here is a short list of external factors that you will need to explore. With each of the factors I am providing a number of questions and observations that I believe can help shape your research in a positive way.

Need

People do not necessarily need a specific service. Instead, they have a need that a specific service might be able to fulfill. For example, parents often choose your school for reasons completely unrelated to your written mission. In fact I would suspect that a majority of parents connected to your school do so. Part of your research obligation, therefore, is to discover the needs that the parents of children currently enrolled in your school and the parents who might consider enrolling their children in your school want you to meet. Here are some questions for you to ponder.

- What are the various needs your school meets?
- How do you know that?
- Would meeting those needs create a conflict with your purpose, mission, or values?
- Which of the needs you have discovered create a genuine sense of urgency within you and your team?

Target audience

Most Christian schools have a specific kind of family in mind, what is called a mission-match family. It is crucial that you identify what you mean by a mission-match family because it will shape virtually everything you do, from curriculum to marketing. Fail to identify an appropriate target audience, and you will find it difficult to keep your everyday practice aligned with your identified purpose.

- Is there a specific kind of family you are trying to reach?
- Describe in detail that specific kind of family.
- Why is reaching that family important to you?
- How large is the pool of those families in your area?
- How do you know that?
- Are there any secondary audiences that you are hoping to reach?
- What have you done to reach those families?
- What have you done that has been successful? Why do you think you were successful?
- What have you done that wasn't very successful? Why do you think you weren't successful with that strategy?
- Is your target audience growing or declining?
- What can you do to increase the size of your target audience?

Location and geography

There is a reason that in the real estate business the three most important factors are location, location, location. Of course the cost of a house matters, but as a real estate agent once said to me, "Alan, if money is a factor, always look for the least expensive house in the neighborhood most attractive to you." Location matters far more than most school leaders would like to admit. Build a school in the wrong location—and I've seen that happen a number of times—and it will likely have a negative impact on your enrollment. When deciding whether to expand your current campus or find a new location, this is a crucial factor to contemplate. Here are some things for you to consider:

- What are the travel habits of your target audience?
  - To work
  - To shop
  - To church

- What are the boundaries, such as rivers or expressways or neighborhoods, that people in your target audience are not likely to cross?
- What housing and retail developments are planned for your community?
- What are the demographics of your area? Is there, for example, a growing or declining number of families with school-aged children?

I can't overemphasize the importance of finding the answers to those questions. I worked with one school that had a thriving preschool program. In fact, the preschool program pretty much subsidized the entire school. In their desire to get out of a less-than-desirable facility, they relocated to what was clearly a building better suited to their needs. Unfortunately, by moving they made it far less convenient for the parents with children enrolled in the preschool. The resulting loss of students was significant enough to put the school at risk.

Another school with which I worked faced a similar dilemma. They had lost access to a facility that they had been leasing for many years, and they found themselves without a home. After two years of renting in an unsatisfactory location, they decided to purchase a piece of property on which to build a new school facility. It was a very affordable piece of property, but the location was more than a bit iffy. The impact on their enrollment was immediate and quite negative. Remember, location matters.

Competition

Only in the rarest of situations will any school find itself devoid of competition. The most obvious competition comes from your local public school. And if you live in a state that allows for public charter schools, that competition has probably become more intense. Here is a key thought I want you to consider: competition is not a bad thing. In fact, as a good capitalist, I believe it is a good thing because it forces us to deliver our service or build our product with ever-increasing excellence. If competition intimidates you, then it is time for you to do some real soul searching.

Here are some questions designed to provoke your thinking a bit.

- Who else does what you do in the area you are trying to reach? Identify every one of your competitors.
- What are the common competitive factors—e.g., curriculum, facilities, faculty, programs, location—by which your target audience will judge you and your competition? (We will explore this concept in more detail in chapter 9.)
- What are the points of pain—the felt needs of your target audience—that are not being addressed by your competition that you can meet without abandoning your purpose, mission, and values?
- Are there any potential collaborators? I'm a big fan of collaborative efforts. Sometimes less (meaning the number of schools in an area) is really more.

Funding

As I argue in my book *Rethinking Sustainability*, I am a big fan of cost-based tuition. When I use that phrase I am referring to the idea that all of a school's operational costs should be funded by tuition and net auxiliary revenue. There are, however, many other costs—what I call program enhancement and capital construction projects—that schools must incur if they hope to deliver a quality education. If, as a result of your strategic planning process, you identify a major program enhancement project such as refurbishing your science labs or a capital construction project such as building a new fieldhouse, then you will need to get a better sense of the funding potential in your school network and community.

Here are some crucial truths to help you as you think through this factor.

- Wealthy people seldom simply give gifts to an organization. Rather, they invest in Kingdom work, and they invest in Kingdom work the same way they invest in the stock market. They want to know what return they can expect from their investment. Thus they need to know if you are worthy of their trust. They will seek to discern whether you do what you do with excellence and whether you are continually innovating, finding better ways to deliver your mission.

- Wealthy people seldom give gifts to advance a mission for which they do not have a personal passion. Sadly, few people of wealth seem to have a passion for Christian schools. To change that reality you've got to find ways to infect people with your passion. You can't do that through mail or e-mail. It's got to be done up close and personal.

- When you charge a fee for the service you provide, the challenge of raising money becomes more difficult. It is the difference between raising money for a church or mission organization and raising money for a school. A good resource that will help explain this reality is Jim Collins' book *Good to Great and the Social Sector*.

- It is important for you to explore your historic efforts at fund-raising and also to explore other fund-raising efforts in your community.

Social and lifestyle factors

Leonard Sax, a practicing physician from West Chester, Pennsylvania, observes (2015), "The challenge of raising children in America today is different from 30 or 50 years ago. Back then popular culture supported the authority of parents, whether it was the 'Andy Griffith Show' in the 1960s or 'Family Ties' in the 1980s. Kids are not born knowing how to be respectful. They have to be taught."

Just spend some time in your local grocery store or at your local mall or in a neighborhood restaurant, and what you observe is likely to reinforce the observation made by Dr. Sax.

The reasons for this are legion, but can be summed up in two observations:
- The stunning and intrusive impact of media and its power to shape how we view ourselves and the world around us
- The increasing failure (for a lot of reasons) of parents to actually parent

Whatever the reasons, however, the impact of social and lifestyle factors on how you do school are enormous. To ignore what is happening all around you is the human equivalent of the proverbial ostrich sticking its head in the sand. The impact of popular culture is huge, and business-as-usual is a prescription for disaster. Here are some questions to consider:

- Given that so many parents are abdicating their responsibilities, what are you as a school going to do to help those parents better fulfill their responsibility?
- What can you do in partnership with your supporting churches to accomplish that goal?
- What are you doing to be more aware of contemporary culture and its impact on your students?
- How does this awareness help shape the design of your Bible curriculum or your instructional strategies in general?

- Are you developing partnerships with your supporting churches to more strategically address the challenges created by the shifting nature of contemporary culture?
- What are you doing to help even your most-engaged parents better understand the impact of culture on their children as well as on themselves?

Political realities

Unless you have been living on a desert island, you are aware that the political and legal climate in our country has become less supportive of, and in some cases openly hostile to, the particular cultural and biblical perspectives and values that shape how you define and deliver your mission. Navigating the cultural and legal minefields that seem to stretch toward an ever-distant horizon will require of you greater awareness and knowledge.

In general it will make sense for you to stay current of local, state, and national legislation. (ACSI's *Legal Legislative Update* is an excellent source for up-to-date information.) There are a number of other legal and legislative organizations such as Alliance Defending Freedom, The Heritage Foundation, and the Beckett Fund for Religious Liberty that publish regular newsletters. I make it a practice to read the *Wall Street Journal* and *USA Today*, as well as my local paper, every day. And even though I don't often agree with the political bent of many of the editorial writers, I do read both the *New York Times* and the *Washington Post* periodically. Also, journals such as *First Things*, the *Daily Standard*, and *National Review* are worth the cost of the subscription.

It is the responsibility of school leaders and board members to stay in touch with the political and legal discussions and decisions that could possibly impact the ability of the school to deliver its mission. Here are some questions to consider:

- Do you know the names of the council members of your local city government? How about the names of your representatives and senators?

- What kind of regular interaction do you have with them? Do you ever call, write, or visit them? If you do, do you do so even when there isn't a particular issue to discuss?

- Are you familiar with the members of your local zoning commission? (When you get ready to pursue a capital construction project, you will wish you were.)

- Do you keep your parents informed about issues that can have a positive or negative impact on your school?
- How often do you and your team actually pray for those in political leadership?
- Do you or any of your leadership team or board take an active role in your local or state government?

It would be nice if none of that were necessary, but it is. You've got to stay constantly informed regarding the political and legal issues and those who will address those issues if you are to make wise decisions during any planning process.

Technology and innovation

Here's both a simple exercise and a silly question. First, the exercise. Brainstorm with your faculty and staff around these questions: In what ways has technology changed your life over the last ten years? What do we do differently today than we did just ten years ago because of technology? Get very specific and detailed. Then after spending some time engaging in that exercise, ask this question: Has technology really had much of an impact on how we think about education? Be honest in the way you answer that question. Here are some more questions to ponder:
- What impact has technology actually had on your instructional strategies?
- How are you addressing the differences between the way your students view and use technology and how your faculty view and use technology?
- What are some of the poor decisions you have made about technology? Why do you think you made those poor decisions? How do you think you can avoid making those kinds of poor decisions in the future?
- What impact do parent expectations have on your decisions regarding technology?
- What impact is continuing innovation in the tech world having on your budget?
- How does technology impact you vis-à-vis your competition?
- What are you doing to stay current with trends in technology and the possible impact of those trends on how you will be delivering education in the short and long term? (There are several journals that will help you in this regard. I am not much of a tech nerd, but I have found *Wired* magazine to be a helpful resource.)

Technology is a tsunami with the potential to sweep across the educational landscape with devastating impact, not all of it good. Education was a lot simpler back in the days of chalkboards, paper, pencils, and virtually complete control of access to academic content. Those days are gone, and it is your task to make wise decisions that help you fulfill your mission with ever-increasing excellence while staying true to your mission.

Staffing

At first glance this factor may appear to be out of place. After all, isn't staffing an internal element? The answer is, of course, yes and no. The composition and performance of your current staff is most certainly an internal issue. But what about your staff of the future—those who are not yet part of your team but will need to be? Consider the following questions:

- What qualities, preparation, knowledge, and skills will teachers need to possess to be successful in the next five to ten years? (And by the way, your current teachers need to be developing those same qualifications now.)

- Where will you find teachers who share a passion for your purpose, mission, and values?

- Given how poorly many of our Christian schools compensate their current teachers, what are your plans for addressing the compensation needs of young teachers who will be graduating from college with thousands of dollars of student loan debt?

As I travel the country I see two common characteristics in the typical Christian school: an aging faculty population and a decline in the understanding of what makes for an education that is truly Christian. Given that the teacher-student relationship is at the heart of education, failure to solve for those two issues will put the entire enterprise of Christian schooling at risk.

Now it's time to get really practical.

The Research Questions

That's a pretty significant list of factors with the potential to shape your decisions and actions throughout any planning process. I've tried to give you a good sense for the meaning and potential powers of each of those factors as well as some observations and questions to help you better understand the potential impact of each factor. Now it is time to take each of those factors individually and engage in some further exploration.

The following questions—what I call key research questions—should be asked in relation to each of those factors.

- *What makes this factor so important right now?* All of the factors listed above will have an impact on your school, but not all those factors will have the same level of impact at this particular point in time.
- *What trends or uncertainties can we discover relative to this factor?* Remember this: What you don't know that you don't know can hurt you—badly at times. Your job involves reducing the uncertainty and evaluating the possible impact of trends.
- *What are the implications for our school?* Wrestling with implications is one of my favorite activities. Knowing something is true or likely to become true is important. Knowing the potential impact on your school is critical.
- *What do we already know about this factor? How do we know that? What are the gaps in our knowledge?* I'm often amazed at how much knowledge is contained in the minds of faculty and staff on a whole host of topics that remains unearthed and untapped. In his book *Where Good Ideas Come From*, Steven Johnson (2011) talks about the concept of adjacent possibilities—the idea that when what one person in isolation knows about a topic has the opportunity to bump up against what another person knows on that same subject in isolation, remarkable insights are likely to emerge. This is a good opportunity to discover what your team already knows on each of these factors and to decide how valuable that information might be.
- *What have we already done regarding this factor? What did we learn? What would we have done differently?* It is quite possible that you have already engaged aspects of each of these factors. In fact, it is highly probable that you have done so. Any marketing efforts would require that you explore the nature of your target audience. Few schools have not wrestled with the impact of technology on classroom instruction. And which faculty has not struggled with understanding the cultural context in which their students live? Sometimes a good place to start is simply to recall and summarize those earlier discussions before moving ahead with new research.
- *Is there a question to which we should find an answer that we have failed to ask to this point?* That is a question we should ask frequently in a whole host of situations. I learned to ask that question when engaged in focus groups. It is always my final question, and I am constantly amazed at how people respond, how perceptive their responses often prove to be. I always learn something I did not know, something that will help the school with which I am working.

The Research Goal

What I am about to ask you to do is a lot of work. I know just how much work it is to do a research report. It is one of the reasons I seek to create a large task force. It is also why I encourage schools to engage in a strategic planning process only when the decks have been cleared—no accreditation activities, no major curriculum revisions, no major construction projects. You simply cannot give the strategic planning process the energy and focus necessary when you and a large number of your faculty and staff are distracted by other major activities. You need everyone focused and fully engaged.

Here is what a research report should include:
- A brief written summary of what you have discovered in the course of your research
- Copies of any articles or chapters that would provide helpful insight into the issues surrounding a particular external factor
- A list of major uncertainties that will require further research
- An impact grid to determine whether what you discovered is
  - Critically important at this time
  - Moderately important at this time
  - Not critical at this time, but should continue to be monitored
  - Not critical at this time
  - Not likely to be critical any time in the near future
- A discussion of
  - the implications of what you have discovered
  - any opportunities that might be created
  - any threats to the school

Some Practical Considerations
- Let people choose the factors they wish to explore. People are usually willing to invest time in what interests them.
- Keep research teams small—two to three people. More than that, and things can get cumbersome. It is also easier for people to sit on the sidelines when there is a large group.
- Someone must take the responsibility for keeping the research moving along. This person is usually someone on the staff, but a committed, capable parent could fill this role. Everyone just needs to know that this person is acting on behalf of the board and task force. That person will need to
  - Ensure that there are clear deadlines, usually no more than a month.
  - Stay in touch with each research team to encourage and respond to questions.
- Provide a common design standard for all reports.
- The head of school and the chair of the board need to review all of the research projects prior to presenting them in a public forum. If you utilize the services of a strategic planning consultant, that person should review all of the work as well.

My grandfather was a rancher in the hill country of Bandera, Texas. It was remarkably hard work, requiring enormous investments of time and energy—and that was true whatever your herd. Whether your herd was sheep, goats, or cattle, they were usually running free over hundreds (and in some cases thousands) of acres. A herder must stay focused at all times because there are numerous potential problems that require constant attention. There are predators that can thin the flock, weather issues that can put the flock at risk, times of drought when water and food are difficult to find. That is why the Psalmist describes the shepherd as one who leads his flock to the still waters and into the green pastures.

In one sense, you are a shepherd. And as difficult a job running a herd of cattle or sheep can be, people and organizations are infinitely more complex and require a huge investment of time and energy. That is especially true during any planning process, which is why so few people are willing to make the investment. As we tried to point out in chapter 1, however, it is a most necessary and worthwhile investment, one that can help you "excel still more."

Let me close this chapter with a thought from Proverbs.

> Know well the condition of your flocks,
> and give attention to your herds,
> for riches do not last forever;
> and does a crown endure to all generations?
> When the grass is gone and the new growth appears
> and the vegetation of the mountains is gathered,
> the lambs will provide your clothing,
> and the goats the price of a field.
> There will be enough goats' milk for your food,
> for the food of your household
> and maintenance for your girls."
> Proverbs 27:23-27

Want your school to flourish? Want your school to remain sustainable well into the future? Want to provide the best for all of your faculty, staff, and students? If so, then doing the hard work associated with "knowing the condition of your flock" is not a burden. It is your calling.

What Is Most Important Right Now?

Years ago I was asked to provide a one-day consult to a school that was struggling to implement the strategic plan they had so meticulously constructed during the previous year. Prior to my visit to the campus I asked the school leadership to send me a copy of their strategic plan. It was an impressive document with a lengthy list of worthwhile initiatives.

On the day of my visit I met with the entire school leadership team. Once we had finished the usual greet-and-meet conversation, I posed this question: "Can you give me a status report of where you are with each of these initiatives?" What followed was a brief period of uncomfortable silence, bowed heads, and diverted eyes. When the acting head of school—did I mention that the head of school responsible for the strategic plan had resigned at the end of the previous school year?—finally responded, it was with this statement: "We've actually only made real progress on one of the initiatives."

Frankly, I was not surprised by that response. After all, in the document before me there was a list of twelve separate initiatives, plus all the additional goals and action steps that had to be addressed if those twelve initiatives were to be accomplished. That is simply beyond the capacity of any school or organization.

As Patrick Lencioni notes, "Most organizations I've worked with have too many top priorities to achieve the level of focus they need to succeed. Wanting to cover all their bases, they establish a long list of disparate objectives and spread their scarce time, energy, and resources across them all. The result is almost always a lot of initiatives being done in a mediocre way and a failure to accomplish what matters most. This phenomenon is best captured in that wonderful adage, 'If everything is important, nothing is'" (2012, 119).

Lencioni goes on to exhort, "Every organization, if it wants to create a sense of alignment and focus, must have a single top priority within a given period of time" (2012, 120). I'm not sure that I fully agree with the idea of a single top priority, but I have learned that once a school gets beyond three key initiatives it becomes nearly impossible to accomplish any of them in a timely fashion with any level of excellence.

Therefore, at this point in the planning process it is crucial to answer the question: How do we decide what is most important right now? It is time to limit and prioritize, but how?

Getting to What Is Most Important Right Now

If you are following the process I've outlined in this book, you have already taken the first step toward answering that question through the SWOT analysis and initial prioritization processes described in chapter 8. While it is not a highly sophisticated process, it can be effective in reducing dozens of issues to a workable handful of possible initiatives.

Some schools choose to expand the list of issues identified by the task force by distributing a survey to the entire school community with questions that would allow this larger group to express their thoughts on strengths, weaknesses, opportunities and threats. I must confess that I am not a big fan of those kinds of surveys. After all, the purpose of a large strategic planning task force is to allow for a broad cross section of input and engagement. I do not see enough additional value from survey results to warrant all of the work it takes to employ a survey.

Christian schools, for the most part at least, are not democracies. In the end the board must give its blessing to the outcome of the planning process. That is why they must be intensely involved from the outset. The board and leadership team must, however, pay attention to the marketplace. They must learn to listen well to the customers who actually fund the mission of the school. That is one of the reasons why I argue for involvement on the task force of parents, donors, and alumni. There is, however, a big difference between being market-aware and market-driven. As we often note during political campaigns, surveys can exert an unhealthy kind of influence.

If you have followed the process well, you identified five to seven possible initiatives during your SWOT analysis. Now comes the hard work. Now comes the time when you must decide to set aside some worthwhile ideas in pursuit of what is truly important right now. That will not be easy. At this point in the process people will, in spite of all your efforts, still have different priorities, driven by their personal beliefs and private agendas. That reality is exacerbated by the fact that at this point in the process no one possesses all of the pertinent information necessary to make a fully informed decision.

Before we move on to the next step in the prioritization process, permit me to make two additional observations about why finishing the prioritization process can be difficult.

The Elephants in the Room

Pay attention to this very insightful observation from Chip and Dan Heath in their excellent book on organizational change, *Switch* (2010, 7–8).

> For individuals' behavior to change, you've got to influence not only their environment but their hearts and minds.
>
> The problem is this: Often the heart and mind disagree. Fervently.
>
> [This] tension is captured best by an analogy used by University of Virginia psychologist Jonathan Haidt in his wonderful book, *The Happiness Hypothesis*. Haidt says that our emotional side is an Elephant and our rational side is its Rider. Perched atop the Elephant, the Rider's control is precarious because the Rider is so small relative to the Elephant. Anytime the six-ton Elephant and the Rider disagree about which direction to go, the Rider is going to lose. He's completely overmatched.
>
> If you want to change things you've got to appeal to both.

It would be nice to believe this is not a problem, but it almost always is. It would be nice to say that every member of our team at every moment in time is fully controlled by the Holy Spirit, but that is seldom the case. We will explore this reality in greater detail in chapter 11 when we look at the challenges of change. For now, let me simply say, don't be surprised by emotional responses as you go through this process. In fact, don't be surprised by emotional responses at any point in the planning process. Anytime you challenge people's comfort zone or add to their stress or decide to move in direction A as opposed to direction B, you are likely to arouse strong emotions.

At times like this it is not a good idea to ask people to ignore their emotions. That is never a healthy reaction. Finding a way to address and channel those emotions is, however, essential to the success of your efforts. Again, more in chapter 11.

The second potential elephant in the room is the person or persons who could, if they wanted to, hijack the process at this point. That person could be the pastor of a church-sponsored school, the chair of the board, a coalition of board members, the head of school, or even a significant donor. Usually there are not ulterior motives at work. Typically the persons in question simply believe they represent better thinking or have a better idea of what matters most at this time.

This is the kind of situation where the checks and balances of engaging a quality consultant can make a huge difference. Often attempts at controlling the outcome of the prioritization process are subtle. Often those attempting to influence the process are rationalizing their efforts with, "I'm just making my case like everyone else." Sometimes that is the case. Sometimes, however, it is a bit more. The consultant's job is to see that "bit more" and intervene.

The Initiative Work Team

At this point in the process it is time to create a work team that will be tasked with performing another level of prioritization. For this task I have created a simple tool called the Strategic Initiative Grid that provides a way to bring a bit of objectivity to this process.

Obviously the strategic initiative work team will have a crucial job to accomplish. Therefore its composition must be carefully considered. It's got to be small enough to actually get work done, but large enough to be representative of the entire team. Its members must be mature enough to accept that in the end the board will make the final decision about which initiatives will be pursued, and strategic and innovative enough in how they think to not fall prey to initiatives that will have little real transformative impact on the school. That is a real challenge. So here are some thoughts on how to build the team.

First of all, the head of school must be a member and probably should have veto power on all other members. If the chair of the board chooses not to serve, he or she should recommend a member of the board to serve on this team. The other three to seven members (always an odd number) should be a selected from among faculty, staff, and parents. If you have a particularly innovative donor, that person could also be a good choice. Here are some key characteristics you will want to look for:

- Does this person "play well with others"? Once again I would refer you to Proverbs 18 for an illustration of who you don't want on this team.
- Does this person stay in touch with current events and trends? Is the person a reader? If not, then the kind of research that will need to be done by this team will likely prove unpleasant.
- Is this a realistic person? Does the person see both the strengths and the weaknesses of the school?
- Is this a "beyond the horizon" kind of person? Can this person get beyond current limitations to see what could be?

There may be other qualities that you would like to see among the members of this team, but you cannot sacrifice any of the qualities I have mentioned. It is always better to have a smaller team of truly exceptional people than a larger group just for the sake of having a larger group.

Strategic Initiative Grid

This team will be tasked with using the Strategic Initiative Grid to determine which of the initiatives identified as a result of the initial SWOT process should be considered as finalists for the strategic plan. To do that, the team will ask the following question: Is this initiative

1. Connected to our "core"?
2. Strategic rather than just tactical?
3. Distinct in a positive way from our competitors?
4. An answer to a specific point of parental pain?
5. Potentially transformative?
6. Student-centered?
7. Grounded in reality?

1. Connected to your core

Your core comprises those nonnegotiables you identified while answering the question "Who are we?" For example, would pursuing a particular initiative accurately reflect your core values or violate them? Would that pursuit violate any of your nonnegotiable beliefs? Would that pursuit better enable you to accomplish your mission, or would it divert from that mission?

Let's say that your school values a "believer only" enrollment policy, meaning that any student who applies to your school must come from a home where at least one parent can give a strong testimony of faith in Christ. And let's say that one of your initiatives is to launch a program to enroll international students—something lots of schools have done with great success and in the process experienced a financial boost to the school.

So, here are some questions you might want to ask yourself as you decide whether this is a strategic initiative you want to pursue:

- How will we surface potential students? Will we do this internally, or will we utilize the services of an outside organization?
- If we use an outside organization, how confident can we be that it will do the screening in a manner that meets our enrollment criteria?
- Have we considered the potential impact that introducing a number of international students might have on our school culture?
- What should we do to effectively prepare our current students for an influx of international students?
- What is driving our thinking on international students? Is it the potential of a new source of revenue, or does it fit a broader part of our mission as a school?

Do you see the challenge? Adding a dozen or so international students to your student body might be a wonderful extension of programs you already have in place. You might arrange annual mission trips for your students to other parts of the world. Your Bible classes might include a substantial cross-cultural component. Or perhaps you have a strong foreign-language program with the intent of preparing your students for life as globally aware adults.

If so, then adding a stream of international students might make all the sense in the world. If, however, your goal is simply to increase your revenue, then a decision to move ahead might create missional conflicts, and that is always unhealthy in any school or organization.

Let me provide a real-life illustration of this element of the process. Several years ago I led a strategic planning process at a Christian school located right on the dividing line between the city of Youngstown, Ohio, and the community of Boardman, which is where the "burbs" begin. The board and leadership team had already made a commitment to a mission of educating a highly diverse student body. Doing that well, however, isn't easy; it comes with lots of challenges.

So, it wasn't surprising to me that during the planning process someone raised the possibility of relocating the campus. It wasn't a completely "out there" idea. To expand the facility in its current location would require the acquisition of some adjacent homes. That was going to be expensive, and some folks on the task force were questioning the fiscal wisdom of expending significant resources on a facility in that location. It was a fair question.

In response, someone asked, "What will happen to the diversity of our student body if we relocate further south in the suburbs?" Another fair question. What followed was a healthy discussion of what really mattered at that Christian school. In the end, the idea of relocation was dismissed as inconsistent with the "core" of the school. That is exactly what should happen during a strategic planning process.

2. Strategic rather than just tactical

One of my favorite reads of the last ten years was a little book by Seth Godin titled *Purple Cow*. Here is an insight from that book (2009, 67):

> Ideas that are remarkable are much more likely to spread than ideas that aren't. Yet so few brave people make remarkable stuff. Why? I think it is because they think that the opposite of "remarkable" is "bad" or "mediocre" or "poorly done." Thus, if they make something very good they confuse it with being virus worthy.

> If you travel on an airplane and they get you there safely, you don't tell anyone. That's supposed to happen. What makes it remarkable is if it's horrible beyond belief or if the service is so unexpected that you need to share.

Now pay careful attention to what he says next: "How soon can you stop?"

I have worked with several schools recently that are doing some truly remarkable things. One school in Florida has developed a program called the RISE Institute. It was a program designed for at-risk middle school students who were simply not, for a variety of reasons, thriving in the normal classroom setting.

What I observed in my brief initial visit was remarkable—transformational, actually. I just assumed that expanding the reach of the RISE Institute would be one of the first things that made it to the list of possible initiatives during our initial SWOT process. That didn't happen. I was both surprised and not surprised. Everyone on campus (well almost everyone) knew it was a good program. It's just hard sometimes for people to see beyond the needs in their own area. That is normal. Strategic things are, however, beyond normal. That is why Seth Godin uses the concept of a Purple Cow.

3. Distinct from competitors

Another way of thinking about what might make a worthwhile initiative is through a process called Blue Ocean Strategy. You may be familiar with the book *Blue Ocean Strategy*; if not, you should probably consider adding it to your leadership library. It is way beyond the scope of this book to thoroughly explore the theory and practice that gives definition to Blue Ocean Strategy, but here are a few thoughts that relate directly to the strategic planning process.

The authors, W. Chan Kim and Renée Mauborgne (2005), argue that most organizations develop strategies based on the assumption that most "industries" that are similarly focused (e.g., automobile manufacturers or airlines) try to compete by being the "best" within that industry. They identify the specific factors within their particular industry and compete with other members of their industry based on how well they perform in each of those factors.

Let's use schools as an example. When parents are considering where to enroll their child, what are the factors that they consider during that decision-making process? Here's a partial list:
• Location
• Overall reputation
• Quality and credentials of faculty
• Price
• Curriculum
• Extracurricular programs
• Facilities
• Educational philosophy

Here's the challenge. If the only ways schools compete with one another are on these common factors, then the only way to win the competition is by offering something that is clearly superior or clearly different. So in the competition between Christian schools and public schools, unless educational philosophy is of critical importance to a parent, then the Christian school will inevitably find itself at a competitive disadvantage. And with the rise of charter schools, most of which market themselves based on a distinct educational philosophy, Christian schools are at an even greater competitive disadvantage.

One way to break out of that competitive clutter is to offer something that is truly distinctive—a program that is so powerfully attractive that it is impossible to ignore, a program so different that there is no real competition—hence the idea of a Blue Ocean Strategy.

I don't know what that might be in your situation. Perhaps it would be an incredible fine arts program, or a remarkable science curriculum, or maybe a Bible program that is not simply more of the same-old-same-old but one that is demonstrably transformative. But it must be something that is truly extraordinary if you ever hope to attract the right kind of attention.

4. Parents' point of pain

A fourth arena for identifying genuinely strategic initiatives is what I call parents' "point of pain." I stumbled across this concept when working with a school in a community where the local public school board had decided, for fiscal reasons, to close one of the two area middle schools, forcing the district to create a rather complicated daily schedule to accommodate all of the students on a single campus. You can imagine the problems this decision created for area families. That is an example of a point of pain.

In fact I have concluded that every parent with a child in middle school is experiencing this "point of pain." Living with a child going through puberty is one of life's more interesting challenges, as I am sure many of you reading this book will attest. Making matters worse is the reality that many middle schools are more holding blocks than educational institutions. (I'm sure some of my readers will disagree with me when I say that I believe that the entire middle school concept is one of the worst ideas to be implemented in the last fifty years.)

Whether you agree with me or not, I suspect that any school with an innovative, effective middle school program would attract a lot of attention if for no other reason than that it would help solve a parent's point of pain. With a bit of discussion, I suspect that the list could be expanded. The point is this. When someone is in pain, if you can provide a solution for that pain, it gives you a competitive advantage. In so doing you are typically taking strategic advantage of a situation.

5. Potentially transformative

Christian schools, for the most part, claim to be in the business of transformation. We claim that what we do, how we do what we do, and the context in which we do what we do are literally transformative in nature. That was certainly my experience as a student in a Christian school. I hope it was the experience of the students who attended the schools in which I taught and led. I must confess, however, that I'm not always confident that what I observe in the schools I visit could be described as transforming.

Rather, what I often observe is mostly typical, not transformative. I seldom see anything that stands out, that says, "Everything we do, every decision we make, every program we implement, all have this as a singular goal: the transformation of our students." Perhaps that's because we don't always have a clear understanding of what we mean when we use words such as *transformation*. Or perhaps we aren't really all that confident that we really can effect transformation in the life of a student. Whatever the case, I suspect that genuine transformation is more rare in our schools than we'd like to think.

Yet, the gospel is the most transformative power within God's creation. And when combined with the Word, the Spirit, and the best efforts of those who themselves have been transformed, we should clearly observe the work of transformation over time in the lives of our students.

Even in the arenas of academics, the arts, and athletics we should grapple with questions about how best to deliver a transformative experience to our students. Indeed, this should be a central conversation during any strategic planning process. Permit me an illustration.

I recently attended a production of *Mary Poppins* in the new fine arts facility on the campus of a large Christian high school in Colorado. It was truly exceptional. I should not have been surprised. Earlier in the year I had taken a tour of that facility with the high school principal. As impressive as was the facility, and it was impressive, what really caught my attention was the rationale behind the design and construction of the facility. It wasn't just about making an impression on the community. Rather it was about the transformative nature of the programs that would take place within that facility.

How many schools envision the opportunity to influence the arts in an entire community? By that I don't mean how many schools envision the opportunity to impress a community with its arts program. What I mean is far different. What I heard during my visit to this school was a desire to literally impact the entire arts community in the Denver area through the efforts of faculty, staff, and students.

That's a transformative goal. We need more of that kind of thinking in the Christian school movement.

6. Student-centered

Here is a phenomenon I have noted in virtually every strategic planning process I've ever led. During the initial SWOT process, the issue of faculty salaries invariably receives a lot of attention. I'm sure that doesn't surprise anyone reading this book. What is equally inevitable is that quality teachers are always mentioned as one of the strengths of the school. When I dig a little deeper, however, I find things are not as simple or obvious as they seem to be.

In reality, many schools often have highly dedicated faculty whose performance by any objective standard would hover somewhere in the middle between poor and exceptional. When leading student focus groups, I often hear something like this: "I know my teachers love me but when it comes to actual instruction it is pretty weak." This frequent assessment is often in stark contrast to the accolades kids give to the one or two truly exceptional teachers in the middle school or high school.

Now let me pull a couple of thoughts together. First of all, I know how poorly Christian school teachers are paid. It is dreadful, actually. Second, poor pay will not necessarily discourage great teachers, though Proverbs teaches us that "Hope deferred makes the heart sick" (Proverbs 13:12). Third, if you are a teacher who is also head of a household, the problem is more acute than if you are not, though veteran single teachers beginning to consider retirement are most often also struggling with the question of compensation. Fourth, as I noted earlier, the emerging generation of teachers will come to your school, if they come at all, with significant student debt that adds additional financial pressure. Fifth, even the most dedicated teachers are vulnerable over time when their hard work, dedication, and innovative instructional efforts earn little more than, "We love you and wish we could do more." And finally, over time that dedicated teacher will likely begin to slide into a holding pattern in which innovation disappears and attitudes grow increasingly brittle. In the end, both teacher and student pay a huge price.

So, why such a long dissertation on faculty compensation in the context of deciding strategic initiatives based on student impact? For this reason. Teachers are crucial to the success of your students. If they are not, then it would make sense to replace them with easily available technology. If, however, teachers really do matter, then you do great harm to your teachers, to your students, and to your entire school culture when you don't do what is the responsible and biblically right thing to do.

Faculty pay raises do benefit your teachers, but the real motivation must be to provide the best quality teachers for your students. If you can't clearly and directly connect an initiative to the positive impact it can have on your students, then you should probably set that initiative aside. This approach to deciding may seem obvious. In my experience that isn't always the case.

7. Grounded in reality

I've lost count of the number of schools who have succumbed to the siren song of, "We've just got to add a high school." You know how it goes. You have a pretty successful elementary school (say, K–5 or K–6), and your parents start to lobby you to add middle school. You reason, "We have a pretty strong fifth grade, so why not add sixth?" And so you do, only to discover that you have lost half of your class to the local public school. You keep moving ahead, however, and before long those same parents are calling on you to add a high school. A decision to move ahead almost always ends badly. Now the entire school is at risk.

I have often encouraged preschools to add the elementary grades because it is relatively easy to build a school at that level. But even then there is much research that must be done before moving ahead. That research is even more important when it comes to a middle school or high school—or building a new facility or adding programs or any number of other high-ticket, high-stress initiatives.

Let's take some real-life situations to illustrate why these questions are important. A Christian preschool has been in operation for twenty years. During that time it has grown to an overall enrollment of 300 children in its various programs. It has a hugely positive reputation in the community, and every year parents are asking the board and leadership team, "When are you going to start an elementary program? The need is real, and we'll be the first to jump on board." For years the board and leadership team of this preschool have resisted these requests. Recently, however, during a planning process, one of the key potential initiatives to surface once again was to start an elementary school. Given the formal nature of the planning process and the deliberate involvement of parents, it had become impossible to simply ignore the question any longer. What steps should the initiative work team take?

What Is Most Important Right Now?

Always begin with these questions:

1. What do you already know about this initiative? Since this is not the first time the question has been posed, it is probably the case that there has been some research done in the past. The first step, then, is to pull out that research and ask, Is this information still current enough to have some validity? In any case, start with what you already know.

2. What are the gaps in your knowledge or expertise? The team assigned to do this research should gather the data and interview those who were involved in the original research. Next, a bit of brainstorming based on what information is already available is in order.
    a. Will adding an elementary school program require that you build a new building?
    b. If so, do you already possess sufficient space to construct a new building?
    c. What do you know about current zoning laws that would impact a decision to build?
    d. What do you know about the cost of building?
    e. Do you know anyone in the building trades who does this kind of work?
    f. Do you know an architect who could help with design questions?

3. What are the key trends related to this initiative?
    a. Do you have any idea what is happening demographically in your area?
    b. What size is the school-age population? Is it growing or in decline?
    c. Have other schools recently entered the market? Is so, were they public or private?
    d. Is the homeschool population increasing or declining?
    e. What is the health of the churches in the area? Are they vibrant or in decline?

4. Now it is time to wrestle with the implications of those trends.
    a. What do the long-term demographic trends tell you about the future viability of a new elementary school in the area?
    b. What does the current health of local churches tell you about your idea?

5. Do you know what your potential customers might want from you?
    a. How did you gather that information?
    b. How do you know it is valid?
    c. How strongly do people feel about your initiative?
    d. Are there enough legitimately potential customers to make your initiative worth pursuing?

6. Is there anyone else in your area who might be considering the same initiative? If so, would you consider a partnership? Why or why not?

7. Will technology have an impact? If so, what and how?

8. What about the impact on your facility?

    a. Is your supporting organization willing to help fund construction and upkeep?

    b. How are you going to raise the money without going into capital debt, which is almost always a bad idea?

9. What about the impact on your current "ownership" relationship?

    a. If you are a church-sponsored preschool, is the church leadership favorable to pursuing such an initiative?

    b. Have they done their homework?

    c. Is there real unity of vision about this initiative?

    d. If you are a private preschool, how do you ascertain the level of support for this initiative?

Obviously this is a lot of work for a small work team to complete in what is usually a four-to-six-week period following the initial strategic planning retreat. It is possible that the team will simply not be able to get to all of the questions above. What they must do, however, is give an initial nod toward the "doability" of the initiative. If, for example, one of the potential initiatives is construction of a new fieldhouse and a quick study of typical construction costs puts the figure for the project at $10 million and the school has never had a successful campaign to fund a capital project, then the team would certainly put this initiative into "wouldn't this be nice but it's probably not realistic" category.

It's Now Decision Time

Once the initiative work team has completed its task, it is time for the team to take the recommendations first to the board, then to the full task force. The recommendations go to the board first because it is the board's responsibility to ensure that none of the initiatives would divert the school from its proper path or put the school at financial risk. This is also a time for the board to dig into the research and reasoning of the initiative work team and to offer their own insights and ideas. Unless there is a compelling reason to ignore or significantly modify the recommendations of the initiative work team, it is now time for a presentation to the entire task force.

In this meeting, the entire task force will have an opportunity to ask questions and make recommendations. By this time, unless there is some serious issue, it is time for the task force to voice its approval of the recommendations and move ahead in development of an action plan for each of the strategic initiatives. That will be the focus of chapter 10. Before moving on to that discussion, I need to make three further observations about the planning process: one relates to this thing we call vision, one relates to the impact of strategic planning on the day-to-day life of your school, and one relates to a final understanding of what matters most right now. Let's take them in reverse order.

What Really Matters Most Right Now?

Making this decision is a fearsome responsibility for all involved. It is also an easy decision to get wrong, no matter how careful the process or committed the people. In fact, I have found that the more rigid and complex the process, the easier it can be to make good decisions while missing what is truly most important right now. Making good decisions will rarely hurt you, but failing to make truly great decisions can hinder you in pursuit of your passion. So what can you do to avoid this danger?

First, bathe every step of the process with prayer. I don't mean the kind of perfunctory prayer we often offer up at the beginning and conclusion of our meetings. I mean the kind of prayer that forces us to pause in our headlong pursuit of the good to ponder what might lie just beyond the surface.

Candidly, I haven't often experienced this kind of prayer when working with schools. We just don't have the time, it seems, or perhaps the will, or maybe we just don't know how. When I have been blessed to be in the presence of people who really do know how to pray, it is a remarkable experience. That happened recently while sitting in on a meeting of the board of a Christian school in Taiwan. It confirmed something I said earlier in this book. When a board takes the time to worship together and pray together, it makes the task of dealing with tough issues easier.

The purpose of this book is obviously not about how to pray. It is, however, about how to be successful in the planning process. I would recommend to every board an excellent book by Eugene Peterson, *Working the Angles*, that contains a lot of good thinking on prayer.

Second, asking good questions—probing questions, even uncomfortable questions—is essential to success in the process. Often we ignore that still small voice in our head because we want to keep the process moving along or want to avoid "controversy." Obviously, controversy for controversy's sake or in pursuit of a private agenda is always unhealthy and unproductive. There is, however, nothing wrong with asking critical questions.

Third, giving people the freedom to ask those kinds of probing questions will require that we learn how to properly address the outlier, because sometimes the outlier is the only one in the room who sees what needs to be seen and sometimes an outlier is just a troublemaker. Let me provide a possible strategy for dealing with this challenge.

Dr. John McArthur told the following story at a Shepherd's Conference many years ago. It was customary practice for the elders at Grace Community Church to require 100-percent approval for all decisions. Given that there were forty elders, all of whom were pretty sharp men with their own thoughts and ideas, this could be a challenge. It was, however, not optional, especially since the leadership of the church truly believed that the Holy Spirit would not move them in differing directions.

At the time that decisions were being made about the design and construction of a new sanctuary, one of the issues that created some pointed discussion was whether to include a baptistery or not. Since Grace Community was not a "Baptist" church, most of the elders were opposed to including the typical baptistery on the wall behind the platform as part of the design of the new sanctuary. One of the elders, however, argued that even though Grace Community was not formally a Baptist church, they still practiced baptism of believers only by immersion, which requires a full baptistery. After some increasingly heated discussion, the elders had reached an impasse. What to do next was the question. Not wanting to short-circuit an important discussion, but also not wanting to get bogged down in what might be nothing more than a private agenda, they came up with a solution that I have found helpful in a number of situations.

They commissioned the one individual who was continuing to make the case for a baptistery in the sanctuary the task of coming up with a solution that would address everyone's concerns. His job was to win the hearts of the elders or to submit himself to their decision. What he devised was nothing short of brilliant.

Instead of building a baptistery in the typical fashion, on the wall behind the platform, he suggested that the baptistery be built under the platform. Thus it was not immediately visible upon entering the sanctuary, which addressed the concerns of those who didn't want to be identified as a Baptist church by such a powerful visible symbol.

But by including a baptistery in the design of the sanctuary, he was ensuring that the church acted consistently with its theological practice. In addition, that particular design actually forced the church to make each baptismal service a special event, which gave the act of baptism an appropriate level of importance. Thus at Grace Community Church, baptism periodically becomes the entire focus of a service. I attended several such services while serving as the provost at The Master's College, and I can tell you that they were incredibly powerful services, providing a tremendous opportunity for those being baptized to share their faith with family and friends.

Sometimes the voice crying in the wilderness has the best idea. In any strategic planning and thinking process, you've got to provide for that possibility.

The Whirlwind

I love how McChesney, Covey, and Huling describe what they call the "whirlwind." "The real enemy of execution is your day job! We call it the whirlwind. It is the massive amount of energy that's necessary just to keep your operation going on a day-to-day basis; and, ironically, it's also the thing that makes it so hard to execute anything new. The whirlwind robs from you the focus required to move your team forward" (2012, 6).

They go on to observe, "Leaders seldom differentiate between the whirlwind and strategic goals because both are necessary to the survival of the organization. However, they are clearly different, and more important, they compete relentlessly for time, resources, energy, and attention. We don't have to tell you which will usually win this fight" (2012, 7).

And as they further note, "The whirlwind is urgent and it acts on you and everyone working for you every minute of every day. The goals you've set for moving forward are important, but when urgency and importance clash, urgency will win every time. Once you become aware of this struggle, you will see it playing out everywhere, in any team that is trying to execute something new" (2012, 7).

Yes, the whirlwind is relentless, and it won't subside while you develop and implement your plan. And some of your daily challenges are of nearly equal importance to the strategic initiatives that you have identified. In fact, one or more of the strategic initiatives identified by the task force will often relate directly to a particularly persistent tactical challenge such as enrollment, marketing, resource development, faculty compensation, or curricular or instructional innovation.

Whatever the case, it is imperative that the daily whirlwind not become an excuse for failure to accomplish strategic goals or for pursuit of strategic goals to become an excuse for ignoring legitimate and necessary tactical tasks. In his book *The Advantage* (2012), Patrick Lencioni describes a process that I have found helpful in keeping an appropriate balance between your school's strategic and tactical efforts. It is built around the idea of strategic anchors, those things that you do every day that are crucial to your continuing success, things that if you ignore while in pursuit of your strategic plan could put your school at risk.

Rather than try to reproduce Lencioni's strategic anchor exercise here I will encourage you to add *The Advantage* to your library and that you take the time to study his approach to the identification of strategic anchors and how to connect those daily tasks to your strategic plan.

Vision, Vision, Where's the Vision?

I've put off a discussion of vision until now because candidly it is, for me, a difficult topic. I say for me because there are hundreds of articles and books on the topic by some very bright people who would argue that vision is the most powerful element in any organization.

Consider, for example, the following quotes from the respected business writer Burt Nanus.

> Quite simply, a vision is a realistic, credible, attractive future for your organization.... Vision always begins with the future. Indeed, vision is where tomorrow begins, for it expresses what you and others who share the vision will be working hard to create. Since most people don't take the time to think systematically about the future, those who do—and who base their strategies and actions on their visions—have inordinate power to shape the future....
>
> Vision is a picture in your mind's eye of the way things could or should be in the days ahead.... In suggesting that vision deals with that which is preferable, we are insinuating that vision entails change. Vision is never about maintaining the status quo. Vision is about stretching reality to extend beyond the existing state (1995, 8).

I agree; vision is important. Every organization should and must have a sense for what they hope to become over time. I'm just not sure that there is a common understanding about what we mean when we use that word *vision*. Let me see if I can explain what I mean when I use the word.

This past December, in what has become a Christmas tradition, my wife—along with our daughter and her family—attended a presentation of Charles Dickens' holiday classic *A Christmas Carol*. It was quite a sumptuous production, beautifully capturing the essence of Dickens' tale of redemption and transformation. What caught me a bit by surprise, however, was the clarity with which Dickens also gave life to the meaning of vision.

You remember the story, of course. Scrooge receives a rather unsettling visit from his long-deceased former partner, Jacob Marley. Marley, who appears as a pathetic-looking creature encumbered with a long, heavy chain forged, as he explains, during a life focused on the self-centered pursuit of wealth, delivers a foreboding message. During the coming night Scrooge will receive visits from three beings: the ghosts of Christmas past, present, and future. Marley warns Scrooge that how Scrooge responds to the messages of those three ghosts will determine his fate.

First comes the ghost of Christmas past, bringing scenes of Scrooge's childhood, early career, joyous first romance, and initial decline into a single-minded pursuit of more—whose first casualty is a future with his beloved. Second comes the ghost of Christmas present, during which we catch glimpses into the loving family life of his faithful employee Bob Cratchett and that of his happily married but financially struggling nephew Fred, both of whom know how to celebrate Christmas well.

It is during the visit from the ghost of Christmas future that Dickens provides one of the clearest illustrations of vision I've seen anywhere. After viewing a pretty bleak future, including a glimpse into the sorrow of a family responding to the death of a young son, and finally the sight of Scrooge's name etched into a gravestone, Scrooge turns to the specter guiding him and implores, "Is this a vision of what must be or a vision of what could be?" In other words, he is asking this simple question: Can I change the future? In one sense that is exactly what we mean when we talk about vision.

For many people, vision is about *more*—more students, more buildings, more money, more acclaim. For Dickens, vision was about *better*—a better person, a better life, a better impact, a better reputation. It isn't that more and better are mutually exclusive. Sometimes more is better—more students graduating with better grades, more students engaged in life-on-life ministry, more quality programs that better equip your students for lives of positive influence upon graduation, more students attending your school so that your impact in the lives of those students can be multiplied. Hopefully you get the idea. But more for the sake of more seems a poor excuse for vision.

One of the best pieces of advice I ever received when I served as a pastor was this: "Alan, focus your energies on deepening the church you serve and let God decide how much He wants to broaden the impact of the church you serve." You've probably heard something similar.

It was not a call to fatalism. It was, however, a call to focus on what I could really influence: how I did my job and how I could continually encourage excellent effort from those who were part of the church and school God had called me to shepherd. And here's what I discovered. Do what you are called to do with excellence and, all things being equal, you will experience numerical growth. Focus on numbers, and you will soon find yourself driving people rather than leading people. That inevitably ends badly.

I do believe that vision is born in the heart of a leader. I also believe that it is God who gives that vision to those He calls to lead. I further believe that a strategic planning process done well is a powerful means to both shape that vision through the insights of others and to spread that vision fully across the breadth of a school, church, or other organization. I just caution leaders to remember three things:
1. It's God's vision, not yours.
2. Vision can't be expressed simply in numerical terms.
3. Mission is not vision, but it is the foundation upon which vision is built.

Documents 9.1, 9.2, and 9.3 (downloadable from https://www.acsi.org/tradebooks/psr/6518) contain prompts that can help you discover and articulate God's vision for your school.

An Inexact Science

Remember, the process is the plan. Whatever you identify as "what's most important right now" is more of a snapshot in time than something engraved in stone. There is always a bit of the impermanent with every decision we make. Circumstances change, new information alters your understanding of the landscape around you, and sometimes you just come to understand that you made a mistake. Learning to move boldly forward in pursuit of your goals while holding everything loosely is a tension that everyone in leadership must learn to manage.

Now it is time to move on to the really hard stuff. It is time to develop a sound, workable action plan to implement the initiatives that you have identified during your process so far.

10

Create a Road Map

Years ago I was traveling with a friend through New York City when we made a wrong turn and got hopelessly lost. It was late at night, and we found ourselves in an area of the city that, to put it nicely, was a bit worn—lots of broken windows and bottles. To avoid driving into even more dangerous territory we pulled into a 24/7 convenience store to ask for directions. Fortunately for us there was a police patrol car parked in the lot, so we approached the officer and shared our predicament. After shaking his head at our poor decision-making and navigational skills, he gave us clear directions back to the expressway—and even followed us to make sure we got on our way safely.

That experience is but one reason why I love my GPS. It has come to my rescue time and time again. Once I plug in my destination it gives me clear turn-by-turn directions along with a map showing my progress. And when, as sometimes happens, I miss one of those turns it immediately recalculates the remaining part of my journey and gives me a new set of driving directions, keeping me on the right path until I arrive safely at my journey's end.

What you are about to do now is to program your strategic planning GPS. You are going to develop a step-by-step, turn-by-turn tactical plan to implement your strategic initiatives. To accomplish this task, you will need to answer the following series of questions:
• Are we sure this is the right thing to do?
• Do we have the right team in place?
• Who will be the team leader?
• Have we identified all necessary action steps?
• What is our timeline?

- What will it cost?
- How will we fund this project?
- How will we track our progress?
- Will this "grab" the hearts of our people?

That's a pretty long (but necessary) list. In this chapter I will walk you through the answers to each of those questions and provide you with the tools necessary to "program your GPS." Before we jump into that task, I'd like to address an additional, related question—one raised by McChesney, Covey, and Huling in their exceptional book *The Four Disciplines of Execution*: "There are two principal things a leader can influence when it comes to producing results: your strategy (or plan) and your ability to execute that strategy…. So stop for a moment and ask yourself this question: Which of these do leaders struggle with more? Is it creating a strategy, or executing the strategy?"

They then go on with this observation: "Every time we pose this question to leaders anywhere in the world, their answer is immediate: 'Execution'" (2012, xxiii).

I find exactly the same thing in working with schools. Defining who you are is a challenge, but it is something you and the members of your task force think about all the time. Identifying what is most important right now is also a challenge, but with a sound process in place it is something you and your task force can agree on after some healthy discussion. Achieving your goals, however, requires something very different. It requires the ability to identify necessary action steps and the discipline necessary to execute those action steps.

That, however, doesn't come so naturally to most people in school leadership, primarily because those in school leadership are seldom equipped with the skills necessary to ensure effective execution. Hopefully, what I share in this chapter will give you some solid ideas for bringing your initiatives to life. In addition I will suggest several excellent books on the topic of execution as part of the bibliography at the end of the book. Reading those books will further deepen your understanding and sharpen your skills. So, let's get started.

Question 1: Are we sure this is the right thing to do?

Obviously you can't program a GPS until you have your final destination firmly in mind. At this point it is imperative to give final approval for the projects that will be driven by each of the strategic initiatives that have been identified during the strategic planning process. Hopefully this question has already been answered, but it is crucial to ensure full agreement that the initiatives you have identified are what are most important right now. Without complete clarity and full ownership, successful execution is unlikely.

Question 2: Do we have the right team in place?

Finding the right team members who can construct and implement an effective plan is crucial. How to go about putting a team together is not always so obvious, however. Our first impulse is often to simply assign people to each work team. I prefer that people self-select based on their personal passion, interest, and experience.

Typically at this point in the process I invite each task force member to volunteer to serve on one of the project teams. It is often fascinating, and sometimes surprising, to see what choices are made by the task force members—for example, the elementary teacher who chooses to work on the enrollment initiative or the parent who chooses the faculty compensation initiative. The fact is that given the choice, people will almost always follow their interests or passions.

It is surprising how often the composition of the project team requires few, if any, changes. I do, however, insist that the head of school and chair of the board review the make-up of all of the teams. On occasion they will suggest some "horse trading"— moving a person or two to ensure that there is good balance of faculty, staff, board members, and parents on each project team. This can all be accomplished in a matter of minutes at the end of a group meeting of the task force.

With the project teams in place, I address two further issues before providing some basic instruction on next steps. First I ask them to identify a team leader. Qualifications for that team leader are listed below. The head of school and chair of the board must endorse those decisions. Second, I suggest that as a team they consider the possibility of adding additional project team members. Those additional team members would typically be individuals who can add some real-world knowledge and expertise that would help in developing the action plan.

One school with which I worked identified a real deficiency in both the instructional and administrative use of technology. It was a crucially important initiative, but everyone on the task force recognized that outside help would be needed. I suggested that they put feelers out to their various networks to see if anyone was interested in helping develop the technology action plan. Two parents, both of whom were professionally engaged in research and application related to technology, responded, joined the team, and ended up playing a crucial role in development of the action plan.

Question 3: Who should be team leader?

For every strategic initiative team you need a team leader. Anyone who has served on a committee or task force knows how easy it is for the group to wander in circles without someone to keep everyone moving effectively in the same direction. However, the best team leader is not always the obvious choice. Our tendency is to choose someone based on the person's position on the organizational chart. Sometimes the head of school or a department head makes the most sense for team leader; sometimes, depending on the focus of the initiative, it doesn't.

Choose wisely and you increase the probability of a positive outcome. Choose poorly and your probability of success will be diminished significantly. Typically it makes sense for this person to be a member of the school staff, but that is not always the case. On occasion, for example, there is a parent whose expertise and passion make that person the best candidate. Always go with the best choice—meaning the person who is willing, knowledgeable, and able.

To be successful, each team leader must
• Possess the necessary expertise to fulfill the role—expertise related to working with a team and to the specifics related to the project.
• Be given the necessary authority to carry out their mandate. Like the head of school, the person must have clear instructions as to the scope of the task. This is especially crucial when it comes to addressing potentially rogue or unengaged team members.
• Recognize that there will be a sound review and accountability process in place.
• Be able and willing to communicate …
   ◦ Up—to appropriate levels of supervision
   ◦ Out—to team members and colleagues
   ◦ Honestly—never hiding any critical information
   ◦ In a timely manner—never catching team members or school leaders by surprise

There is one additional thought to consider when developing project work teams and choosing team leaders. One of the benefits of developing project work teams as I am suggesting is that it allows you to break through the typical organizational barriers, what the business literature calls silos (Lencioni 2008). In my experience it is not unusual to visit schools where the elementary faculty have little interaction with the high school faculty or where the fine arts faculty have little real professional conversation with the coaches or where parents are kept at arm's length from every aspect of the school except for fund-raising events. That kind of separation is unhealthy.

Imagine a project work team of parents, faculty (elementary and upper school), and staff—all focused on improving instructional innovation. In your mind's eye, do you see a bit of uneasiness, a potential for a bit of conflict, a bit of posturing for turf management? Of course you do. All of that is to be expected, at least initially. Now imagine this. A team of quality people committed to achieving a common purpose, willing to look past the kinds of barriers we typically erect to keep people in their "proper" place, all seeking the best insight, information, and innovation toward completion of a crucial task. Imagine the increasing level of understanding, ownership, and performance. That is equally possible with this kind of team.

What will prevent the formation of effective teams are parochial self-interest, a lack of genuine interest in addressing the issues related to the strategic initiative, and a strict adherence to the lines of authority on the organizational chart. Hopefully the care with which the task force and project teams are constructed will reduce the possibility of that kind of thinking and behavior.

Question 4: Have we identified all of the necessary action steps?

Here is a simple exercise I use with schools to help them in the creation of an action plan. I call it the "Plan your holiday meal" exercise. I use this exercise because virtually everyone on the task force is familiar at some level with planning a holiday meal of some kind.

It is a brainstorming exercise, so the first thing I do is break the larger task force into four smaller groups. I ask them to consider all of the tasks they must perform and all of the questions they must answer in preparation for the big day, and then to put them in an appropriate order. For example, one of the first questions you would need to ask and answer is this: Whom are we going to invite? With the answer to that question in place, you can quickly identify some necessary actions steps such as, Who will write the invitation? Will contact be made via snail mail, e-mail, text, phone call, or some other means? Will you require an RSVP? And on it goes.

To create an action plan, start with the end in mind and work backward. Obviously, some ends are a bit more complex than others, and thus will require a bit more involved action plan. Putting a man on the moon, for example, is a bit more complex end than planning a Thanksgiving meal. But the contours of identifying the necessary action steps are similar—to reach this end we must ... to reach that end we must ... and so forth until you have identified your initial action step. For a sample action plan, see document 10.1 (https://www.acsi.org/tradebooks/psr/6518).

To ensure that you have developed an effective action plan you must be sure to continually ask yourselves these questions: What are we missing? What are the gaps in our knowledge? Who might help us fill in those gaps? Repeat after me: What you don't know that you don't know will always hurt you. Make sure you've considered every possible question during the development of your action plan.

Question 5: What is our timeline?

The short answer is this: long enough to ensure that quality work can realistically be accomplished, and short enough to keep the level of urgency high. Since I believe that maintaining an appropriate sense of urgency is crucial to the success of any project, I lean toward a shorter rather than longer time frame.

Consider this observation from John Kotter: "We have a problem. The problem is complacency. We have all seen it. Yet we underestimate its power and its prevalence.... With complacency, no matter what people say, if you look at what they do it is clear that they are mostly content with the status quo. They pay insufficient attention to wonderful new opportunities and frightening new hazards" (2008, 4–5).

The solution, as Kotter points out, is learning to maintain a true sense of urgency. "When people have a true sense of urgency, they think that action on critical issues is needed *now*, not eventually, not when it fits easily into a schedule. *Now* means making real progress every single day. *Critically important* means challenges that are central to success or survival, winning or losing" (2008, 7; emphasis in the original). Those are the kinds of challenges you are, or should be, addressing through your strategic initiatives.

Putting yourself on the clock, and doing so publicly, is absolutely essential to creating that sense of true urgency and to achieving ultimate success. If you don't put yourself on the clock, I guarantee that the daily whirlwind we discussed earlier will prove too powerful. If you doubt me, consider the latest round of accreditation in which you engaged. Accreditation creates a huge amount of work for your entire team. It is time-consuming and intrusive, and it requires gathering together all kinds of detailed information. Yet it gets done in spite of the whirlwind. Why do you think that is so? Let me suggest two primary reasons.

The first reason relates to the importance of accreditation. It affects your enrollment efforts. It impacts your fund-raising efforts. It shapes everything you do in the realm of instruction. It shapes public opinion about your school. Accreditation touches every aspect of your school. Because it is worth the effort, you will choose to resist the force of your school's daily whirlwind.

Second, however, is that ticking clock. You know that on a particular day the accreditation team will be arriving on your campus. And you know that if you aren't ready, that if all the required tasks have not been completed and completed appropriately, then you will fail to achieve your goal. That is a pretty powerful motivation.

Can you imagine attending an athletic contest in which there was no specific end game? In professional basketball there are four quarters; in baseball, nine innings; in soccer, two halves. How often have you watched your favorite team facing the relentless ticking of the clock? Talk about urgency! Nothing keeps your sense of urgency at an appropriate level like a clear objective tied to a specific time.

As McCheshney, Covey, and Huling note, "... in 1961, President John F. Kennedy shook NASA to its foundations when he made the pronouncement 'land a man on the moon and return him safely to the earth before this decade is out'" (2012, 39). They then ask this question. What do you think happened to accountability within NASA when the challenge of putting a man on the moon was publicly announced?" (2012, 41). You need that same kind of accountability with each of your strategic initiatives.

In much of the strategic planning literature, great emphasis is placed on setting very specific short (three months), intermediate, (usually six months) and long-term (usually one year) goals for each identified action step. That is probably helpful if for no other reason than it keeps you from drifting further and further behind. If you choose to mark out your progress in that way, you will need to identify landmarks that you hope to achieve within those time frames, much as your GPS continually gives you updates on your progress toward your ultimate destination.

Setting those specific timelines is absolutely crucial because "We constantly see goals ... that no one can achieve because there is no finish line; no way of telling whether you completed the goal or not and where you stand at any given point" (McChesney, Covey, and Huling 2012, 37).

Question 6: What will it cost?

Prior to this point in the process I would have already met with the senior leadership team of the school, as well as with the board, to address potential costs of each particular initiative. Some initiatives will come with a modest price tag; others can cost millions. For example, an initiative to encourage instructional innovation may cost a few thousand dollars (though it could require a lot of time in research and actual implementation), whereas a strategic initiative to construct a new fieldhouse, fine arts facility, or science wing will likely come with a substantial price tag.

Having this information in hand prior to taking the strategic plan public is crucial. I have a rule of thumb for this situation. Never take an initiative public unless you have a high degree of confidence that you can actually fund the initiative. As Jim Collins wisely observes, "There is nothing worse in leadership than to hold out false hopes" (2001, 65). Sadly I've witnessed the loss of credibility that can occur when leaders make promises that they simply cannot keep.

Because so much is riding on whether you can actually bring your strategic initiatives to life, it is crucial that you identify people with the experience and skill to accurately assess the potential cost of a project. This is especially true when it comes to major capital projects. Let's be honest: projecting construction costs is not a skill most school leaders learn in graduate school. That lack of knowledge can, and almost always will, put you at risk. That is why you must utilize the skills of highly qualified people to help you develop your cost projections.

Let me emphasize the phrase "highly qualified people." The board chair's best friend's best friend may or may not be "highly qualified," but even if that person is qualified, you need to exercise great care in looking for someone to provide you with accurate numbers. Take your time and do your homework.

No matter what the project, here are some realities for you to consider in developing cost estimates:
• Every action step has a price tag, in either money or time.
• It almost always costs more than you think it will.

- You don't get to keep going back to your donors asking for more money because you didn't do your homework well.
- Make sure that you get the right people involved in the cost-estimating process. Make sure that you ask the right questions—and you will need the right people to help you ask the right questions.
- Some project costs are capitalized over time, such as equipment and furniture.
- Some project costs require cash now, such as materials and labor.
- Some projects will have future budget impact, such as depreciation, maintenance, and replacement.
- Projects can have other hard costs such as these:
  ° Consulting
  ° Additional staff
  ° Fund-raising
- Projects can have soft costs, such as reassigning current staff to new or additional roles.

Once the numbers get crunched, a decision is sometimes made to postpone a particular project. Sometimes, in spite of the final price tag, a decision is made to move ahead because the value of achieving the goals connected to the project is so important. In either case, however, a clear-eyed decision can be made with accurate information in hand. Whatever the case, it is important to "count the cost."

Question 7: How will we fund this project?

Have you ever purchased something you really wanted but couldn't afford? I know I have. A decision to purchase a new set of golf clubs or to take a weekend trip to a nice resort destination will crimp your lifestyle for a few months. But the decision to buy a car or a house way beyond your means can mean financial catastrophe. It might feel nice for the first month after you drive the car off the dealer's lot, but once those payments become a continuing reality competing with a long list of other financial realities, it doesn't seem quite as wonderful anymore.

The same is true of the strategic planning process. As I've noted several times already, you simply can't do everything you might want to do or even believe you must do. Part of the planning process is always about deciding from among a number of worthwhile projects. It is also about deciding whether to fund a particular project from your operational budget, from your program enhancement budget, or from a capital budget. In my book *Rethinking Sustainability*, I carefully distinguish the purpose and funding source of each of those budgets.

For example, if increasing faculty and staff salaries is one of the initiatives that emerge from the strategic planning process, then you will need to develop an action plan that will allow you to fund those increases from your operational budget. To do that you will need to ask the following questions:

- How much of an increase do we want to make to staff salaries? Will the increase be a modest 5 percent or a more robust 20 percent?
- Over what time frame are we planning to make those increases? Will we increase salaries in a single year or phase them in over a period of two, three, or four years?
- Are we agreed that the increase should be funded fully from increases in tuition?
- If so, how much will we need to increase tuition on a yearly basis to cover this specific increase in operational cost?
- Have we ever done a multiyear budget? Do we know how?
- Is this a realistic goal?
- What is our plan to communicate these tuition increases—and the reason behind the increases—to our parents?

The same kinds of questions would be asked for any strategic project that you intend to fund directly from your operational budget.

If you plan to fund a strategic project from either your annual fund or through a capital campaign, you will need to consider the following questions:

- Do we have a healthy annual fund strategy already in place?
- Have we historically used income from the annual fund to pay for program enhancement projects or to cover a gap in our operational budget?
- If we have used annual fund income to fund the gap and we now want to use that revenue to fund a particular project, are we willing to increase tuition to ensure full coverage of our operational costs?
- How will we communicate this decision to our parents?
- Have we ever run a capital campaign? Is so, was it successful?
- If we decide to run a capital campaign, are we willing to do necessary precampaign research to determine our fund-raising potential?
- Have we considered any potential ongoing operational costs that will arise from the completed project, e.g., maintenance and utility costs of that new facility?
- Will we build into the capital campaign an endowment to cover those annual costs, or will we cover those costs from our operational fund? Have we considered the impact on our tuition?

Getting better at what you do requires, at minimum, three things. First, you've got to learn to think creatively about everything you do. In education it is easy to do one of two things—to constantly chase after the next new thing or to cling comfortably to familiar patterns. Both choices will typically end badly for you. Careful, creative thinking, on the other hand, can open the door to continuing success as a school.

Second, creative thinking must always be coupled with quality execution. Ideas, no matter how great, refuse to self-execute. Quality execution requires strong leadership and teamwork, a willingness to be held accountable, focused effort balanced by flexible responses to changing circumstances, and full awareness of whether efforts are achieving the desired outcomes.

Third, creative thinking always comes with a price tag. Sometimes that price tag has dollar signs attached. It is highly unlikely that in a creative, growing organization the cost of doing business will ever decline. Thus, counting the cost is truly important. You simply can't waste limited resources in pursuit of bad ideas and pipe dreams. That is another reason why the strategic planning process is so important.

There is, however, another potential cost that is often associated with genuine creative thinking. There will be occasions when some long-time faculty or staff simply are not able or willing to make the kind or level of change driven by your strategic initiatives and resulting action plan. When that happens, it is almost always painful. At those times, however, you must remember that it is the best interests of your students that must take precedent.

Question 8: How will we track our progress?

Name a game. Any game. Chances are there is a way to keep score. In fact, the great sports announcers all have this in common. They never let more than ten minutes go by without telling their audience two things: how much time is left in the game and the score. Without a way to keep score, what's the point? Even in soccer (which I must confess seems pointless to me) every goal scored is greeted by wild cheers (perhaps because there are so few goals).

You are not playing a game. What you do is deadly serious. A means of keeping score, however, is crucial if you truly want to keep track of your progress or, in some cases, lack of progress. Entire books have been written on this important topic. My goal here is to ensure that you grasp at least the contours of a strategy for staying on course and evaluating your progress.

My thinking on the importance of effectively tracking progress has been influenced significantly by a number of people such as Peter Drucker, Jim Collins, John Kotter, and Patrick Lencioni. For me, perhaps the most compelling and helpful description of how best to ensure that everyone stays on course and on time is found in *The Four Disciplines of Execution* by Chris McChesney, Sean Covey, and Jim Huling. In that book they suggest how to design what they call an organizational "scoreboard." (2012, 70).

Here are the components of that scoreboard.
- *Is it simple?* While a coach may need a lot of complex data for game preparation and management, the information needed to keep everyone engaged is rather minimal. You've got to decide which bits of information should be visible to everyone at all times.
- *Is it easy to see?* Scoreboards are public. I find great value in keeping essential information in a public space—your conference room, for example—so that anyone, anytime, can at a glance determine your progress on each of your strategic initiatives. It is important to remember, "Visibility ... drives accountability" (2012, 70).
- *Is it specific?* McChesney, Covey, and Huling use the concept of lag and lead measures.
  - ∘ "A lag measure is the measurement of a result you are trying to achieve. We call them lag measures because by the time you get the data the result has already happened" (2012, 46). (We have raised the $5 million we need to build our new fieldhouse.)
  - ∘ "Lead measures are different; they foretell the result. They have two primary characteristics. First, a lead measure is predictive, meaning that if the lead measure changes, you can predict that the lag measure will change. Second, a lead measure is influenceable; it can be directly influenced by the team" (2012, 47),

Here is an illustration. Let's say that you are trying to raise $5 million for the construction of a new fine arts facility. That $5 million would be your ultimate lag goal—a goal you have set to achieve over a three-year period. To achieve that ultimate goal you know that there are certain steps (lead measures) that you must accomplish if you hope to reach your ultimate lag goal. Those lead measures might be things like these:
- The hiring of a general contractor and a design team, and final design of the fine arts facility including building design, site preparation, zoning, and engineering issues among others
- Completion of a precampaign study

- A certain number of personal contacts with potential donors within a specific amount of time
- A certain number of pledges from potential donors within a certain time frame
- Planning for and executing some kind of public event related to achieving your lag goal
- A follow-up strategy with all of your donors
- Development and implementation of an ongoing communication strategy

Each lead measure must have its own specific timeline and specific way of measurement. For example, "We have identified twenty potential major donors, and we will make contact with each of those donors within the next 45 days. Our goal is to raise 50 percent of the total lag goal from these fifteen donors."

You can see how helpful that would be in tracking your progress. If, for example, after contacting all twenty donors you have received promises of only $1.5 million, then you know that achieving your ultimate goal of $5 million will require revision or you will need to identify and contact a significant number of new donors. In either case, you have a clear understanding of your progress.

- *Can we tell at a glance if we are winning?* For some reason, many people in leadership have an aversion to taking bad news public. That is foolish and clearly counterproductive. Imagine playing in a game where you have no idea of how well you are doing. Being behind in the third quarter of a football game does not mean that you will lose. What it does mean is that you will probably need to make some adjustments in your strategy and step up your level of execution—neither of which you would do without knowing the score.

Let me provide another illustration of the compelling power of a public scoreboard coupled with the power of lag and lead indicators.

Upon arriving at The Master's College in 1996, I was given the task of reversing a long-term year-to-year decline in enrollment. That was my strategic initiative. I must confess I knew virtually nothing about marketing and enrollment management in the higher education world. Immediately I did two things. I first took my enrollment and financial aid team away for a three-day strategic planning retreat during which we identified our strategic initiatives (lag goals).

Second, I set out to learn as much as I could about the art and science of higher education enrollment management. This was important because at my first board meeting I had been asked to give a projected enrollment for the fall of 1996. Here was my response: "I have no idea. I don't even know how to do that." I added a few more observations, none of which, I am sure, endeared me to the board. I did tell them, however, that I would be prepared with answers to all of their questions in our next meeting—answers based on solid data.

At that time, schools used something called the enrollment funnel. Using that funnel, we were able to track the key bits of data that allowed us to make quality enrollment projections for the coming year. At the bottom of the funnel was our lag measurement—our desired enrollment for the coming year. At every other level of the funnel were the lead measurements. When comparing those lead measurements with previous years we could, even as early as January, get a good sense of whether we would achieve our lag goal in September.

Then, to take that simple means of measuring our progress, I could add a couple of equally simple, clear measurements. For example, I knew that by following a specific follow-up protocol with individuals who made an inquiry about TMC, we increased the probability of producing an application from that student. So we carefully tracked and recorded all of our follow-up actions.

We also knew that if we could get a student on campus, we increased the probability that the student would enroll. Therefore, we worked hard to get every student who filled out an application onto the TMC campus. And from year to year we evaluated the effectiveness of our "get out the vote" strategies. All of our decisions were driven by the data we generated, and all of our predictive data (lead indicators) were publicly tracked and discussed in our weekly staff meetings.

In doing this we were not only able to keep track of our progress but to constantly revise how we did what we did to achieve ever better results. Tracking your progress and doing so in a public way is absolutely essential to your success in achieving your goals.

Question 9: Will this "grab" the hearts of our people?

I've saved this question for last even though it is something that must be considered at every step of the strategic planning process. Quite simply, what people don't understand they can't "own," and what they don't "own" they aren't likely to support. Because it takes significant resources of time, energy, and money to bring a strategic plan to life, it is crucial that you do all you can do to "grab" the hearts of everyone associated with your school.

Unfortunately, that often doesn't happen, even when schools spend the necessary time, energy, and money. In *Made to Stick*, their exceptional book on communication, Chip and Dan Heath explain why: "We are wired to feel things for people, not abstractions" (2007, 18). For instance, "Research shows that people are more likely to make a charitable gift to a single needy individual than to an entire impoverished region." Think of all those World Vision "specials" you've seen on TV. What is the focus of each of those specials? Is it the country of Honduras or Ethiopia or the Philippines? Of course not. It is a specific child in a specific village, and the result is often a pledge of support.

It is important to understand that people give first to people. That isn't to say that people won't give to their alma mater. They often do. The greatest motivator, however, is a powerful emotional connection between the gift and a specific project that will have direct impact on people. In the case of a school, those people are usually the students.

Over the years I have made a relentless argument for moving people from the lower form of motivation (emotion) to a higher form of motivation (intellectual support for the purpose of the organization). I still believe such a goal is worthwhile. What I failed to appreciate is the power of emotion to "grab" people by the gut. I don't want to depend on emotion alone because emotion has limited staying power. But appealing only to the intellect is nearly impossible to do with the kinds of communication strategies we employ today. To get to the intellect, people have to trust you and like you and believe that you have the best interests of others at heart. Once you've won their hearts, you can now win their minds.

Winning their hearts doesn't mean you will automatically be able to win their minds. Failure to win their hearts, however, almost always dooms you to failure in any attempt to win the battle for their minds. What should excite you and motivate you is the reality that a truly worthwhile project—one that if achieved can genuinely make a difference in the educational experience of your students—can, if you craft a compelling story and communicate it with excellence, capture the hearts and imagination of people.

What Could Go Wrong Now?

Actually, a lot of things. We live in a fallen world, and not everyone will be excited about what you are hoping to accomplish through your strategic plan You can have the greatest strategic plan in the world with the clearest road map programmed into your GPS and still fail to reach your destination. It happens all the time, especially when you are trying to implement new programs or new approaches to the way you are already doing things. Change always looks better on paper than it does in the trenches. In the next chapter I will explore the challenges you must address as you seek to implement change in your school.

The Challenge of Change

Change is hard—not always, not for everyone, but most of the time for most people. As Chip and Dan Heath note, "In our lives, we embrace a lot of big changes ... [while] other behaviors are maddeningly intractable" (2010, 4). For example most of you have been or currently are married. Marriage is a big-time change, yet most people willingly choose to get married. They choose to embrace change. Try to implement a new evaluation process at your school, however, and I promise you there will be resistance. Interesting, isn't it?

While not all people resist change, it is the rare person who doesn't at some time resist some kind of change. Even the most adventuresome people get accustomed to doing things in a certain way or become comfortable at using a particular tool for a certain kind of task. Here's reality, however—and this will surprise you I know!—change is inevitable. And in the day in which we live it is not only inevitable; it is relentless, daunting, and often chaotic.

Here's another reality. Change is not only inevitable, but failure to change in a timely and appropriate fashion puts the organization you lead at risk. Few organizations, however, are as resistant to change as are schools, even as schooling is being turned on its head by what is happening in the world of technology.

As I've often said to teachers, if you view your primary responsibility as delivering information to an audience, then know this: nobody needs you anymore. Everything you know and everything you "deliver" to your audience is available on the Internet. Fortunately for teachers, schooling is not just about information delivery. Unfortunately, far too many teachers haven't figured that out yet.

I don't want to get bogged down here in a philosophical discussion on the role of teachers in the classroom, but I do want to make this point. The world is changing—not just minor changes around the edges of life, but massive changes that will result in major rewrites of how we do just about everything. If the strategic planning process in which you engage doesn't address this probability, it isn't a very good process. If it does, it will prompt you to consider some fundamental changes in how you do school.

Knowing you need to change some things, however, doesn't mean that things will change. You've got to manage the change process. That's likely to test your leadership skills in ways you've not yet experienced. In this chapter you will be introduced to some key organizational change concepts—concepts you will need to know and master as you seek to lead your school through necessary, but perhaps disconcerting, change.

Let me be honest. This topic is way beyond the scope of a single chapter. There is, however, a lot of quality research on the subject of organizational change. I highly recommend that you purchase two books. The first is *Leading Change* by John Kotter, professor at the Harvard School of Business. Based on sound research, his thoughts and suggestions should be taken seriously.

The second book is *Switch: How to Change Things When Change Is Hard*, by Chip and Dan Heath (authors of my favorite book on communication, *Made to Stick*). Chip is a professor at the Graduate School of Business at Stanford University, and Dan is a senior fellow at Duke University's Center for the Advancement of Social Entrepreneurship. Their approach to the topic of implementing change follows a different tack than does John Kotter's, but taken together the common threads will provide you with significant help as you try to lead your school through the many obstacles that litter your path on the way to healthy change.

Obstacles to Change

My goals in this chapter are modest. First, I want to identify some of those obstacles and suggest some strategies for dealing with them. Second, I want to encourage you to invest a bit more time in the topic of organizational change. It is something that you will be dealing with at some level throughout your tenure as a leader.

Here are two questions that have helped me think through the complex issues surrounding the challenge of change:

- What makes people so resistant to change?
- Are there things we can do to reduce that resistance?

Before we jump into this conversation, let me make two additional observations about change.

Sometimes forces completely beyond our control thrust shifting conditions upon us. Think of the images you've seen of refugees fleeing war or famine or political upheaval. Lots of pain. Lots of turmoil. Lots of grief. In those kinds of situations there is often little that can be done to change a current reality. In these cases there are no manuals on how best to adjust to the reality that your home is gone, along with your way of life and probably a number of family and friends. You have been thrust into a level of turmoil and change that certainly was not your choice but to which you still must respond.

Organizational change, however, is considerably different. In organizational change efforts, someone is choosing change over the status quo. Someone is suggesting that the proposed change makes sense, that it will lead to something better, that it will prove to be superior to what has been. When that someone is not you, when that someone is perfectly happy with the current status quo, when that someone views the nature of the change under consideration as the work of the devil or at least the work of a crazy person—well, then you have a very different kind of pain, but pain nonetheless. In this more typical change context, you will need to consider a number of possible obstacles, each of which will need to be addressed.

Obstacle 1: Past experience

Here is a rather lengthy quote from John Kotter to introduce this obstacle.

> To date, major change efforts have helped some organizations adapt significantly to shifting conditions, have improved the competitive standing of others, and have positioned a few for a better future. But in too many situations the improvements have been disappointing and the carnage has been appalling, with wasted resources and burned-out, scared, or frustrated employees.
>
> To some degree, the downside of change is inevitable. Whenever human communities are forced to adjust to shifting conditions, pain is ever present. But a significant amount of the waste and anguish we've witnessed in the pasts decade is avoidable (1996, 3–4).

I've been there, and so I suspect have you. I was part of a major effort to change the ministry philosophy and focus in a local church of which I was a part. I experienced exactly what Kotter describes in that quote. No real blood was spilled, but a lot of people's lives were upended, friendships destroyed, and sadly, the reputation of Christ in the community was tarnished. And in this case not a single genuine theological issue was in question.

There were no discussions on the nature of redemption, the incarnation of Christ, or the authority of Scripture. The entire conversation revolved around the focus of the church's mission and the strategies the church would employ in pursuit of that mission. In response to the changes suggested by the pastor and staff, many people just opted to leave the church. There was no single massive church split, just dozens of splinters, all of which were painful. Having lived through that experience, I can understand why people with a similar experience would be a bit resistant to any discussion of change.

What could you do to lessen the impact of past experience in current change efforts? I suggest that you begin by gathering historical data about past change efforts. It is one of the first things I do when working with a school.

I want to know who was behind the formation of the school. I want to know, as much as possible, the motives behind the founding of the school. I want to know about the great successes and the great failures. I want to know the philosophical and theological beliefs that were part of the foundation of the school. I want to know the aspirations, disappointments, assumptions, and fears of those who are currently in leadership at the school. Without all of that historical understanding in hand, I can almost guarantee that any change effort will founder.

Obstacle 2: The failure of people to distinguish between form and function, between absolute and nonabsolute

Consider the following observation. Wherever people live in community, there are things that must be done in order for that community to function. For each of those functions, forms are developed. Over time, as Gene Getz (1984) points out, people tend to confuse form and function so that the form actually becomes the function in the minds of people.

Here's an illustration. In the late 1970s our church in Delaware, like many other independent Baptist churches, launched what was called the "bus ministry." Each week our church would send buses into neighborhoods all over New Castle County to provide transportation to our church on Sunday morning. On each bus was a team of people who would visit families in the area with the intent of increasing the number of riders each Sunday. It was viewed as a significant part of our evangelistic ministry. Over time, however, it became apparent that the increasing cost of operating the bus ministry was unsustainable. As a result, the pastoral staff looked for ways to continue reaching kids in their neighborhoods without using such an expensive strategy. Once consensus was reached on how to do that, we announced to the church that we would no longer be running buses on Sunday morning.

The response was immediate and ferocious. People were angry and accused the pastoral staff of abandoning our commitment to reach kids with the gospel. That, of course, was not the intent; and indeed we had developed what seemed to be a very sound, but very different, form for accomplishing the same function. People, however, were not convinced. They had so confused the function of reaching kids with the form of the bus ministry that in their minds to abandon one was to abandon the other.

Now substitute "bus ministry" with discussions on curriculum, spiritual formation, instructional strategies, or any other long-term program at your school. Do you see the potential for misunderstanding and conflict?

Regardless of the topic, however, people's thinking is often shaped more by their assumptions than it is by careful analysis. Not all differences of opinion, however, arise from flawed or unchallenged assumptions. Often those differences arise from honest disagreement on the fundamentals, on what is absolute as opposed to something that is a nonabsolute. For example, educators who embrace a more classical approach to education are simply not going to see curriculum and classroom instruction in the same way that someone from the Waldorf school of thought or the Montessori approach to education will see those things.

In those cases, sometimes the only course of action may be separation. But that should be a last resort and should emerge from a thoughtful, informed discussion, not from privately held assumptions based on little more than personal experience and preference.

Obstacle 3: Parochial self-interest

Let's say I've been teaching third grade for twenty-five years and doing so with some degree of success. And let's say that I've been using a particular curriculum for that entire time. How amenable do you think I'm going to be if a particular strategic initiative calls for an evaluation and possible revision of the entire elementary curriculum? Let's be honest. I suspect that enthusiasm for that kind of change in that context will be less than overwhelming.

As Chip and Dan Heath observe, "When people try to change things, they're usually tinkering with behaviors that have become automatic" (2010, 11), and who among us wants to learn a new way of doing something that has become second nature to us? "If you want people to change," the Heaths note, "you've got to simply make the journey easier. Create a steep downhill slope and give them a push. Remove some friction from the trail. Scatter around lots of signs to tell them they're getting close" (2010, 181). It's a concept they call shaping the path.

Much of shaping the path can be accomplished through proactive training and provision of resources. There are times, however, when parochial self-interest has less to do with the how-tos of education and more with the potential loss of power, prestige, or influence. In those cases you've got to get to what we call "the heart of the matter."

The leaders of the Sanhedrin, for example, didn't call for the crucifixion of the rabbi from Nazareth simply because of some minor theological differences. After all, the Pharisees and the Sadducees were not exactly on the same page theologically. No, the decision to execute Jesus of Nazareth came about because He was seen as a genuine threat to their position of influence and power in Roman Palestine. No amount of discussion over theological differences would have resolved that conflict.

There are lots of ideas on how best to address this kind of situation. I have found, however, that you cannot avoid a face-to-face conversation with those who are resisting change for personal reasons. You can't ignore that conversation any more than you can ignore a cancerous tumor in your body. You don't negotiate with a tumor. You kill it or cut it out. People aren't tumors, but sometimes you do have to put the proposition to people this way: Get on board enthusiastically, or leave graciously. Hopefully they will choose the latter option.

Obstacle 4: Lack of trust

As Steven Covey notes, "Low trust is the greatest cost in life and in organizations, including families. Low trust creates hidden agendas, politics, internal conflict, interdepartmental rivalries, win-lose thinking, defensive and protective communication—all of which reduce the speed of trust. Low trust slows everything—every decision, every communication, and every relationship" (2006, xxx).

It actually doesn't take long to "feel" the lack of trust in most organizations. That was my experience in my first ministry position; sadly, I have repeatedly seen the same in churches and schools all across the country. Trust is hard to build, easy to lose, and essential to your ability to fulfill God's call in your life. It isn't that leaders are purposefully dishonest. As Covey notes, "It's the little things—a day at a time, a weak or dishonest act at a time—that gradually weaken and corrode credibility" (2006, 47).

Those little things count because over time they erode trust so thoroughly that the organization grinds to a halt—or worse, implodes in the face of another unnecessary crisis. "You cannot prevent a major catastrophe," Peter Drucker notes, "but you can build an organization that is battle-ready, that has high morale, that knows how to behave, that trusts itself, and where people trust one another. In military training, the first rule is to instill soldiers with trust in their officers, because without trust they won't fight" (cited in Covey 2006, 47). And that doesn't just apply to the military.

If you want to build trust within and about your organization, here is a brief list of behaviors that must characterize you and the school you lead.

• *Always tell the truth.*
  Never lie, distort or hide the facts, or misuse information. We see that kind of thing all of the time in our current political discourse. It's one of the primary reasons why we just don't trust our leaders much anymore. You've heard the saying, "If his lips are moving, he's lying." That is a pretty cynical view of the world, but one that currently holds currency among much of the American electorate. You'd think that leaders in a Christian organization would understand something so fundamental. Unfortunately, they often don't.

  I repeat, always tell the truth, even when doing so will cause temporary pain. If someone has to be fired for a moral failure, don't tell people that they resigned for personal reasons. If a decision you made backfired, tell it like it is. People will more quickly forgive you for a bad decision (unless it happens too frequently) than they will for trying to cover up or misdirect. *Integrity is essential to trust.*

• *Be good at what you do.*
  As Covey notes, "A family doctor might have integrity and his motives might be good, but unless he's trained and skilled to perform the task at hand (brain

surgery, for example) he'll be lacking in credibility" (2006, 55). This is an affliction in many organizations, but it is especially true in a lot of Christian schools. The reason is simple. Far too many Christian school leaders come to the task woefully underprepared.

If that is the case in your situation, you need to do two things immediately. First, you need to get the necessary training. There are lots of ways to do that—from graduate school programs to tons of reading and reflection to taking advantage of programs such as ACSI's Leadership U or the Van Lunen Fellowship, both of which are dedicated to raising the bar of leadership in the world of Christian schooling. Second, you need to honestly ask yourself, "Is this, leading a school, something I can really do with excellence?" In asking and answering that question, you need to look beyond your own evaluation. You need to get honest, outside, objective feedback from a trusted friend who has the experience necessary to help you make that judgment. *Competence is essential to trust.*

- *Don't play favorites.*

  I once worked at a school where the new elementary principal fired her best friend. It wasn't an easy decision, but it was a necessary one. It was, however, a decision that would not be made in a lot of schools. As a leader you must always do what is best for your school. Personal preferences must never be allowed to influence any decision-making process, whether it has to do with staffing or resource allocation. *Fairness is essential to trust.*

- *Stay on point.*

  My grandfather once remarked to me, "Son, you're like a duck waking up on a new pond every day." He was referring to my rather scatter-brained approach to life at that time. While that may be nothing more than a bit of an annoyance in a ten year old, it is devastating when it characterizes someone in leadership. It's what happens when, every time you return from a conference or read a new book, you end up announcing to your staff a new initiative—one that moves the school in a different direction from the last idea you promoted, the one that caught your attention after the previous conference you attended. It's also what happens when you make decisions that are inconsistent with how you have chosen to define yourself.

  As Patrick Lencioni notes, "All too often leaders underestimate the impact of even subtle misalignment at the top and the damage caused by small gaps among the members of the leadership team" (2012, 74). People just can't do their jobs when the leadership team is not on point with one another or when the senior leader seems confused and unable to sustain a particular direction for the school. As Jim Collins notes, better a hedgehog focused on one good idea than a fox bounding aimlessly through the woods (2001). *Consistency is essential to trust.*

• *Keep your promises.*

Solomon pretty well sums up the problem that arises when we make promises we don't keep: "A brother offended is more unyielding than a walled city" (Proverbs 18:19). When you tell people you are going to do something, do it even if it costs more than you thought it would. That is why whenever I work with a school on strategic planning I always caution them about what they choose to make public. My constant counsel is this: Never put something into print unless you are absolutely confident that you can make it happen. To do otherwise creates great harm to how people view you as a person and as a leader.

The problem actually goes deeper than a loss of confidence in leadership. If our goal is to accurately and robustly represent the person and nature of God, then keeping our promises is crucial. As Peter reminds us, "The Lord is not slow to fulfill his promise" (2 Peter 3:9), and neither should we be. If you make a promise, even a foolish one, do what needs to be done to honor that promise.

I had to deal with that exact situation when I had to confront a board member about promises he had made about some rather significant financial contributions. He would make the promise in a public meeting, then never follow through. I can't recall a more uncomfortable situation in all of my leadership history. I wish I could say it ended well, but it did not. People don't like being called out, and I probably could have handled it in a better way. Having said that, I can tell you that at that moment in time I lost all respect for and trust in that particular individual. Worse, projects that we needed to address and intended to address with those promised gifts were left undone, which hurt everyone on campus. *Keeping your word is essential to trust.*

Obstacle 5: Lack of clarity

If you've ever driven your car during a pounding rainstorm or blinding blizzard, you have a sense for what it is like to function in an organization where leadership tends to speak unclearly and inconsistently. "Clarity is," as Patrick Lencioni observes, "about creating alignment" (2010, 73). Schools, like any organization, have alignment only when every action taken by leadership and staff is consistent with and reflective of what that school or organization says about itself.

For example, if a school claims to believe in delivering every aspect of its mission with excellence, then failure to do something with excellence is an obvious misalignment. As Lencioni notes, "No matter how many times executives preach about the 'e' word in their speeches there is no way that their employees can be empowered to fully execute their responsibilities if they don't receive clear and consistent messages about what is important from their leaders across the organization. There is probably no greater frustration for employees than having to constantly navigate the politics and confusion caused by leaders who are misaligned" (2010, 74–75).

Jim Collins echoes this kind of thinking in his best-selling book *Good to Great*: "The good-to-great companies built a *consistent* system with clear constraints," and then "they hired self-disciplined people who didn't need to be managed, and then managed the system, not the people" (2001, 125; emphasis added).

However, as Collins notes, "Most companies" (and I would add most schools) "build their bureaucratic rules to manage the small percentage of wrong people on the bus, which in turn drives away the right people on the bus, which then increases the percentage of wrong people on the bus, which increases the need for more bureaucracy to compensate for incompetence and lack of discipline, which further drives the right people away, and so forth" (2001, 121). This is what I mean by the dreadful drag of bureaucracy.

A better approach, however, as Collins points out is to, "Avoid bureaucracy and hierarchy and instead create a culture of discipline. When you put these two complementary forces together—a culture of discipline with an ethic of entrepreneurship—you get a magical alchemy of superior performance and sustainable results" (2001, 122).

Sadly, many Christian schools do the exact opposite. They either give in to anarchy, essentially allowing teachers to do what they please regarding curriculum and discipline, or they create a life-strangling, creativity-killing bureaucracy. Neither approach will produce excellence.

If you want to experience true, long-term success, you've got to create clarity about who you are and what you hope to accomplish. Then you've got to find people who not only share your passion but who also bring to the task the necessary self-discipline, spiritual maturity, knowledge, skill, and creativity.

Obstacle 6: Failure to reach both the heart and the mind

I love how Chip and Dan Heath talk about the role of the rational mind and the emotional heart in the planning process. As I mentioned in chapter 9, they cite research done by University of Virginia psychologist Jonathan Haidt, who observes that in decision making and action our emotional side is an Elephant and our rational side is its Rider. "Perched atop the Elephant, control is precarious because the Rider is so small relative to the Elephant. Anytime the six-ton Elephant and the Rider disagree about which direction to go, the Rider is going to lose, He's completely overmatched" (2010, 7).

Now I know what you are going to say. "But, Dr. Pue, we are followers of Jesus Christ, and we have the Holy Spirit, who gives us the capacity to overcome our emotions." That is true. I've seen my dear and godly wife, however, lose the battle over whether to eat another piece of chocolate time and again. Chalk up another win for the emotional over the rational. I'll not mention my long list of weaknesses. The Heaths are just warning us that we ignore the power of emotion to our peril. We've got to learn to appeal to both the mind and the heart, to reason and emotion.

John Kotter, in his wonderful book *Leading Change*, makes the same point. "The core of the matter (in any planning process) is always about changing the behavior of people, and behavior change happens in highly successful situations mostly by speaking to people's feelings." He goes on to say, "This is true even in organizations that are very focused on analysis and quantitative measurements, even among people who think of themselves as smart in an MBA sense. In highly successful change efforts, people find ways to help others see the problems or solutions in ways that influence emotions, not just thought" (cited in Heath and Heath 2010, 105).

Need further proof? Consider how the apostle Paul makes his case for the transformative power of renewing the mind. In closing out his brilliant presentation of the gospel in chapters 1–11 of his letter to the church at Rome, Paul breaks into song. Romans 11:33–36 is actually one of the earliest hymns of the church, and the language Paul employs here is theologically sound but far more evocative and laden with emotion than his earlier words.

Oh, the depth of the riches and wisdom and knowledge of God! How unsearchable are his judgments and how inscrutable his ways!
 "For who has known the mind of the Lord,
 Or who has been his counselor?

Or who has given a gift to him that he might be repaid?"
For from him and through him and to him are all things. To him be glory forever. Amen.

From there Paul moves on to make one of the most powerful arguments for change found anywhere in Scripture. "I appeal to (I personally love the language of the KJV, "I beseech") you, therefore, brothers, by the mercies of God, to present your bodies a living sacrifice, holy and acceptable to God, which is your spiritual worship. Do not be conformed to this world, but be transformed by the renewal of your mind, that by testing you may discern what is the will of God, what is good and acceptable and perfect" (Romans 12:1–2).

Do you see the marvelous way that Paul moves from the mind through the heart to behavior? It is powerful, and it should serve as a model for us as we seek to implement essential changes within our organizations. Simply put, if you can't make an argument that not only satisfies the minds of people but also wins their hearts, then any change effort, no matter how crucial, is likely to fail.

Obstacle 7: People just don't see the upside

Did you ever participate in sports or play an instrument in a band or orchestra, or try to win a competition of any kind? If so, you will quickly get what I am about to say. As a kid in high school I spent countless hours on the concrete pad in my backyard shooting hoops while a silent narrative played relentlessly in my mind. In that narrative I would inevitably take the final winning shot in a game of huge importance. I was always the hero, I always got the girl, and I always basked in the glow of admiration that was the result of my highly developed skills.

That narrative, as totally unrealistic as it was, drove me up and down the court until I thought my lungs might burst and my legs might simply refuse to take another single step. In a word, I was willing to pay whatever price necessary, even endure real pain, in pursuit of something I truly desired. I suspect that you have a similar story.

If you want people to embrace the challenge of change, you've got to help them "see" what lies beyond the pain. Until they do, it is unlikely that they will be willing to pay the necessary price.

Obstacle 8: A low level of urgency

I am not talking about the frantic, panicked activity that often characterizes an organization in the midst of crisis. Rather I am talking about the quiet determination to always "press toward the mark for the prize of the high calling of God in Christ Jesus" (Philippians 3:12–14, KJV). This should be an attitude of the heart and mind that we fully understand and embrace as followers of Jesus Christ.

That same attitude of continuous improvement should also characterize how we think about the organizations we lead. I like to use the phrase "holy dissatisfaction" when talking about how we should view our schools. As a leader, I think you need to wake up every day and ask, How can we do what we do better today than we did yesterday? And how will we be able to do it better tomorrow than we did today? It won't be enough, however, to ask yourself that question; you must help your team think the same way.

That will open you to accusations that you are never satisfied, that you just aren't appreciative of how hard it is to do this thing called school. In response you must simply say, "No, I'm not satisfied; and yes, I know this is hard. Hard is OK. Hard is the price we must be willing to pay to do anything well, to do anything that really makes a difference." The way of the cross is always hard. Christ warned His followers to "count the cost" because He knew that there is always a cost when attempting to do anything worthwhile and right, especially in the face of opposition.

Remember this. The enemy of excellence is not lack of resources; it is indifference masquerading as contentment. Every believer should learn to be content with the resources God makes available to us. But no believer should ever be content with past or current effort on behalf of the King and His kingdom. While it is true that the Master doesn't always provide the same level of resources to everyone, He does have the same level of expectation on how those resources are used in pursuit of Kingdom purposes (Matthew 25:14–30).

(That is one of the great truths C. S. Lewis underscores in his marvelous book *The Screwtape Letters*. The demons are to be little concerned about a believer who is content with a life of indifference, a life of that never challenges the status quo, a life that is quite willing to flow downstream, meandering along sluggishly with a late summer's current.)

Let's be honest, however: slipping into a kind of indifferent contentment is as easy to do as slipping into hammock on a warm, sunny, summer afternoon. Keeping the level of urgency at an appropriate level at your school is always a challenge. Here are some thoughts to help you with that task.

First of all, you must make sure that everyone on your team knows what it is that you are trying to accomplish. Are we trying to increase the creativity of our instructional efforts? Are we hoping to increase our retention numbers? Are we working to improve test scores or the quality of a particular program? Whatever it is, make it clear as to what you are hoping to do, how you are going to accomplish your goal, and what success will look like along the way and when it is finally achieved.

Second, you've got to continually update everyone on your progress. You've got to decide what data helps you do that, and then you've got to communicate that data to your team. Here's what we are trying to accomplish. Here's the ultimate target. Here's where we are at present. Here's what we've learned during the process, the unexpected challenges we've had to address. Here are the adjustments we've made as a result of what we've learned.

Stay hungry. Stay limber. Keep moving forward. Don't allow your school to be lulled into a false sense of contentment.

Obstacle 9: A disengaged leadership team

In a book review on *Team of Teams* by General Stanley McChrystal, I made the following observation: "Our tendency, as popularized by Taylor [Frederick Taylor, father of modern management theory], when thinking of leaders is to imbue them with nearly supernatural powers. We expect them to possess a nearly limitless capacity for acquiring knowledge relevant to their profession and an equally limitless capacity for always making the right decision. That of course has always been a fantasy. In the world we now inhabit it has become a dangerous one."

As McChrystal notes, "Where once an educated person might have assumed she was at least conversant with the relevant knowledge on a particular field of study, the explosion of information has rendered that assumption laughable" (2015, 223).

Instead of the leader as chess master able to counter every possible move of his or her opponent, McChrystal argues for adopting a different metaphor: the leader as gardener. This metaphor will require a very different way of thinking about leadership. It required McChrystal to "shift [his] focus from moving pieces on the board to shaping the ecosystem" of his organization, from making all of the decisions to "creating and maintaining the teamwork conditions we needed." Thus he writes, "Tending the garden became my primary responsibility" because "I found that only the senior leader could drive the operating rhythm, transparency, and cross-functional cooperation we needed. I could shape the culture and demand the ongoing conversation that shared consciousness required" (2015, 226). And that description of leadership is more compatible with what I read in the New Testament.

It is also a description more compatible with Kotter's research on change-ready organizations: "In an environment of constant change, individuals, even if supremely talented, won't have enough time or expertise to absorb rapidly shifting competitor, customer, and technological information. They won't have enough time to communicate all the important decisions to ... others. They will rarely have the charisma or skills to singlehandedly gain commitments to change from large numbers of people" (1996, 163–164).

Exceptional leadership is crucial to the health of any organization. Exceptional leaders, however, recognize their own limitations and the value of team efforts. It has been my observation that the more people who are invested—not just involved, but invested—in the effort to improve the effort and impact of an organization, the greater the potential for success and the greater level of urgency driving those efforts.

"Highly controlling organizations often destroy leadership by not allowing people to blossom, test themselves, and grow. In stiff bureaucracies, young men and women with potential typically see few good role models, are not encouraged to lead, and may even be punished if they go out of bounds, challenge the status quo, and take risks. These kinds of organizations tend either to repel people with leadership potential or to take those individuals and teach them only about bureaucratic management" (Kotter 1996, 166). Those kinds of organizations seldom build strong teams. Those kinds of organizations seldom flourish in times of change.

If you want a change-ready organization, you need a change-ready leadership team.

Obstacle 10: Lack of a clear, consistent, compelling, effective communication strategy

Are you the greatest story never told? As I often tell schools, "Remain the best kept secret in town and you will soon become nothing more than a footnote lost in the distant fog of history."

This is not a book on communication. It is, however, a book on how to become a school of significance, a school that makes a difference, a school that refuses to descend into mediocrity. You will find it increasingly difficult to do what you want to do unless you build a strong team of supporters, and you will find building that team difficult unless you are able to keep them reminded of what they do and why that matters.

As I've often noted, marketing is simply a compelling story well told—and not just well told, but relentlessly told. As Patrick Lencioni observes, "Leaders confuse the mere transfer of information to an audience with the audience's ability to understand, internalize, and embrace the message that is being communicated. The only way for people to embrace a message is to hear it over a period of time, in a variety of different situations, and preferably from different people. That's why great leaders see themselves as Chief Reminding Officers as much as anything else" (2012, 142).

If you want a change-ready organization, you need to constantly remind people what you do and why that matters.

Obstacle 11: Failure to celebrate short-term wins

The Old Testament is filled with instructions about feasts and festivals—including the weekly Sabbath. Jesus attended so many social gatherings that it earned Him a reputation as a friend of sinners (Luke 7:34). When was the last time you attended a wedding ceremony that lasted an entire week, like the one described in John 2? That was the way first-century Jewish people celebrated weddings. Celebration was woven into the fabric of Jewish life; it must also be woven into the fabric of your school's life.

As Kotter noes, "Real transformation takes time. Complex efforts to change strategies or restructure business risks losing momentum if there are no short-term goals to meet and celebrate. Most people won't go on the long march unless they see compelling evidence within six to eighteen months that the journey is producing expected results. Without short-term wins, too many employees give up or actively join the resistance" (1996, 11).

That reality is, I believe, the reason we as followers of Christ are instructed to "do this in remembrance of me." There are few moments in the life of the church as compelling as our common receiving of Communion. Our journey through life in this fallen world can be painful, frustrating, even terrifying. Yet in that moment we are reminded of the sacrifice and triumph of our Lord—His sacrifice on our behalf and His triumph over death. We all need that kind of reminder, and that is just as true for us as we journey to "better become what God has called us to be" as it is on our journey of faith.

Obstacle 12: Celebrating victory too soon

It is important to celebrate short term-wins. It is, however, always a mistake to prematurely declare victory. One of the most powerful examples of this took place in May 2003 on the deck of the aircraft carrier *USS Abraham Lincoln* in the early days of the Iraq war. You may remember the scene. President George W. Bush bounded onto the deck of the carrier and declared, "Mission accomplished." He then went on to declare, "Major combat operations in Iraq have ceased." It was a great photo op—and a terrible mistake. It was a political miscalculation and tactical error that was to haunt the remainder of his presidency.

Again, I quote Kotter: "In the final analysis, change sticks only when it becomes "the way we do things around here," when it seeps into the very bloodstream of the work unit or corporate body. Until new behaviors are rooted in social norms and shared values, they are always subject to degradation as soon as the pressures associated with a change effort are removed" (1996, 14).

I watched that very kind of thing unfold after I left a school that I had led for fifteen years. It was among the most painful experiences of my life. I mistakenly believed that because I understood the importance of certain things and had managed to win the hearts of my faculty and staff, the changes we had worked so hard to implement would last into the future. And they did for a while.

What I didn't realize was how poorly the core operating philosophy of our school was understood and embraced by our board. It was part of my DNA but, using Kotter's metaphor, it had not seeped into the school's bloodstream. The person who followed me got it, but she didn't have the same kind of relationship with the board that I had had. I could push things through by a force of will because there was a high degree of trust in me personally. My successor didn't have that same kind of relationship with the board. Within three years she resigned, frustrated over that lack of relationship. It wasn't her fault. It was mine.

Kotter discusses two key practices that must be employed if key changes are to become part of the organizational DNA. First of all, there must be "a conscious attempt to show people how specific behaviors and attitudes have helped improve performance." This is important because, as he notes, "When people are left on their own to make the connections, as is often the case, they can easily create inaccurate links" (1996, 14). When change is attributed to the style or ability of a particular leader rather than to different ways of thinking and acting, the impact of change efforts will typically be short-lived.

Thus it is crucial to keep the focus on that different way of thinking and those different ways of acting. To do that you would be well served to use every possible means of communication—from newsletters to staff meetings to parent meetings—to not only highlight and celebrate short-term wins but to purposefully connect those wins to those different ways of thinking and acting.

Second, Kotter makes this crucial observation: "Anchoring change also requires that sufficient time be taken to ensure that the next generation of management really does personify the new approach. If promotion criteria are not reshaped, another common error, transformations rarely last." And then he makes two additional critical observations: "One bad succession decision at the top of an organization can undermine a decade of hard work. Poor succession decisions at the top of companies" (and I would add schools) "are likely when boards of directors are not an integral part of the effort" (1996, 14).

Kotter could have written that after a visit to the Christian school following my resignation. It is exactly what happened, because I had failed to adequately involve the board in the transformation efforts at the school and I had not equipped the board to think about the purpose of Christian schooling. The consequences of my failure soon became apparent and eventually led to the closure of the school. That was a truly painful day for me, even after having been gone for twenty years.

Creating clarity around core questions—such as, What is our purpose? What is our mission? What are our beliefs and values?—is absolutely crucial in the planning process. Without that clarity, and without continued consistency in living out the implications of the answers to those questions, most schools will likely drift from their roots.

Schools also need to create clarity about the reasons behind any change efforts; about the strategies that will be employed in pursuit of those changes; and about the staffing implications, resource allocation decisions, and the impact of those efforts. Without that kind of clarity, coupled with the discipline to stay on target, change efforts will inevitably fail to take root deeply enough in the organization to withstand the stress of daily life over time.

Don't make the mistake President Bush made in declaring that victory had been achieved. His failure arose out of a flawed understanding of the realities on the ground and a failure to adequately define what victory would really look like. Don't make the same mistake I made as head of school. My failure was in not realizing that change will not take root simply because I willed it to. For change to become embedded in any organization, everyone must understand and own both the reasons for the change and the nature of the change process.

Since change is inevitable and necessary, do it right. Otherwise, you will likely experience the pain of change without the benefit of change.

Afterword

A Holy Dissatisfaction

I've struggled my entire life with contentment. I'm not—content, that is. Never. Nothing I do is ever good enough. Everything I write could be better. I go back and reread articles and book reviews I've written and shudder. Then I make the mistake of picking up a book by C. S. Lewis or Tim Keller or Jim Collins, and I just want to go away and hide. I edited and reedited every chapter in this book several times and yet was filled with discontent the day I transmitted the initial manuscript to Purposeful Design.

Is discontent sin? At times, yes. At times, no. When I become discontented with the way God has made me or with His provision in my life or with the status I have achieved, then yes, discontentment is sin. When my car isn't nice enough or my house isn't big enough or my retirement fund won't allow monthly trips to exotic locales, then yes, my discontentment is sin.

If, however, I take an honest look at my personal spiritual maturity and conclude, "I'm a long way from where I could be," then no, my discontentment is not a sin. When I consider the quality of my work, whatever that work may be, and conclude, "I can do better," then no, my discontentment is not a sin. Now if I compare my situation with someone else's and believe I've drawn the short straw, then yes, I've probably slipped from an attitude of holy dissatisfaction into ugly covetousness.

If you are reading this and thinking, "Wow, keeping the right balance on this thing called contentment can be a challenge," then you get it. It is a tough tension to maintain. Let me try to help with that. After all, this entire book is about holy dissatisfaction. It is the premise of this book and of my entire ministry that you and I can be better and can do better what God has call us to be and do—to "excel still more," as the apostle Paul encourages the church in Thessalonica. So let me

191

conclude this book with some brief thoughts on how to maintain the right balance between holy dissatisfaction and ugly covetousness.

God didn't call you to be "that" guy or "that" gal.

While serving as pastor of a Baptist church I heard John McArthur preach a sermon on Isaiah praying in the temple upon the death of King Uzziah. It was powerful, mesmerizing, and memorable. I remember leaving the sanctuary that night thinking, "I could never preach like that." And then thinking, "I probably should pursue another calling—something like a greeter at Walmart."

As my wife would say, "Here's a news flash. You're not John McArthur. You're Alan Pue. And that's quite OK." Remember. God is not the great Photocopier in the sky. He is the great Potter, however, and as the Scriptures remind us, "Can the clay say to the potter, 'Hold on here, I'm not happy with your design'?" (the Alan Pue version). The answer, of course, is "no, you can't"—or really, "no, you shouldn't."

Your holy dissatisfaction will soon degenerate into ugly covetousness the moment you start comparing your situation with that of others who may appear to be more successful, more talented, or more blessed. You are right where God wants you at this moment in time. Give thanks for what you have; don't seek someone else's success.

You can, however, become better at what God has called you to be and do.

Here's what I discovered. I may never be as good at delivering a sermon as John McArthur or Andy Stanley or any number of other exceptional speakers. What I can be, however, is a bit better tomorrow than I am today. I can observe great speakers and ask, "What makes them so good?" As leader of a school I can study great schools and ask, "What makes them great?" Of course that requires me to dig a bit beneath the surface, below the glossy language often used of "great" schools.

I can read good books, ask probing questions, and seek wise counsel. I can observe and identify principles and practices that underlie good performance and then determine to act on what I learn. I can invite sharp, capable people with proven track records into my life to observe my efforts and recommend modifications to how I do things. I can set realistically higher standards and continually strive to meet those standards. I can be better tomorrow than I am today simply by making small, continuous improvements.

Change always begins inside of you, not with your circumstances.

How often have you heard someone say, "If only this would change, or that would change, then our school could really take off"? Forgive me for speaking so bluntly, but that is "loser language." That is what you say when you don't possess the will or you fail to acquire the wisdom to do the hard work required when building something from nothing. When you adopt that posture, you will always have an excuse for why your efforts are not producing positive results.

If you want to see nothing, travel to Haiti or to the Congo or to the massive refugee camps in the Middle East. Yet, in the midst of enervating poverty and relentless turmoil, kids manage to learn. Now I know that your parents' expectations are a bit higher than the parents of kids in the Sudan or Afghanistan, but creativity and grit are free. Start there. Don't fall prey to the litany of excuses that are often raised in defense of failure—we don't have enough money, we don't have very supportive parents, our facilities aren't quite what they need to be, our location is poor, the economics of our community are in decline, etc. All of those external facts may be real, but they can't keep you from getting better at what you do.

Start with what you have: love, passion, hope, creativity, fortitude, discipline. Insist that both you and your teachers come to school every day prepared to do remarkable things. Encourage your teachers while providing quality professional development opportunities. Mobilize your parents. Relentlessly promote your school in every possible place and way. Pray with passion, importuning your Lord daily. Design great projects that can make a difference in the lives of your students, and then pursue donors with the capacity to fund those projects. Start small. Prove yourself. Repeat. Stay sharp. Keep growing. Because for your school to get better, you've got to get better first.

Change can't be about you; it must be always be about others.

If you want a formula for success, pay careful attention to these words from our Lord: "the Son of Man came not to be served but to serve and to give his life as a ransom for many" (Matthew 20:28).

As J. Oswald Sanders (1992, 70) reminds us, "Jesus was no revolutionary in the political sense, but in no area was His teaching more revolutionary than in that of spiritual leadership. In the contemporary world the term *servant* has a lowly connotation, but Jesus equated it with greatness: 'Whoever wants to become great among you must be your servant, and whoever wants to be first must be slave of all.' (Mark 10:43-44)." Your success will be dependent on your willingness to serve. Forget that, and you will struggle continually.

Not every great leader spends his or her entire life in a single place. Sometimes God does have another place for you to use your gifts. Now and again, it is just time to move on. However, when one place simply becomes a stepping-stone to something bigger and better, then you are probably not being driven by holy dissatisfaction or by a desire to serve. Other people must never be merely the means to your success; rather, they must be the focus of your deepest concern and greatest effort.

Few people have exemplified that for me as clearly as my dear friend George Janvier. George, as I noted in my comments on purpose and mission in chapter 6, served for over thirty years in the country of Nigeria. George is one of the most gifted people I know. He is a skilled writer, able speaker, adept leader and administrator, and tireless advocate for the work of the seminary that God called him to lead. For George it was never about the next opportunity. It was always about better serving his students and the people of Nigeria.

It is unlikely that George will ever be the subject of a glowing biography read by tens of thousands. What is certain, however, is that his biography has already been written in the lives of the hundreds of people he has faithfully served. For George, as for thousands of others who have served as leaders in obscure, out-of-the-way places, it was always about serving others, never about being the center of attention.

What I find fascinating is that this concept of servant leadership is foundational to success in the secular world as well. It's what Jim Collins, Peter Drucker, Steven Covey, and more recently Patrick Lencioni have all observed about great leaders. Pay careful heed to what Jim Collins says about what he calls Level 5 Leaders: "Level 5 leaders channel their ego needs away from themselves and into the larger goal of building a great company. It's not that Level 5 leaders have no ego or self-interest. Indeed, they are incredibly ambitious—but their ambition is first and foremost for the institution, not themselves" (2001, 21). Remember: begin with others in mind.

Stuff happens; learn to get over it.

Failure is the inevitable result of effort. Try enough new things and sooner or later something will go "boom!" We live in a fallen world, and none of us is exempt from the consequences of that fallenness. Not every new idea will bear fruit. Not every decision will end well. The journey to better seldom takes place on the long straightaway of a superhighway. Most often it's like the switchback road you travel to the top of Pike's Peak—winding, tortuous, with more than a bit of danger involved.

Failure may be inevitable, but it doesn't have to be the end of you. That is the point of one of my favorite quotes from Theodore Roosevelt: "It is not the critic who counts, not the man who points out how the strong man stumbled, or where the doer of deeds could have done them better. The credit belongs to the man who is actually in the arena; whose face is marred by dust and sweat and blood; who strives violently; who errs and comes short again and again; who knows the great enthusiasms; the great devotions; who spends himself in a worthy cause; who, at the best, knows in the end the triumphs of high achievements; and who, at the worst, if he fails, at least fails with daring greatly" (cited in Fox 1976, 104).

Don't allow failure to define you; rather, let it spur you on to "better." Let it fuel your sense of holy dissatisfaction.

Change is a team sport.

I resonate with these words from the pen of the author of the New Testament book of Hebrews: "Let us hold fast the confession of our hope without wavering, for he who promised is faithful. And let us consider how to stir up one another to love and good works, not neglecting to meet together, as is the habit of some, but encouraging one another, and all the more as you see the Day drawing near." (Hebrews 10:23–25) Simply put, we need one another. We can't get from here to there without one another. Change is a team sport.

John Kotter makes that clear when he writes, "Major transformations are often associated with one highly visible individual.... This is a very dangerous belief.... Because major change is so difficult to accomplish ... A strong guiding coalition is always needed—one with the right composition, level of trust, and shared objective. Building such a team is always an essential part of ... any effort to restructure, reengineer or retool" (1996, 51–52).

To do that you have to "win the hearts" of other people. That takes time, patience, and grace. I've always loved this quote from Abraham Lincoln. And with it I will close.

If you would win a man to your cause, first convince him that you are his true friend. Therein is a drop of honey that catches his heart, which say what he will, is the greatest highroad to his reason, and which when once gained, you will find but little trouble in convincing his judgment of the justice of your cause, if, indeed, that cause be really a just one. On the contrary, assume to dictate to his judgment, or to command his action, or to make him as one to be shunned or despised, and he will retreat within himself, close the avenues to his head and heart; and though your cause be naked truth itself, transformed to the heaviest lance, harder than steel and sharper than steel can be made, and though you throw it with more than Herculean force and precision, you shall be no more able to pierce him than to penetrate the hard shell of a tortoise with a rye straw." (cited in Fox 1976, 83)

Appendix

Needs Assessment for Strategic Planning

Lynn E. Swaner

When most school leaders hear the term *needs assessment*, one of two things often happens: either their eyes glaze over, recalling a boring graduate course on assessment that had little practical application in their work, or they immediately see dollar signs—imagining they need to hire an expensive consultant who will take months to produce a glossy and complicated report, and exhaust the annual fund in the process. It's not surprising that many school leaders take a pass on needs assessment, even though they intuitively know it would be of great benefit in the strategic planning process. In fact, if you're one of the brave readers who dared open up this chapter of Alan's book, you're to be commended for overcoming such negative feelings—and for caring deeply enough about strategic planning that you're committed to doing it well. And needs assessment is an *essential* part of doing strategic planning well.

There's an entire science behind needs assessment and a superabundance of business textbooks that go along with it, but most texts are cumbersome and unhelpful for educators. This chapter attempts to remedy that by making needs assessment accessible—and perhaps even interesting!—for Christian school leaders engaged in strategic planning. My goal and prayer is that this chapter will help school leaders do three things: (1) recognize the value of needs assessment to strategic planning; (2) understand how needs assessment can work practically in their settings; and (3) walk away with some doable strategies for conducting needs assessment, with the teams and resources that God has already entrusted to them.

By way of full disclosure, I'll start by saying that in many years as a graduate professor, my absolute favorite courses to teach were on research and assessment. While most faculty viewed these as the least desirable courses to teach—probably because students walked into class already petrified, in full-blown math phobia—I loved the challenge of surprising students with how useful and engaging these topics were for their work. The key was helping them to see assessment as a valuable tool for solving real-world problems they cared about, and that they were certainly capable and competent (with some information and a little coaching) to attack those problems with confidence.

My purpose in writing this chapter is not much different. If you're a Christian school leader, that means you're already skilled in identifying problems, setting priorities, and finding solutions. Needs assessment offers you a powerful blueprint for going about those tasks. And with needs assessment in your leadership toolkit, strategic planning becomes an even more effective process for fulfilling God's plan and purpose for your school.

What Is Needs Assessment?

A good place to start in talking about a concept is to define it. Gupta (2007) defines a *need* as a "gap between the current condition and the desired condition" in an organization, and *needs assessment* as "a process for figuring out how to close" that gap (14). In other words, needs assessment involves figuring out what *really is* at a school, and comparing that with what stakeholders think *ought to be*. Although a school can conduct a needs assessment on any number of things (a STEM program, communication with parents, the pay scale for faculty), when done in the context of strategic planning, the focus of needs assessment is identifying the gaps in the school's attainment of its mission statement. This is because the mission statement is the ultimate picture of what the school considers "ought" to be at the school. And if the school finds there's room for improvement in achieving its mission, the needs assessment process provides the background information needed to set strategic goals and figure out how to do a better job going forward. Thus, needs assessment is fundamentally "a diagnostic process that relies on data collection, collaboration, and negotiation to identify and understand gaps ... to determine future action" (Gupta 2007, 15).

While that's a helpful definition, what does needs assessment actually *look like* in practice? While the next few pages of this chapter provide a picture of just that, I've found it's often a good idea to start off in reverse: to define a concept by describing what it's not. To this end, below are four illustrations of activities in which schools regularly engage, but that do not qualify as true needs assessment.

1. Needs assessment is not a list of what everybody thinks is wrong at the school.

I don't doubt for a minute that all school leaders can tick off a long list of problems at their school (for that matter, any parent, student, teacher, or board member can do the same). However, needs assessment is not developing a comprehensive list of problems and concerns from every stakeholder at the school. (Keep reading to find out why.)

2. Needs assessment is not an assessment of "wants."

Kaufman and Guerra-Lopez (2013) explain that "many so-called needs are not needs at all, but rather preferred wants. Likewise, many so-called assessments are not needs assessments, but rather a survey of wants" (9). It's very important to understand the distinction between a want and a need. Gupta, though using business terminology, explains the difference well: "A want is something the client would like to have even though it does not contribute to the long-term learning or performance goal. By contrast, a need, when addressed, contributes to achieving the desired learning or performance goal by closing the gaps between the current condition and the desired condition" (2007, 30–31). Rephrased in educational terms, a want—though it can be positive and beneficial—is something that does not contribute to the overall mission and desired outcomes of the school. That's why generating a long list of everyone's perceived problems at the school is not needs assessment, because it will inevitably end up being a wants assessment instead! Every school leader knows that the school cannot be "all things to all people," even though they wish it could. Ultimately, the school mission serves as the litmus test for parsing out needs and wants. If addressing an issue will advance the school's mission and contribute to better attainment of the school's desired outcomes, it's a need. If not, it's a want. Schools must strategically allocate their resources (no matter how expansive or how limited) toward addressing real needs, as doing so will automatically advance the school's mission.

3. Needs assessment is not obtaining casual or anecdotal information.

Needs assessment relies on more formal data collection than teachers' remarks about the spring concert the morning after, or comments overheard about the football program from parents at last night's game. It may be helpful to think of it this way: have you ever asked anyone in passing if they think your new haircut is a good one?

Very few people will tell you anything short of "I love it!"—and probably only your immediate family or those who have it out for you will tell you it's horrible. When schools rely on information gathered this way ("Mr. Smith told Principal Jones this or that"), there are all kinds of issues with the data they collect. Such feedback is often off-the-cuff (meaning based on how people are feeling that exact minute, without reflecting carefully on it) and is often self-serving (meaning they want their response to get you to like and agree with them—or get you to dislike or disagree with someone else). In addition, it's difficult to tell whether the issue is widespread or is really just Mr. Smith's concern. How many times have you heard someone say, "I'm not the only one who feels this way!" and you find out it's really just that person plus the spouse—not a horde of people as they seemed to suggest? These concerns aren't mitigated by amassing a lot of anecdotal feedback, because a pile of bad data isn't any better than a single piece of bad data. Instead, needs assessment requires systematically gathering data from a fair representation of stakeholders, and making sure people have opportunity to give thoughtful and thorough feedback on issues that are important for the school.

4. Needs assessment is *not* something school leaders can do on their own.

At the top of the list of Christian educators' fears, somewhere just under downward-spiraling enrollment (for administrators) and six separate preps (for teachers), is "death by committee." Many school committees are poorly scaffolded (meaning they have very broad and unclear agendas, with little guidance and monitoring) and poorly managed (meaning they don't meet regularly enough, and when they do meet, they get very little done). Understandably, school leaders often try to protect their faculty from having to serve on yet another committee. However, there are very few tasks at a school that are more important to tackle as a group than needs assessment, and particularly when it's done in the context of strategic planning. Needs assessment simply cannot work effectively if it's done by just one or two people (e.g., the head of school and a board member). Let me ask you a question: have you ever stopped to think about why there are four Gospels in the Bible, three of which are synoptic (meaning they basically tell the same stories in pretty much the same sequence, albeit with different emphases)? If it's all the same story—and it is, since there is only one Christian gospel—why are there four different accounts? We often explain this in terms of these specific audiences needing to hear the gospel in a way they would best understand. I agree, but I think there's another fundamental point here: for humans to understand something in its fullness—and particularly something that is very significant and impactful—*we need to view it from multiple vantage points*. If the most important news in the history of humanity had to be told by multiple authors sharing from their unique perspectives, it stands to reason that so too must the central story of your school—which is its mission and vision, or why it exists and where it's headed. Needs assessment, and strategic planning in general, is not a one-person task. In order to get it right, it has to incorporate empowered representation from all school stakeholders, meaning that they can truly speak into the process and be heard when they do. It's messier to manage and may create work for more people, but it's well worth the effort (given that nothing short of the school's future is at stake).

In contrast to these pictures of what needs assessment is *not*, when schools engage in true needs assessment, they "define, justify, and create the future by providing hard and soft data for the identification of … gaps between current and desired results. Additionally, they help identify the best solutions for closing these gaps, and thereby ultimately reaching the organizational vision" (Kaufman and Guerra-Lopez 2013, 10). I conceptualize this process in terms of three steps, which are woven into and throughout the overall strategic planning process at a school. These steps are: (1) **developing a needs assessment map**, which will guide the needs assessment process; (2) **conducting assessment using this map**; and (3) using the resulting data to **prioritize and plan** to address the gaps identified by needs assessment (and ultimately improve the school's ability to fulfill its mission). Then, there's a fourth step further down the line, which involves comparing data gathered during needs assessment with data gathered after strategic initiatives have been implemented. This last step usually occurs years later, when the school is (4) conducting **evaluation** of the plan's impact. The diagram below depicts the steps of needs assessment, as they relate to strategic planning:

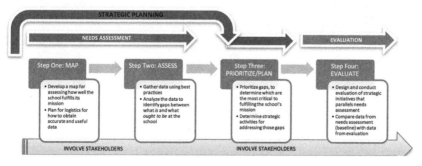

The remaining sections of this chapter will focus on the nuts and bolts of the first two steps of needs assessment. The school begins by examining its mission statement, which is the key picture of what "ought" to be at the school. From there, the task is to develop a comprehensive **assessment map** that identifies expected student outcomes, missional activities, acceptable indicators of success, and specific assessment methods. The second step involves **implementing** this assessment map, by using best practices to gather, collate, and interpret data on how the school is doing relative to its mission.

The third step—**prioritizing and planning**—is where needs assessment converges with and informs the strategic planning process at a school. In this step, schools look at the data gathered during the needs assessment and identify the most crucial gaps between what *is* and what *ought to be* at the school. Those gaps then become the focal point for identifying strategic activities, which—if selected and executed properly—should not only close those gaps, but also help the school to better achieve its mission. Certainly, not every effort within a strategic plan is geared at closing gaps; some strategic plans may involve an expansion of the school's mission, with corresponding new initiatives. However, becoming more effective at fulfilling the school's mission and its existing programs should be a priority of any strategic plan. Accordingly, so should prioritizing and planning to address the gaps identified through needs assessment.

The needs assessment process comes "full circle" in the fourth step—future **evaluation**. In this step, data gathered *during* needs assessment can be compared against data gathered *after* strategic initiatives have been implemented. This is important because the school can gauge progress in how it is fulfilling its mission as a result of the strategic plan. Cast in research terms, needs assessment data can serve as a baseline for evaluating the success of the strategic plan. Practically, this means that when schools are looking to evaluate the success of the strategic plan at the end of its lifespan, they should design the evaluation to mirror (in whole or in part) the needs assessment methods that informed the plan. For example, if a parent survey was used during the needs assessment, schools should consider surveying parents again (either with the same survey, or a new survey that uses many of the same questions), so that data from both can be examined for changes and improvements. In this sense, needs assessment data gathered today is gold in the bank for future evaluation.

Finally, **involving stakeholders** in the needs assessment process is a constant, regardless of the step. Kaufman and Guerra-Lopez (2013) explain why. "Any successful organizational improvement effort is dependent on the involvement and buy-in of its organizational partners. Needs assessment is no different. You will want to include representatives of all relevant stakeholder groups in your needs assessment. If the very same people charged with defining and accomplishing the results that the organization commits to deliver are not part of the process, it is doubtful that they will be a willing partner after the fact" (10).

Note the language here: *representatives of all relevant stakeholder groups*. I'm amazed by the number of times school leaders have told me they've given up on asking for stakeholder feedback because people never respond. It's unrealistic to get feedback from 100 percent of school constituents; it requires more persistence than trying once or twice to get a representative sample. If you've ever planned a wedding, you know that virtually no one responds by the RSVP date listed on the invitation. But because it's such an important event, you don't throw your hands up on that date and resign yourself to no one coming. Instead, you persist—and even find diplomatic ways to get as many responses as possible. Likewise, persistence is key to involving stakeholders in needs assessment.

Ideally, opportunities for feedback can be built into regular school life (such as orientation and meet-the-teacher night) instead of special occurrences that require busy constituents to commit further time. In this way, schools can not only take advantage of "captive audiences" to obtain feedback, but also can proactively cast vision for strategic planning, validate the importance of stakeholders and their perspectives, and market the school as future-thinking and forward-thinking. In this way, needs assessment—and the strategic planning process as a whole—becomes one of the most powerful PR activities in which a school can engage.

When conducted under the umbrella of strategic planning, the four steps of needs assessment enable schools to examine how well they fulfill their mission, and strategize for how they can do it even better. When conducted collaboratively, as Gupta (2007) explains, "A needs assessment frames the problems or opportunities of interest and builds relationships among the people and groups who have a stake in the issue. It also provides the foundation for planning and action.... More specifically, a needs assessment can align resources with strategy, build relationships among those who have a stake in the situation, clarify problems or opportunities, set goals for future action, and provide data for decision making" (20).

Needs assessment can provide the important information school leaders need in order to create strategic plans that will carry their schools into the future. Just as any long journey requires a map and directions (whether printed, or the spoken GPS kind), the first step is to develop a needs assessment map.

Building a Needs Assessment Map

While certainly no two Christian school mission statements are identical, there is often a great deal of commonality. Most include goals like preparing Christian leaders, developing a biblical worldview in students, providing strong academics, creating a caring community, having faculty who disciple students and teach with excellence, preparing students for life beyond graduation, and inspiring students to Christlikeness and service to others. These are all admirable elements of a mission, but they are incredibly complex. It is difficult to know if and when a school "arrives" in any of these, let alone a combination thereof. Unfortunately, this means that most schools don't know where to start with assessing how well they are doing at carrying out their mission. The problem is that, left unmeasured, there is little formal accountability for accomplishing the mission statement. Even worse, the mission statement can become more aspirational than directive in nature. After all, if we don't know and can't tell whether or not we're achieving our mission, we can default to saying that it's something we're shooting for—and leave it at that. As the saying goes, what gets measured gets done—and the inverse is often true.

But as educators, we know the key to accomplishing any complicated task is to break it into smaller, more manageable tasks. This applies for studying for a test, choosing a new textbook, or planning homecoming—and the same is true for determining whether and how well a school is accomplishing its mission. A powerful tool in this process is a needs assessment map.

The key elements to be developed in an assessment map are the following:
1. **Mission components (MC):** the mission statement broken down into a set of its essential components
2. **Expected student outcomes (ESO):** what the school expects students to do or be, relative to each mission component, as a result of their time at the school
3. **Missional activities (MA):** the activities (e.g., programs, curriculum, actions of people) the school utilizes to produce or effect the student outcomes
4. **Indicators (I):** data that indicate the state or level of producing or effecting the student outcomes
5. **Assessment methods (AM):** the collection methods used to gather data relative to the indicators

This is a sequential list, as each of these is essentially a building block upon which the next rests. Thus, the assessment map must be carefully constructed, one element at a time.

Such a map provides not only a starting place for schools looking to conduct needs assessment, but also an organizing principle for determining what data to collect and how. Further, like any visual tool, it can help engage and communicate with those involved in the needs assessment process, as well as track progress over time. Although it may be tempting to simply write out an assessment plan in narrative form, I strongly recommend producing a visual map or flowchart for these reasons (and there are many easy-to-use software programs available that can help). The rest of this section will lay out the steps to developing a needs assessment map, and will provide an example of a fictitious school—"Cornerstone Christian School"—for illustration.

Identifying Mission Components

The first task in developing an assessment map is to examine the school mission statement and identify the major **mission components (MCs)** therein. As discussed earlier, the mission statement is the starting point for needs assessment, because it is the most comprehensive picture of what the school says "ought" to result from its efforts. Much like sentence diagramming, this task involves dividing the mission statement into its key parts. Using our fictitious school, an example is provided below:

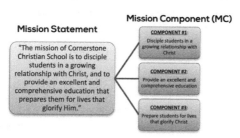

In this example, Cornerstone Christian School's mission statement has essentially three MCs: (1) discipling students in a growing relationship with Christ, (2) providing an excellent and comprehensive education, and (3) preparing students for lives that glorify Christ after they graduate. Of course, these are not completely discrete, encapsulated components, and some may overlap or depend on one another. (For example, one could argue that a "growing relationship with Christ" necessarily means learning to love God with one's mind, which also relates to obtaining "an excellent and comprehensive education.") Separating out the mission statement in this way does not deny or negate the interrelatedness of the various components. Rather, it is the first and necessary task in creating an assessment map; this will become more apparent as we add additional building blocks to the map.

It should be noted that some schools' mission statements may be much longer, or may be written in such a way that it's harder to parse out the essential components. (Note: this is one of many compelling reasons for bringing clarity to school mission statements, as unwieldy ones do not lend themselves to planning for needs assessment.) For a school that finds itself with a less-than-elegant mission statement, stakeholder involvement becomes all the more crucial at this early point. It will require a group effort—employing different perspectives from various stakeholders—to analyze the school mission and identify MCs that are conducive to assessment. This is essential, as a lack of clarity at this foundational level will result in further confusion down the line.

Identifying Expected Student Outcomes and Missional Activities

Once schools have identified the key components of their mission statement, the next task is to link **expected student outcomes (ESOs)** to them. ESOs are what that the school expects students to be able to do or to be as a result of their time at the school. While many ESOs are academic in nature, they can also fall into several other domains of learning and development, such as social, physical, and spiritual. ESOs are a critical building block in the assessment plan, as they translate the more abstract MCs into concrete "deliverables" (of the educational process at the school). Whereas it's still difficult to see a path for assessing MCs, it's much easier to see how ESOs might be measured. (It should be noted that this task is considerably easier for schools that already have a list of ESOs, particularly if they developed those ESOs directly from their mission statement; if not, they will need to spend time developing ESOs for each MC.)

At this point in the mapping process, stakeholder involvement becomes essential. Representatives from all parts of the school—administrators, teachers, parents, students, board members, others—must together ask what it *really means* for that particular mission component to be achieved. For the sake of time and ink, let's look at the third of Cornerstone's MCs, "preparing students for lives that glorify Christ." Here the school needs to ask what it really means for students to be prepared to live a life that glorifies Christ. In outcomes language, the question becomes, "What should our students be able to do—or who should they be—if they are to live lives that glorify Christ once they graduate?" This is not an easy question, and the answer will probably vary from individual to individual, let alone school to school, or even denomination to denomination. That is why stakeholder engagement, dialogue, and consensus are critical in translating MCs to ESOs.

Let's imagine that after much dialogue, representative stakeholders at Cornerstone have determined that this means three things: being spiritually, academically, and vocationally ready for life after graduation. By spiritually, the school means that students have made a commitment to Christ, regularly engage in the spiritual disciplines, and evidence a biblical worldview in their thinking. By academically, the school means that students are prepared for college-level work. Finally, being prepared vocationally means that students know their strengths and giftings, and they have an emerging sense of God's calling and direction in their lives. In the group's deliberating, they agreed that if students are ready in these three areas, they will be prepared to live lives that glorify Christ—in whatever environment or vocation they may find themselves.

After identifying these ESOs, it's time to map **missional activities (MAs)** to each outcome. An MA is an activity (which can be a program, curriculum, or actions of people) that the school utilizes to produce or effect the desired student outcomes. In other words, what is the school actually doing that would result in these outcomes? This is not always an easy task, as mentioned earlier. The reason is that for every activity a school does, there's at least one person who thinks it's mission critical (hence, why an elementary teacher at one school nearly resigned when her principal suggested she find a less expensive Mother's Day craft than the annual $30-apiece handmade pins). Groups conducting needs assessment must stare down challenges like tradition, inertia, and tyranny of the convenient when trying to separate out MAs from everything that goes on at a school.

Thus, schools need a litmus test to determine whether an activity is truly missional. I always suggest asking the following three questions of any activity:
1. Why are we doing this?
2. Do we need to do this in order to best fulfill our school's mission?
3. If we stopped doing this, would we be neglecting something God has called us to do?

If no one can point to the "moral why" for the activity somewhere in the mission statement, that should be the first clue that it may not be a missional activity. (Hint: "Because students like to have fun" is rarely in the mission statement.) If the answer to the next two questions is in the affirmative—the activity helps fulfill the school mission, and stopping it would mean neglecting God's calling on the school—it is most likely a missional activity. Note that none of these questions asked whether people would be upset if the school stopped doing it. Making everyone happy is never a good metric for identifying mission-critical initiatives. (There will always be *somebody* who gets upset whenever something is eliminated.) Remember that a Christian school does not exist to be all things to all people. Rather, it exists to fulfill the mission with which God has entrusted it, and that means focusing resources—no matter how limited or expansive—on activities that support and further that mission.

Continuing with building our sample assessment map, Cornerstone once again involved stakeholders in extensive dialogue to identify MAs that map directly to ESOs. For the ESO of spiritual readiness, the school identified two major activities— the Bible curriculum and its robust spiritual life programming—as its primary, mission-centered efforts that aim to effect that outcome. For academic readiness, the school pointed to college-level coursework (APs and dual-enrollment courses) as well as SAT/ACT prep programs, all of which serve to prepare students for the academic rigor of college. Finally, for vocational readiness, Cornerstone linked its guidance department and staff and its integrated K–12 guidance curriculum.

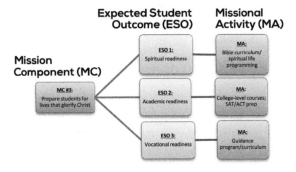

Now that the school has drawn clear lines from its mission to related expected student outcomes, and then to missional activities that work toward producing those outcomes, it's finally time to start building in the actual assessment pieces to their needs assessment map.

Indicators and Assessment Methods

The next step is identifying **indicators (I)** that will help gauge the effectiveness of the school's missional activities (MAs) in producing the expected student outcomes (ESOs). Indicators are "observable phenomena that are linked to something that is not directly observed and can provide information that will answer an evaluation question" (Kaufman and Guerra-Lopez 2013, 111). In other words, an indicator is a piece of data that we would accept as indicating the state or level of producing an outcome.

It's sometimes helpful to think of this in terms of economic indicators, with which most Americans are familiar. Virtually everyone—from politicians, to businesspeople, to workers—would agree that a healthy economy is a desired "outcome" of both our political and economic system. We know that many activities contribute to the health of the U.S. economy (Federal Reserve policies, government budgeting and spending, and U.S. trade policies, just to name a few). But evaluating any one of those activities in isolation will not fully answer the question of how well the economy is doing. So, to answer that question, economists have identified indicators that they will accept as data points. These include things like the national unemployment rate, gross domestic product (GDP), strength of the dollar, interest rates, national debt, bankruptcy filings, and new housing construction. By looking at these and other indicators, economists can determine with some degree of confidence—based on analysis of current as well as historical data—that the economy is expanding, contracting, or doing something in between. They can even issue warnings based on trends they see in the data, which can serve as the basis for legislative or corporate course-corrections.

While schools are not exact microcosms of the U.S. economy, there are indicators that schools can—and regularly do—use to determine whether their activities are truly effective in producing the outcomes they desire. One example that requires little explanation is a school's graduation rate. Schools that have abysmally low graduation rates simply cannot be said to be doing a good job. Certainly there are often many factors (socioeconomic, geographic, etc.) that contribute to those rates. However, the school still has the basic responsibility of providing a K–12 education, which it isn't doing well if most students aren't graduating. This is why billions of dollars are spent to improve "failing" schools—defined by low graduation rates and other indicators (e.g., poor standardized testing results)—because it isn't acceptable that these schools are not producing the most basic outcome of a K–12 education.

It's important to note that while many educational indicators are purely quantitative in nature, some used in educational settings are not. For example, schools that do a senior thesis may gauge the quality of student work, such as written communication and research skills, as an indicator for student outcomes. Schools still need to develop a rigorous and consistent way to evaluate qualitative indicators. In the case of the senior thesis, this might include an evaluation rubric, the results of which are tracked over time for entire classes. The results of this rubric—particularly if it is robust and includes a lot of qualitative feedback—may not be reducible to a single number. However schools can still track student performance using these rubrics; further, if students are underperforming, the school can add remedial activities and track whether there is improvement.

As with the earlier building blocks of the needs assessment map, identifying indicators must be done collaboratively. A representative group of stakeholders is needed to ask and answer the question, What indicators will we accept that our school's activities truly result in the ESOs? I've often found that parents and students will say something very different from teachers and administrators when it comes to acceptable indicators. (Just mention "athletic program" and see what happens!") Acceptable indicators need to be negotiated and consensus built before a school can proceed to the next step, which involves assessing the school's performance on those indicators. Once these indicators are established, schools can then add **assessment methods (AM)** to their map—the specific data collection methods used to gather data relative to each indicator. Principles for selecting and designing assessment methods are discussed more in depth in the following section.

Turning again to Cornerstone, our sample school continued building its map and identified eight indicators across their three ESOs and MAs. The indicators for spiritual readiness include commitment to Christ, regular engagement in spiritual disciplines, and a senior thesis that evidences a Biblical worldview. Those for academic readiness include grades in college-level courses and SAT/ACT scores; college acceptance, matriculation, and graduation rates; and alumni self-reports of their preparedness for college. Finally, for vocational readiness, the indicators are high-quality career portfolios developed by the end of the senior year, and the seniors' articulation of an emerging sense of purpose. The school is confident that these indicators will provide a good gauge of how well the school is doing in fulfilling this component of its mission—preparing students for lives that glorify Christ.

In addition, the school mapped a corresponding eight assessment methods that will address all of its indicators for this mission component: (1) student interviews (including senior exit interviews); (2) student focus groups (including ones with just seniors); (3) parent interviews; (4) parent focus groups; (5) analysis of senior theses using a rubric; (6) institutional data on grades, SAT/ACT scores, and college acceptances; (7) an alumni survey; and (8) analysis of career portfolios using a rubric.

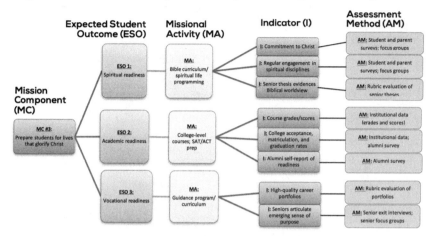

With both indicators and related assessment methods added, the school's needs assessment map is complete. This completed map helped the school to identify key components of its mission, link those components to student outcomes, and identify missional activities at the school that are designed to produce those outcomes. Next, the map enabled the school to plot the indicators that will be used to gauge whether or not the outcomes are being produced, as well as identify the assessment methods the school will use to obtain data for those indicators.

Logistics Planning

A final piece of an assessment map is to develop a logistics plan, which details the logistics for each of the assessment methods (AM) listed on the map. This can be done as a companion piece to the needs assessment map. For each assessment method, the schools need to specify the following:
• Stakeholders to be sampled
• Administration timeline
• Data analysis approaches
• Identification of responsible parties
• Funding/resource considerations

As space does not permit for a detailed presentation of an assessment plan for our sample school, just Cornerstone's intention to use an alumni survey will be highlighted. For this survey, the school would need to design a logistics plan that addresses each of the above bulleted logistics, which might look like this:

Data Collection Logistics	ALUMNI SURVEY
Stakeholders to be sampled	• Sample drawn from past five years of Cornerstone graduates (n = 250 total graduates) • Current e-mails, available in alumni database, to be used for invitation (total e-mails available = 180; thus sample size of n = 180 graduates)
Administration timeline	• Online survey developed and administered during the month of October • Invitation sent on October 1, with a reminder e-mail to be sent each week until survey close
Data analysis plan	• Online survey program providing data analysis and reports (with graphs, charts) • Reports to be run first week in October • Results to be presented to needs assessment steering committee second week of October
Responsible parties	• Director of admissions, with support from IT director
Funding or resource considerations	• Annual fee for online survey program of $250 (already budgeted by administration for current year) • Total number of anticipated work hours: 10 hours for admissions director; 2 hours for IT director

The logistics plan serves several functions: first, it serves as "marching orders" for those who will be carrying out the assessment. It can also provide an accountability measure that a steering group or committee can use to track needs assessment activities. Finally, it can serve as a log of the school's needs assessment activities, which will be important for the fourth step of needs assessment (evaluation) some years later. At that point, the logistics plan can be replicated in whole or in part, providing comparative data from before and after strategic plan implementation.

Needs Assessment Principles and Methods

Once a school has developed an assessment map and corresponding logistics, it's time to start gathering data on indicators, analyzing the data, and then synthesizing and reporting the findings. Certainly there is no one "right" way or set formula for going about needs assessment. In fact, each school's assessment map should look different from those of other schools, since its mission, culture, programs, and people are unique. However, here are two overriding principles that should guide any school's efforts in this area. First, when it comes to data collection, schools must work to **triangulate data sources**; second, they should use a **jury approach** when conducting data analysis, synthesis, and reporting. The first principle will ensure that schools collect useful and accurate data during needs assessment; the second will help schools to interpret and effectively utilize the data they collect. These principles also have important implications for specific needs assessment methods.

Triangulating Data Sources

An important consideration in needs assessment is ensuring the data collected is valid—meaning it is a true and accurate picture of reality at the school. The key to doing this is triangulation, which is a complicated-sounding research term that actually describes a simple concept. Have you ever driven by a land surveyor looking through a transit, with another surveyor doing the same thing a few feet farther down the road? If so, you've seen triangulation in action. Land surveyors triangulate a measurement of a specific distance by taking measurements from two other points, with the idea that three measurements of the same thing—from three different vantage points—will provide a more valid measurement in the end. (This concept is not dissimilar from the earlier discussion about the synoptic Gospel accounts.)

Triangulation in educational research does much the same, with researchers gathering data on the same thing by using different measurement methods. Practically speaking, this means assessment cannot be a "one-and-done" event. For example, if a school wants to get parent feedback, a good way to make sure that feedback is valid is to (1) conduct a parent survey of all school families, (2) hold a focus group with a subset of parents, and (3) analyze exit interview data for information on why families have left the school. Most Christian schools conduct a regular parent survey, but few go further to validate survey data by obtaining data from other vantage points. And it's particularly important to ensure that self-report data—such as that obtained through a survey—is validated through other, more objective measures. As Kaufman and Guerra-Lopez (2013) explain, the findings on a given survey "reflect reality according to each individual. For that reason, you should triangulate people's perceptions with other forms of data" (130).

Triangulation also helps to ensure that the methods used to collect data are well-suited to the indicators under examination. A principle of assessment that I regularly share with schools is this: the complexity of the data collection methods should roughly match the complexity of the phenomenon under investigation (Swaner and Finley

2007). Consider the question, "Was Johnny successful in mastering the concept of fractions this year?" This is a relatively straightforward question, in that it really only addresses one area of interest (Johnny's math performance in a given unit). As such, it could be answered fairly easily by looking at Johnny's unit tests for fractions. Johnny's teacher also could be consulted briefly if Johnny's scores seem out of place with his performance in other math units. By way of comparison, consider the question, "Is Johnny succeeding in school?" That's far more complex and can't be answered by looking at a single piece of quantitative data (e.g., a unit math test). Rather, it would take a few years' worth of academic transcripts and standardized testing results, as well as discussions with all of Johnny's teachers and interviews with Johnny and his parents, before you could confidently answer that question. As discussed earlier, school mission statements are often extraordinarily complex (and their implementation involves hundreds of Johnnys, plus their parents and teachers). Triangulating data sources automatically ensures that a variety of methods are used in data collection—which, taken together, are far more sufficient for capturing the complexity of the school mission and the school's multiple efforts to fulfill it.

If triangulation sounds like more work, it is! But, it's far better to put in the extra effort and get usable data, than a smaller amount of work and get data that is inaccurate (which, by the way, is what we tell our students all the time about studying). One surefire way to ensure that triangulation occurs is to utilize mixed methods, which simply means employing both quantitative and qualitative measures. As a refresher, *quantitative* methods involve quantifying something with numerical data, and as such tend to be broader in nature (e.g., sending out a survey to all stakeholders). *Qualitative* methods involve gathering descriptive, nonnumerical data about something, and tend to yield more detailed and in-depth data (e.g., conducting a small focus group with just a few stakeholders). From a practical standpoint, it's a reasonable goal to use at least one quantitative and one qualitative measure for each indicator that is to be assessed. That isn't to say that a school needs to develop two separate measurement methods per indicator. Rather, a single measure (like a survey or focus group) can kill several birds with one stone, by addressing multiple areas and indicators at the same time. This means that each measurement method should be carefully designed to maximize both the quantity and quality of the data to be collected.

When selecting both qualitative and quantitative measures as part of a mixed-methods design, it's important to know that there are established best practices when it comes to specific methods of collecting data. It is beyond the scope of this chapter to enumerate all of them, but there are many books available on the topics of survey construction, as well as conducting focus groups and interviews. It's a good idea for those in charge of needs assessment to obtain some of these resources before designing the school's assessment plan (which for many of us means locating them among our graduate textbooks and dusting them off!) and either read them together as a group, or divide and conquer among the team. Though an in-depth discussion of methodology is not possible in this chapter, I do want to share some best practices I've identified over the years for three specific methods: (1) surveys, (2) focus groups and interviews, and (3) analysis of institutional data.

Surveys

The data obtained from surveys is only as good as the clarity of the questions asked and the representativeness of the sample that responds. In terms of **question construction**, it's key to avoid confusing or technical language and to offer clear answer choices to participants. The way to establish the clarity of a survey's questions is not for the survey designers to determine whether they think the questions are good! Rather, there are two helpful approaches to this. First, schools should use established, already-tested questions from other schools or published surveys when possible. Discussion boards, professional networks, and even sample surveys (offered by many online survey design sites) are good sources for these ready-made questions. Second, before sending the survey out, it's important to test and retest questions with a small group of representative individuals. For example, before sending out a survey to all faculty, schools can have the department chairs take it and provide feedback on the survey itself. They can be asked whether the questions were clear or confusing, and if the survey was a reasonable length. (If it's too long, "survey fatigue" can set in and participants will quit before they reach the survey's end.)

Next, once a quality survey has been constructed and is ready for administration, it is critical to ensure that there is a **broad representation** of participants. In the case of a school, where the size of stakeholder groups is usually measurable (e.g., number of students, teachers, or families), the goal should be as close to 100% participation as possible. As mentioned earlier, the best way to do this is to find times when stakeholders are "captive audiences." With the ubiquitous nature of cell phones, parents can be asked to complete a survey during meet-the-teacher night or during orientation. Teachers can likewise complete a survey during a faculty in-service. Students can be surveyed during a specific subject or class period either in a computer lab, with a mobile computing cart, or on their own devices. Thankfully, today's technology makes survey administration unprecedentedly easy; many free or low-cost programs allow for instant analysis of results, and will even generate graphs and smart art from the data collected. That being said, just because a school can send out a survey every month, doesn't mean it *should*. It's important to not "over-survey" constituents, just like it's important to not send out three e-mails from the school office in the same day. The same principles apply to surveys as to communication with stakeholders: make it intentional, meaningful, and to-the-point.

A final consideration for designing and administering surveys is whether a school should hire an outside consultant, which is a popular option in Christian education. There are a few positives for doing so. Consultants are often experts at survey construction, which spares busy school leaders the challenge of designing and testing a survey. Donors may also be inclined to give toward efforts like hiring a consultant, if they are assured that the survey results will truly help the school to plan and improve. Of course, consultants' reports can look more professional. Finally, sometimes data from an established survey can be compared with the results from other similar schools that have also participated. The most obvious drawback of hiring an outside consultant is that it can be expensive, but that's not the only concern. First, many professional surveys are cookie-cutter, and may contain language that is foreign to a specific school. Even if the survey can be customized for a specific setting, the consultant may not have the time required to really get to know the school and to design questions that are tailored to the school's unique culture. Second, some professional surveys are complicated to the point that they are difficult to interpret without extensive help from the consultant. This is problematic not only at the time of survey administration, but also years down the line when the school is looking to compare data from multiple years. For these reasons, I've had a number of school leaders tell me that they've hired a consultant to conduct an expensive survey, only to find that the results "weren't really that useful." In order to avoid these pitfalls, I recommend that school leaders ask prospective consultants to provide references for at least three schools—preferably of similar size and setting—that can be contacted regarding their experiences with the consultant and with the survey on offer.

Focus Groups and Interviews

Whereas there is (literally) a science to survey construction, conducting focus groups and interviews is more of an art. Qualitative measures take much more time than quantitative measures to conduct, and they require a more significant investment of effort on the part of those conducting the research. I like to say that these kinds of measures require four "Ps": people skills; patience; persistence; and practice. There are seminal resources that will help school leaders with the mechanics of qualitative research (e.g., Creswell 2013), but in years of conducting and teaching qualitative research methods, I've developed the following brief list of helpful practices:

- *Don't just invite your friends.* It's sometimes hardest for friends to give honest feedback, and in most cases, you already know what their opinions are. A balanced group (in terms of demographics and viewpoints) is best for obtaining valid feedback.

- *Never do just one.* One focus group or one interview simply won't generate enough data to determine whether feedback is valid. In fact, multiple focus groups or interviews allow for a "cascade" effect; the next one can be used to gain clarity or further insight on what was heard in a previous one. There are different schools of thought on how many are enough, but a general rule of thumb is that you're close to that point when you stop hearing any new responses to the same questions.

- *Don't go it alone.* Unless you have prior consent to record a focus group, try to have two people in the room—one to facilitate, and one to take notes. It's virtually impossible to do both well at the same time. Make sure both individuals introduce themselves and their roles at the beginning.

- *Plan ahead.* Design a small set of questions (approximately six to eight questions, for an hour-long session) beforehand. Questions should be open-ended (not lending themselves to a simple yes-or-no response) and should be sequenced from easier to harder (e.g., from "What do you love about the school?" to "What really needs to change for the school to get better?"). Be sure to avoid complex, multi-part, or lengthy questions, as there's a limit to how much auditory information participants can retain while trying to formulate cogent responses. In some cases, it works well to give participants the questions beforehand, so they can have more time to think about their responses.

- *Lay the ground rules.* Participants in focus groups and interviews need to be told up front about how their responses will be kept confidential, as well as how the data will be used and reported—and to whom. In focus groups, it's important to set a group expectation that what's said in the room stays in the room.

- *Check for understanding.* It's a good idea to occasionally restate or rephrase something participants say, and then ask if you got it right. This will help not only ensure that your understanding is accurate, but will also give participants an opportunity to expand or clarify.

- *Attend to interpersonal dynamics.* Determine beforehand how you will handle common issues, like one person monopolizing the conversation in a focus group (try giving everyone a turn to speak) or dead silence in an interview (have additional prompts prepared beforehand).

- *Debrief immediately.* Schedule an extra ten or fifteen minutes after a focus group or interview is over so you can jot down impressions, themes that were noted, or questions that arose. If you don't, the valuable data you obtained is just a student crisis or facility issue away from being recalled inaccurately.

Institutional Data

Most Christian schools have a treasure trove of data they routinely gather, but often they fail to harness this data for more than a single purpose. For example, schools that conduct standardized testing may look at the results to determine if certain students need additional help, or if adjustments are needed in the curriculum. However, they may not think to review this data during strategic planning and in overall institutional needs assessment. Institutional data sources are ideal because in most cases the school has already allocated funding for them in their operating budget, and schools often have years of data that can show longitudinal trends. Standardized testing results are one example; schools can also analyze data from course-level tests and assessments, course grades and GPAs, student portfolios, AP results, admissions data, financial aid information, and retention data.

Institutional data is also particularly important because it can be used to triangulate data obtained from other methods such as surveys, focus groups, and interviews. For example, over years of conducting accreditation visits, I've noticed a generally positive correlation between stakeholder perceptions of a school's academic quality and student performance on standardized testing for the preceding five years. Just recently I visited two schools that had very different profiles. The constituents at School A noted in focus groups that while academics were "solid" at the school, improvements were needed in the rigor and "one-size-fits-all" approach in the school's academic offerings, as well as additional AP courses (the school offered less than five per year). Constituents at School B, however, consistently praised the high level of academic expectations coupled with individualized support offered by teachers, and the school offered over two dozen AP courses from which students could choose. Interestingly, standardized testing data from School A showed that on average, students performed at the 55th percentile as compared with their peers nationwide; at School B, students performed close to the 85th percentile. This is a prime example of how I've used institutional data to confirm the perceptions of parents, students, teachers, administrators, and board members. The same approach can be used to look at areas like college readiness (by examining college acceptance and alumni graduation rates) and parent engagement (e.g., by tracking attendance at school events).

Often, school leaders aren't aware of all the data that is collected, so a good place to start is to brainstorm all of the sources of institutional data that the school currently has. It's important again to do this exercise with a cross-section of stakeholders, so that no data source is missed. Once this list is developed, schools can intentionally map institutional data sources to specific indicators on their assessment plan. Wherever possible, an institutional data source should be used to complement quantitative and qualitative methods (e.g., surveys, focus groups, and interviews) and triangulate the data from those sources.

The Jury Approach

By now, it should be obvious that it takes a good deal of effort to develop and implement a needs assessment plan. And once the results are rolling in, it's very easy to get bogged down in data and ask in exasperation, "Now what?" The way to prevent data overload is to strategize for data analysis *beforehand*, by including data analysis in the needs assessment logistics plan (as outlined in the previous section). A key task of data analysis will be to do "reverse mapping," which means flipping the order of the needs assessment map: the results are placed on the left, and then the implications of those results are analyzed and worked through the building blocks of the map, in reverse. Returning again to our sample school, we can see how Cornerstone can do this with the results of their alumni survey.

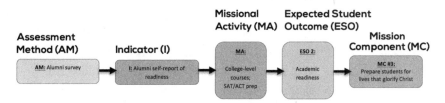

Here, we can see that the survey asked alumni to rate how prepared they felt for college-level work, specifically by the college-level courses and SAT/ACT prep at the school. Their responses provide the data needed to determine whether and to what degree the expected student outcome—academic readiness—is being produced by the school. If we imagine that there is an excellent response rate to the survey, and 95 percent of respondents indicate they felt extremely prepared by the school and all its efforts, Cornerstone has one piece of evidence that it is doing a good job of academically preparing students for lives that glorify Christ. When combined with institutional data on college acceptance, matriculation, and graduation rates (which will also be gathered, per the school's assessment map) the evidence may become even more compelling. Thus, the needs assessment map can be reversed, and can be utilized as a helpful tool for organizing, analyzing, and reporting data.

Of course, many times data is not as conclusive as in the previous example. This can be compounded by the number of data sources used, which—as discussed previously—is the very goal of triangulation. When dealing with complex ecosystems such as schools, reality is sometimes not straightforward. Nonetheless, we are consistently exhorted in Scripture to seek the truth. To this end, I appreciate Douglas Reeves' (2008) discussion of a "jury" approach to interpreting data, and have found it to be very helpful in working with school leaders as they try to understand how to analyze the data they've collected. Although writing specifically and very briefly about action research data, Reeves explains:

> Juries confronted with circumstantial evidence seldom recognize the proverbial smok-ing gun. Rather, they must piece together fact patterns… We trust the jury to make a high-stakes decision, however, based on the preponderance of evidence in a civil case or evidence beyond a reasonable doubt in a criminal case. (35)

I believe the jury metaphor is equally helpful when discussing needs assessment data, for a number of reasons even beyond Reeves' statement.

First, schools must look closely and carefully at the data collected to detect where patterns exist and where the truth ultimately lies. In a trial, with all of the data sources and points laid out in a systematic fashion by attorneys, the jury must decide which story makes the most sense. They must parse out whether multiple sources corroborate or diverge from each other—and where the latter occurs, dig deeper for understanding. Let's revisit the Cornerstone alumni survey, which indicated that the vast majority of alumni felt their time at the school prepared them for college. What if institutional data revealed that almost all Cornerstone graduates attended a local community college, but that very few went to four-year state or private institutions—either upon graduation, or after attaining their associates degrees? How would those conducting needs assessment interpret the full set data? Would it change or in some way nuance conclusions about students' academic readiness? These are the kinds of deliberations that schools may face when looking at data from multiple sources, and when trying to discern the full picture of what is occurring at the school.

Second, serving on a jury also means maintaining objectivity as much as possible. This includes not dismissing data that is less than favorable, or making assumptions when interpreting data. With regard to the latter, I encountered a distressing example from a school that conducted an extensive survey of faculty experiences. One department chair responded in the comments section that she wished faculty would "just be left alone to teach the way we know is right." The administration assumed that this comment had to do with the chair's outspoken desire for the school to withdraw from state mandated testing, and didn't give it a second thought. A couple years later, however, the chair assembled and led a coalition of faculty to the school board to protest the "top-down" approach of administration, and demanded more faculty involvement in running the school—including representation at all administration and board meetings. Had the administration paid closer attention to the earlier survey feedback, and probed further for understanding rather than making assumptions about how to interpret the data, it's possible they could have built bridges or—failing attempts at that—removed the chair from an influential leadership position. This example underscores the importance of taking all feedback seriously and without a "grain of salt."

Third, the jury metaphor also provides support for the ongoing involvement of school stakeholders in needs assessment. Juries are typically composed of twelve people— no small number! The size of a jury reflects the idea that multiple perspectives are necessary to get the full picture of what is true and of what has occurred. Likewise, as discussed earlier, needs assessment simply cannot be done well by one or a handful of people. Further, jurors are representatives of the community who have been called upon to serve that community (as anyone who's received a jury summons can attest). Jurors are carefully vetted before being selected to serve, with care given to ensure they demographically reflect both the defendant and the community in which the crime occurred. Similarly, members of needs assessment teams should be a cross section of school constituents. A steering-committee structure is often well-suited to manage the needs assessment process; even though subcommittees are assigned to work on specific tasks or elements of the process, the larger group convenes regularly to share and discuss findings.

Finally, just as with juries, those leading the needs assessment effort at a school must keep working diligently—analyzing, discussing, and deliberating—until they reach a consensus from all of the data. And just as juries require more time to reach a verdict when the case is more complicated, the needs assessment process at a school requires time-on-task, spread over multiple months, to reach conclusions regarding the school's effectiveness in accomplishing its mission. Of course it's impossible to sequester a group of school stakeholders from the beginning to the end of the needs assessment process. But it's fair to say that the process requires a significant investment of resources and time allocation on the part of school staff, as well as involved parents, board members, students, and others. It's important that time be built into people's schedules so they can make needs assessment a priority.

Concluding Thoughts

At its core, strategic planning involves making decisions about how Christian schools will fulfill the unique mission with which God has entrusted them. Put simply, the role of needs assessment is to provide the data necessary for schools to make good decisions. Needs assessment accomplishes this by gathering and analyzing data, with the purpose of identifying gaps in the school's attainment of its mission statement. Once those gaps are understood, schools can make collaborative, informed decisions as to whether and how the strategic plan should attempt to close those gaps. Furthermore, the data gathered during needs assessment can serve as the baseline against which future evaluation of the strategic plan can be conducted. This is critical given not only the current era of accountability in education, but also the importance of continuous school improvement to excellence in Christian education.

While recently visiting a Christian school near Washington, D.C., I heard the chapel speaker remark how God designed the human body entirely for forward movement—all the way from the placement of our eyes, to the movement of our joints and muscles, to the orientation of our feet. We are built to move forward, not backwards or sideways. (As a runner with a chronic injury from twisting my knee, I can attest to this fact!) As importantly, we're not designed to stay still, either; if we don't continue to move forward, our muscles will atrophy and we will lose strength. This image struck me as a powerful analogy for Christian schools in general, and for strategic planning specifically. As a movement, Christian education needs strong schools that are mission-focused and forward-moving if it is to thrive. If done well, strategic planning—supported by needs assessment—keeps schools oriented and moving in the right direction.

References

Barker, Joel A. 1993. *Paradigms: The business of discovering the future*. New York: HarperBusiness.

Beckwith, Harry. 2003. *What clients love: A field guide to growing your business*. New York: Warner Business.

Boice, James Montgomery. 1983. *The Gospel of John: An expositional commentary*. Vol. 4. Grand Rapids, MI: Zondervan.

Brooks, David. 2015. *The road to character*. New York: Random House.

Buckingham, Marcus. 2001. *Now, discover your strengths*. New York: Free Press.

Carr, Nicholas. 2011. *The shallows: What the Internet is doing to our brains*. New York: W. W. Norton.

Case, Steven. n.d. Cited in Garten, Jeffrey E., *The mind of the CEO*. Wikipedia.

Chin, W. Chan, and Renée Mauborgne. 2005. *Blue ocean strategy: How to create uncontested market space and make the competition irrelevant*. Boston: Harvard Business Press.

Collins, Jim. 2001. *Good to great: Why some companies make the leap ... and others don't*. New York: HarperBusiness.

Collins, Jim. 2009. *How the mighty fall: And why some companies never give in*. New York: HarperCollins.

Collins, Jim, and Morten T. Hansen. 2011. *Great by choice: Uncertainty, chaos, and luck—why some thrive despite them all*. New York: HarperBusiness.

Covey, Stephen M. R. 2006. *The speed of trust: The one thing that changes everything*. New York: Free Press.

Creswell, J. W. 2013. *Qualitative inquiry and research design: Choosing among five approaches*. 3rd ed. Thousand Oaks, CA: SAGE Publications.

Dewey, John. 1897. My pedagogic creed. Wikisource.

Downes, Larry, and Paul Nunes. 2014. *Big bang disruption: Strategy in the age of devastating innovation*. New York: Portfolio.

Drucker, Peter. n.d. Cited in a presentation by Bishop Michael Rinehart.

Drucker, Peter. 2008. *The five most important questions you will ever ask about your organization*. San Francisco, CA: Jossey Bass.

Dubay, Thomas. 2009. *The evidential power of beauty: Science and theology meet*. San Francisco, CA: Ignatius Press.

Eliot, T. S. 1943. *Four quartets*. New York: Harcourt, Brace & World.

Eppler, Mark. 2003. *The Wright way: Seven problem-solving principles from the Wright brothers that can make your business soar*. New York: AMACOM.

Fox, Joseph M. 1976. *Executive qualities*. Reading, MA: Addison-Wesley.

Garber, Steven. 2007. *The fabric of faithfulness: Weaving together belief and behavior.* Downers Grove, IL: IVP.

Gardner, John Elliott. 2013. *Bach: Music in the castle of heaven.* New York: Vintage.

Getz, Gene A. 1984. *Sharpening the focus of the church.* Wheaton, IL: Victor Books.

Gladwell, Malcolm. 2005. *Blink: The power of thinking without thinking.* New York: Little, Brown and Co.

Godin, Seth. 2009. *Purple cow: Transform your business by being remarkable.* New York: Portfolio.

Gupta, K. 2007. *A practical guide to needs assessment.* 2nd ed., updated by C.M. Sleezer and D.F. Russ-Eft. San Francisco: John Wiley & Sons, Inc.

Heath, Chip, and Dan Heath. 2007. *Made to stick: Why some ideas survive and others die.* New York: Random House.

————. 2010. *Switch: How to change things when change is hard.* New York: Crown Business.

————. 2013. *Decisive: How to make better choices in life and work.* New York: Crown Business.

Johnson, Steven. 2011. *Where good ideas come from.* New York: Riverhead Books.

Kaufman, R., and I. Guerra-Lopez. 2013. *Needs assessment for organizational success.* Alexandria, VA: ASTD Press.

Kidner, Derek. 1964. *Proverbs: An introduction and commentary.* Downers Grove, IL: IVP.

Kotter, John. 1996. *Leading change.* Boston: Harvard Business Press.

————. 1999. *John P. Kotter on what leaders really do.* Boston: Harvard Business Press.

————. 2008. *A sense of urgency.* Boston: Harvard Business Press.

Lencioni, Patrick M. 2002. *The five dysfunctions of a team: A leadership fable.* San Francisco: Jossey-Bass.

————. 2004. *Death by meeting: A leadership fable about solving the most painful problem in business.* San Francisco: Jossey-Bass.

————. 2008. *Silos, politics and turf wars: A leadership fable about destroying the barriers that turn colleagues into competitors.* San Francisco: Jossey-Bass.

————. 2012. *The advantage: Why organizational health trumps everything else in business.* San Francisco: Jossey-Bass.

Lockerbie, D. Bruce. 1980. *Asking questions: A classroom model for teaching the Bible.* Fenton, MI: Mott Media.

Macaulay, Ranald, and Jerram Barrs. 1998. *Being human: The nature of spiritual experience.* Downers Grove, IL: IVP Academic.

McChesney, Chris, Sean Covey, and Jim Huling. 2012. *The four disciplines of execution: Achieving your wildly important goals.* New York: Free Press.

McChrystal, Stanley. 2015. With Tantum Collins. *Team of teams: New rules of engagement for a complex world.* New York: Portfolio/Penguin.

Mudd, Philip. 2015. *The HEAD game: High efficiency analytic decision-making and the art of solving complex problems quickly.* New York: Liveright Publishing.

References

Nanus, Burt. 1995. *Visionary leadership*. San Francisco: Jossey-Bass.

Peters, Tom. 2016. Personal e-mail on July 22. Used by permission of Tom Peters. Tompeters. com.

Peterson, Eugene H. 1987. *Working the angles: The shape of pastoral integrity*.

Philbrick, Nathaniel. 2006. *Mayflower: A story of courage, community, and war*. New York: Viking Adult.

Reeves, D. B. 2008. *Reframing teacher leadership to improve your school*. Alexandria, VA: ASCD.

Roth, John D. 2011. *Teaching that transforms: Why Anabaptist-Mennonite education matters*. Scottsdale, PA: Herald Press.

Sanders, J. Oswald. 1992. *Shoe-leather commitment: Guidelines for disciples*. Chicago, IL: Moody.

Sax, Leonard. 2015. Parenting in an age of awfulness. *The Wall Street Journal*, December 18.

Schermer, Michael. 2015. Do the right thing. *The Wall Street Journal*, May 7.

Sinek, Simon. 2009. *Start with why: How great leaders inspire everyone to take action*. New York: Penguin.

Swaner, L. E. and A. P. Finley. 2007. The scope of BTtoP research: Design and findings from the demonstration project. *Peer Review* 9(3): 22–29.

Warren, Rick 2002. *The purpose driven life: What on earth am I here for?* Grand Rapids, MI: Zondervan.

Westminster Shorter Catechism, www.reformed.org/documents/WSC.

Willard, Dallas. 2009. *The great omission: Rediscovering Jesus' essential teachings on discipleship*. New York: Harper Collins.

Wilson, Ian. n.d. From scenario thinking to strategic action. http://horizon.unc.edu/projects/ seminars/futurizing/action.asp.